BEDFORD SQUARE

40
E.C. '89.

Andrew Byrne

Bedford Square

An Architectural Study

For Sid,
Many thanks for
Ludlow May/June 2006,

Andrew Byrne

THE ATHLONE PRESS
London & Atlantic Highlands, NJ

First published 1990 by The Athlone Press Ltd
1 Park Drive, London NW11 7SG
and 171 First Avenue, Atlantic Highlands NJ 07716

FOR MY LATE COUSIN AIDAN

British Library Cataloguing in Publication Data
Byrne, Andrew
Bedford Square: an architectural study.
1. London. (London Borough) Camden. Public places.
Squares. Architecture
I. Title
720′.9421′42

ISBN 0 485 11386 4

Library of Congress Cataloging-in-Publication Data
Byrne, Andrew.
Bedford Square: an architectural study/Andrew Byrne.
p. cm.
Includes bibliographical references.
ISBN 0 485 11386 4
1. Architecture–England–London. 2. Bedford Square (London, England) 3. Architecture, Georgian–England–London. 4. London (England)–Buildings, structures, etc. 5. Bedford Square (London, England)–Buildings, structures, etc. I. Title.
NA970.B9 1990

720′.9421′42–dc20

Produced for the publishers by
John Taylor Book Ventures
Designed by Alan Bartram
Made and printed in Great Britain by
BAS Printers Limited, Over Wallop, Stockbridge, Hampshire

FRONTISPIECE No.40 Bedford Square, entrance doorway.

Contents

The author and publishers are grateful to Gardiner & Theobald, the present occupiers of several houses in Bedford Square, who commissioned this book to celebrate 150 years of practice – initially as architects and surveyors and latterly as chartered quantity surveyors. During this period their principal offices have always been located in Bedford Square or in the streets of the Bedford Estate immediately adjacent.

Acknowledgments
I wish to thank all those people who have helped in the compilation of this book. In particular, the following: Marie Draper at the Bedford Estate, and also Brian Wynn-Higgins and Clive Chester; Richard Knight of the Camden Local History Library, for his constant help; Dorothy Abel Smith, for showing me around Woodhall Park; Peter Walne, archivist at the Hertfordshire County Record Office, for information on Sir Lionel Lyde and the New Church at Ayot St Lawrence; John Hardy for information on classical mythology; Clive and Basil Leverton for information on Thomas Leverton; Sarah Tillotson for allowing me to look at her thesis on Thomas Leverton; Barry Holloway for showing me around the central gardens in the Square; Paul Gilby and James Thorp for their cooperation; Susie Brooke and Francesca Gilby for their help in typing part of the manuscript, and especially Pam Cotterill for typing the bulk of the manuscript with such patience and good humour; Ali Bernstein, Jane Briginshaw, Jim Carroll and Rupert Bound, for taking such care with the measured drawings; Ted Cullinan and Glynn Boyd Harte, for donating their time so generously to supply a drawing; Caroline Ryan, Michael Coombs and Alan Baxter for their help, and Jamie Whitehead for drawing the axonometric view of No.32 Bedford Square; Neil Burton and Treve Rosoman of English Heritage for their tips. Especial thanks go to Susie Barson of English Heritage for editing the text and to Frank Kelsall, also of English Heritage, who has done so much work on Bedford Square that perhaps he should have written this book; the generous imparting of the results of his research has added greatly to the book. Lastly, my thanks to the partners of Gardiner and Theobald for their sponsorship, for trusting my decisions and for their lack of interference.

The houses in Bedford Square are private. The author gratefully acknowledges the help given by all the tenants in the preparation of this book and asks that readers restrict their interest and curiosity to the pages of this book.

Preface

This book came to be after I was approached by the publisher with a request for some sort of architectural study. It was a vague brief but no less exciting for I was given a completely free choice of subject. A general study was immediately ruled out – there are far too many of them already – and I concentrated instead on coming up with something that would deal with a particular building or group of buildings. Although I had never contemplated researching it before, almost at once I decided that Bedford Square would be a good subject. It had always been dear to me, it had never been adequately researched though it had so much to tell, and it clearly warranted a book. I reported back, got on with other things, made the occasional excursion in optimistic anticipation and then received the go-ahead. I hope my efforts will prove useful.

My relationship with Bedford Square began some time in the early 1980s when I came to London to study. An interest in architecture was forming. I was beginning to enjoy looking at buildings but was more concerned with building styles than architectural history. The first time I walked through the Square, perhaps it was in 1981, I did not take much notice but I did recognise it as Georgian. It must have made an impression because I was soon back there, often going out of my way just to walk through.

The more we became acquainted the more it revealed its secrets – a Gothic balcony, a surviving lamp-holder, a lead rainwater hopper with an ungainly overflow spout, a footscraper, the list proved to be endless and yet the houses were so plain. How could such houses be so full of character? Then one winter's day I was passing by and looked up through some of the first-floor windows. I had to stop and admire the view. I was looking at a most beautiful ceiling, sparkling and luxuriating in a wash of sublime colour. My eyes moved to the next house and there was another ceiling and then another. I walked around the whole Square, unable adequately to take them all in. There were so many of them. I was by now hooked on this tiny part of London that was strangely complete and so self-contained.

It has proved to be a continuing delight to walk here, especially on an autumn or winter afternoon when there is that bonus of beholding these exquisite ceilings. Harley Street, Stratford Place, Mansfield Street and Portland Place are all good, but Bedford Square is magnificent. This is one of the great architectural shows of London.

Our relationship is now so well established that I know I shall never tire of visiting the place. There is a wonderful atmosphere, a restraint and a self-effacement and yet a powerful aura and a bold self-confidence. It exhibits neither the overpowering severity of the sheer terraces of Dublin nor the over-restoration of ivy-clad Belgravia and Chelsea. It bears its age so well and so honestly, quietly demanding and always receiving a universal admiration from all who become involved.

I shall conclude by quoting from an outsider, a man who understood and appreciated London on a level way above that of most Londoners. In the 1930s, his keen sense of the power and drama that architecture can offer took him, for example, into the East End to take photographs of the massive fortress walls enclosing the London Docks. For Steen Eiler Rasmussen 'London is a first-rate architectural city, and Bedford Square is one of the finest squares in the world'.

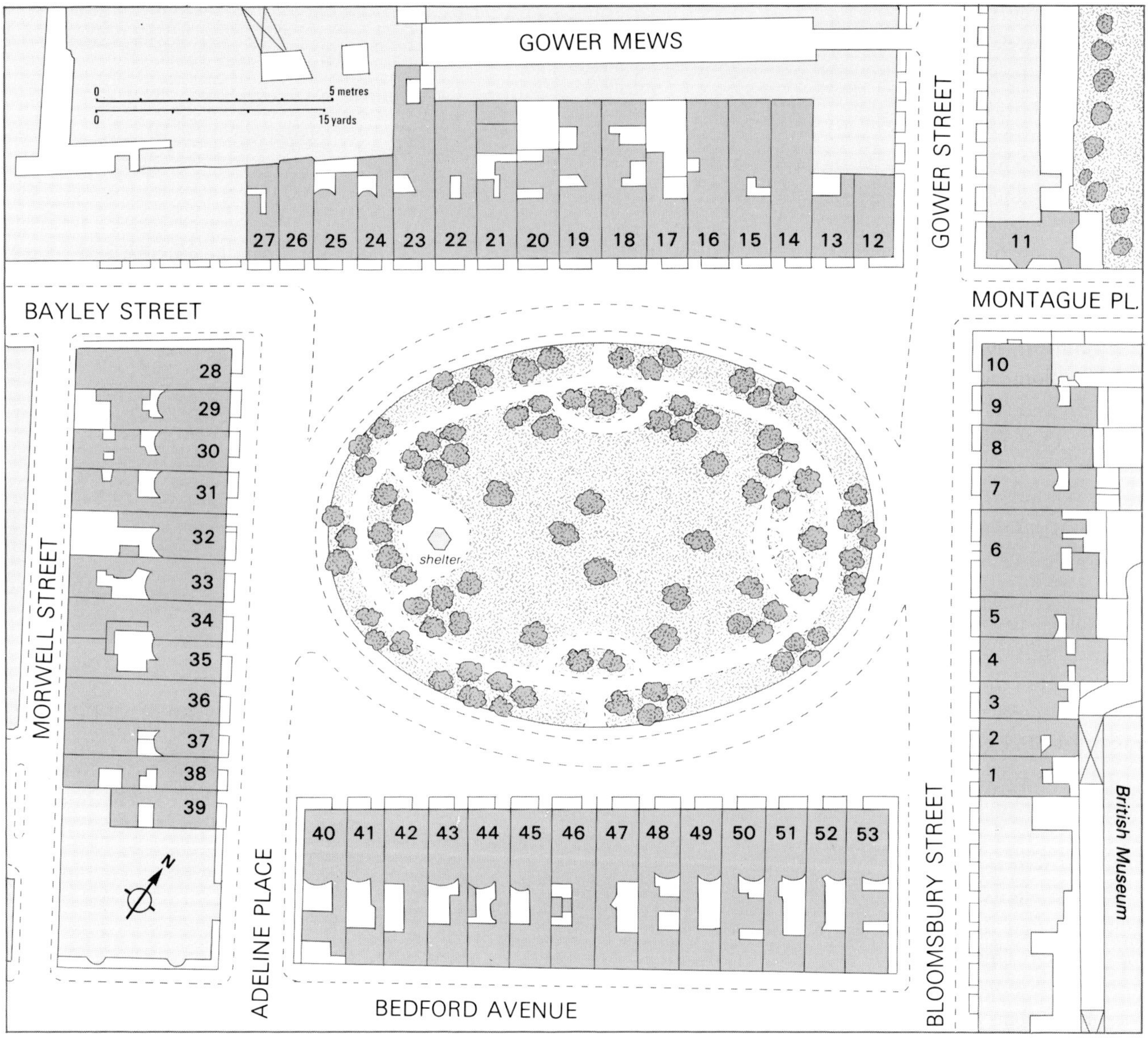

The scales on the measured drawings in this book
are in feet and inches

Introduction

... It is a little surprising that among the great number of squares in London, not one is to be found that is regularly built, on the contrary it is hardly possible to conceive any thing more confused and irregular than the generality of them are.

JOHN GWYNN *London and Westminster Improved* 1766

Bedford Square is unique. It has four sides of uniform palace-fronted terraced houses which form a 'perfect' symmetrical square, with stucco-faced pedimented
1 centres surrounding a leafy garden. Built between 1775 and 1783, its chief importance lies in the fact that it was the first example in London of a square with such consistent uniformity: the builders of the Square managed to achieve what hitherto had been squibbish attempts at some overall coherence. These earlier essays usually comprised four unequal sides: two sides of arcaded terraces, a wall, and a church (Covent Garden, 1630s); three sides of houses, not uniform, with the fourth side taken up by a large house (Bloomsbury Square, 1660s) or with a palace-fronted terrace on one side only (Queen Square, Bath, 1720s). Moreover, the achievement at Bedford Square was never again exactly repeated. Fitzroy Square, for example, had only the south and east sides built to Robert Adam's elevations in the 1790s; by the time building could continue after the French Revolution, taste had changed and the later blocks, influenced by Greek Revival ideas, are, according to Bolton, 'confessedly inferior'.[1] Other squares suffered from being built in fits and starts, and none display the four palace-fronted terraces with pedimented centres and end pavilions that make up Bedford Square. Unlike grandiose schemes in France, where higher authorities governed the appearance of town planning to a larger degree, as with the perfect Place des Vosges, the English system of speculative development under which Bedford Square was created was governed by so many variables – land ownership, money supply, demand for houses – that the exact circumstances were unlikely to be repeated. This system, for better or for worse, accounts for the variation and anomalies found in most eighteenth-century urban development; Bedford Square was no exception.

The year 1768 was important in the architectural history of London, because a renewed taste for coherence and uniformity was initiated in the town planning and architecture of the capital. In the decade that followed that pivotal year, London witnessed a remarkable maturity in its domestic architecture, a maturity that most adequately set the guidelines for the refinement and elegance of the remainder of the Georgian era. Bedford Square belongs at the tail end of those ten years. The building agreements were signed in 1776 (though building probably began the year before), 34 of the 53 houses were leased by 1777 and by the end of 1784 all the houses were occupied.

Bedford Square was conceived at a time when architectural effect depended more on the treatment of complete estates rather than on the design of a particular street or group of houses. Lavish fitting out of the interior was also a priority, and Bedford Square manages to combine both the exterior restraint and austerity of the Palladian years (while hinting at the decorative stucco of the Regency) with the internal magnificence of the 1770s when the influence of Robert Adam was at its height. With so many of its contemporaries all but vanished (for example, the Adelphi and the Minories) or greatly altered (for example, Portland Place and Stratford Place), Bedford Square survives remarkably unscathed. Thrown up at the tail end of the ten-year period in which the influences upon it so clearly lie, the Square stands as the great survivor of the Golden Age of domestic architecture in London.

Bedford Square was certainly not London's first square and in spite of initial impressions it is by no means perfect. Closer inspection reveals a host of stylistic quirks and structural oddities which confound and intrigue; some, not all, of these will be explained in the following chapters. Although many of the problems of building Bedford Square were due to particular circumstances, some were common to other contemporary urban speculative developments.

The years 1775-83 during which the building of Bedford Square took place represent an important and busy period for London's domestic architecture in general. The year 1766 was significant: the number of property transactions recorded in the Middlesex Deeds Register in that year was more than twice the number registered in 1761.[2] It was also a period of great fluctuation in building which reflected the movement and size of the population. After little increase between 1700 and 1760, a substantial increase in the population in the second half of the century meant a larger demand for houses in and around the metropolis. Building had been at a low ebb during the 1740s due to a combination of factors: war against Spain and France, the Jacobite Rebellion, a decline in trade, bad winters, and 'gin mania', and picked up only slowly throughout the 1750s. This trend gained momentum after the Peace of Paris in 1763, and a building boom in London began. Contemporaries commented on the fast rate of building, noting the 'many piles of building that are daily rising in the metropolis' (1764), 'the rage or at least hurry, of building' (1765) and the 'thousands of houses' (1767) that had been built in the last few years. This was the climate in which Bedford Square was conceived.

1. Bedford Square, north side in 1913. Note the tented verandah at No.21, since taken down.

A lull in activity followed from 1767 to 1771, and again during 1772-3 when a severe financial crisis badly affected building (this was when the Adam brothers were nearly bankrupted by the infamous Adelphi development). Between 1773 and 1777 there was another upturn, but the intensification of the American War of Independence, after the entry of France in 1778, brought about a rapid and prolonged downturn in building. The National Debt more than doubled, the price of Consols (Government stock) fell sharply, and because the Government was paying high interest rates, private loans – the life-force in speculative development – became impossible to obtain. Prices were also fluctuating; the price of bread between 1766-7 and 1772-4 was high, and people fell on hard times. Bedford Square, along with other developments, suffered after 1778 from the lack of investment because of the 'unhappy war', yet loans to the builders from the Bedford Estate enabled the scheme to be completed by the end of 1783 (see Appendix 2).

Generally speaking, it was an industrious time in the building world; imports of timber corresponded closely in this period to an increased number of registrations in the Deeds Registry; these were healthy throughout the 1760s, peaking in 1776. With population growth providing a demand for housing, and general prosperity and available credit in the private sector, conditions were good for large-scale development. Blocks of dwellings or terraces began to line newly-formed streets, and the terraces were combined to form crescents, circuses and squares in larger schemes. Several such schemes were contemporary with Bedford Square.

At the south-eastern edge of the City of London, and a stone's throw from the Tower, the younger George Dance was working on a quite remarkable venture. Having succeeded his father as Clerk of the City Works to the Corporation of the City of London in 1768, he submitted to its City Lands Committee in June of that year drawings for a semi-circle of houses in an opening off the Minories. An extended layout was built shortly after as Crescent, Minories, along with Circus to the south and America Square to the north, both linked to Crescent by a straight line no more than four or five house widths

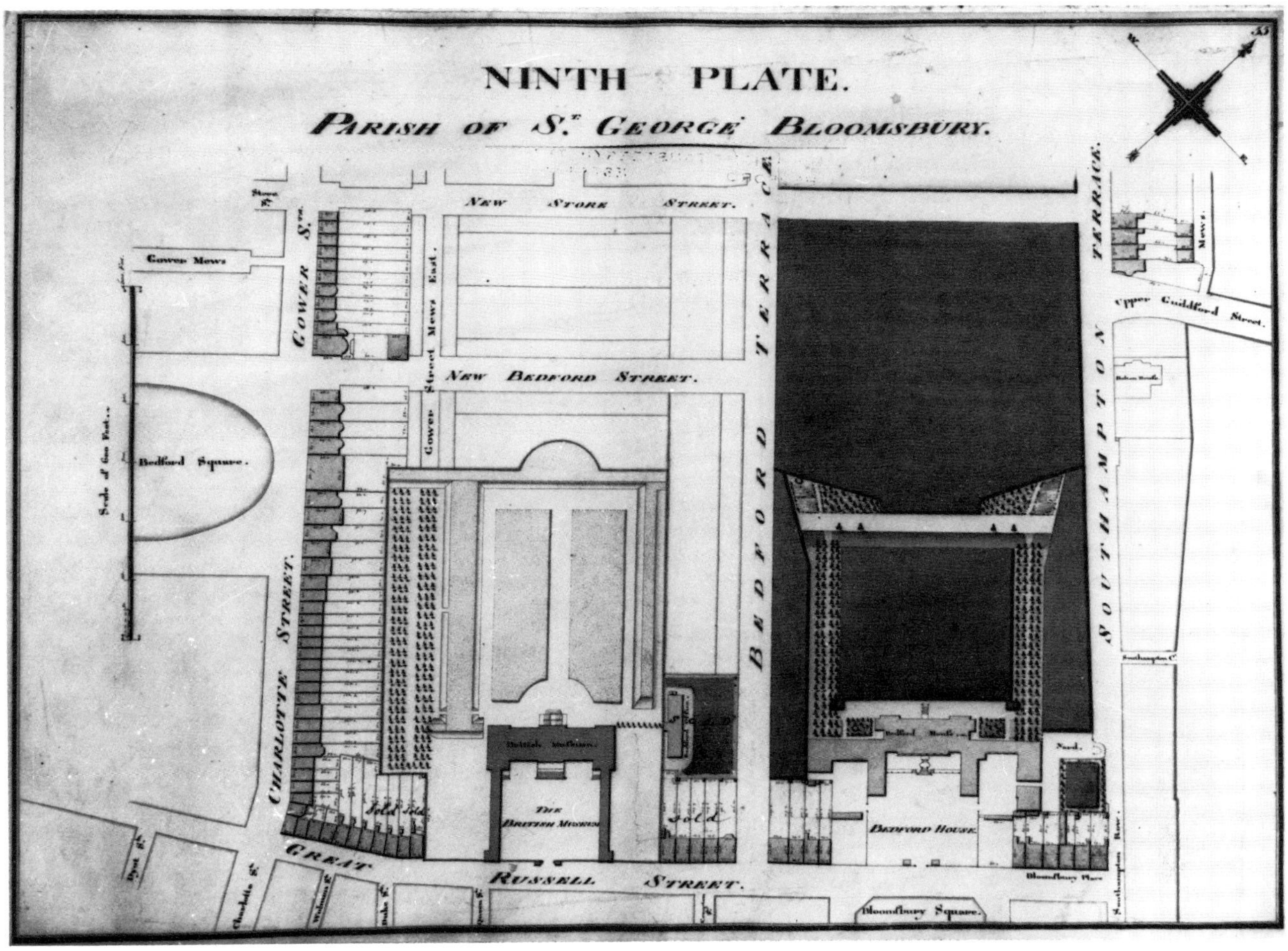

2. Bedford Square, east side, survey of 1795.

3. Bedford Square, north side, survey of 1795.

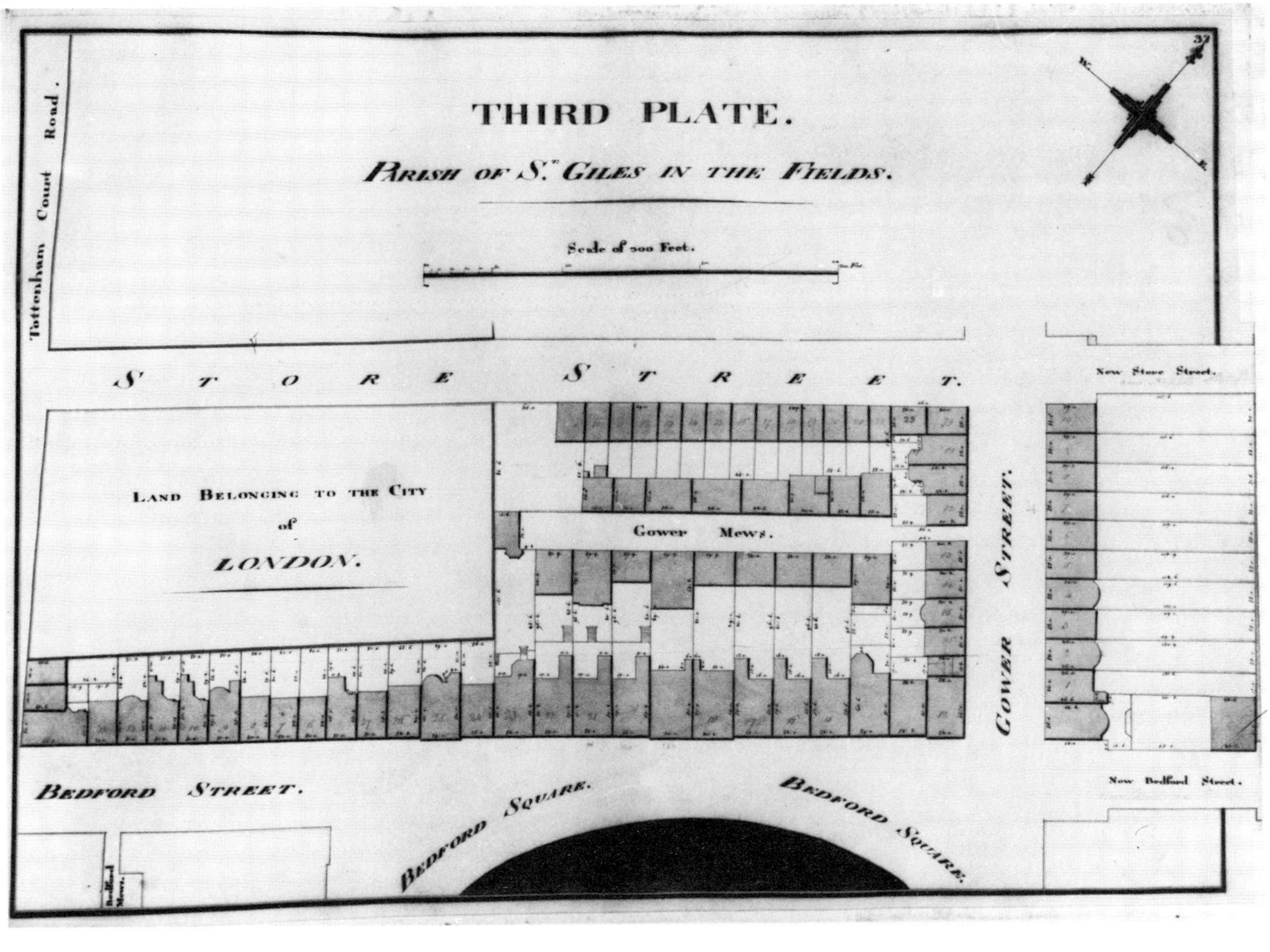

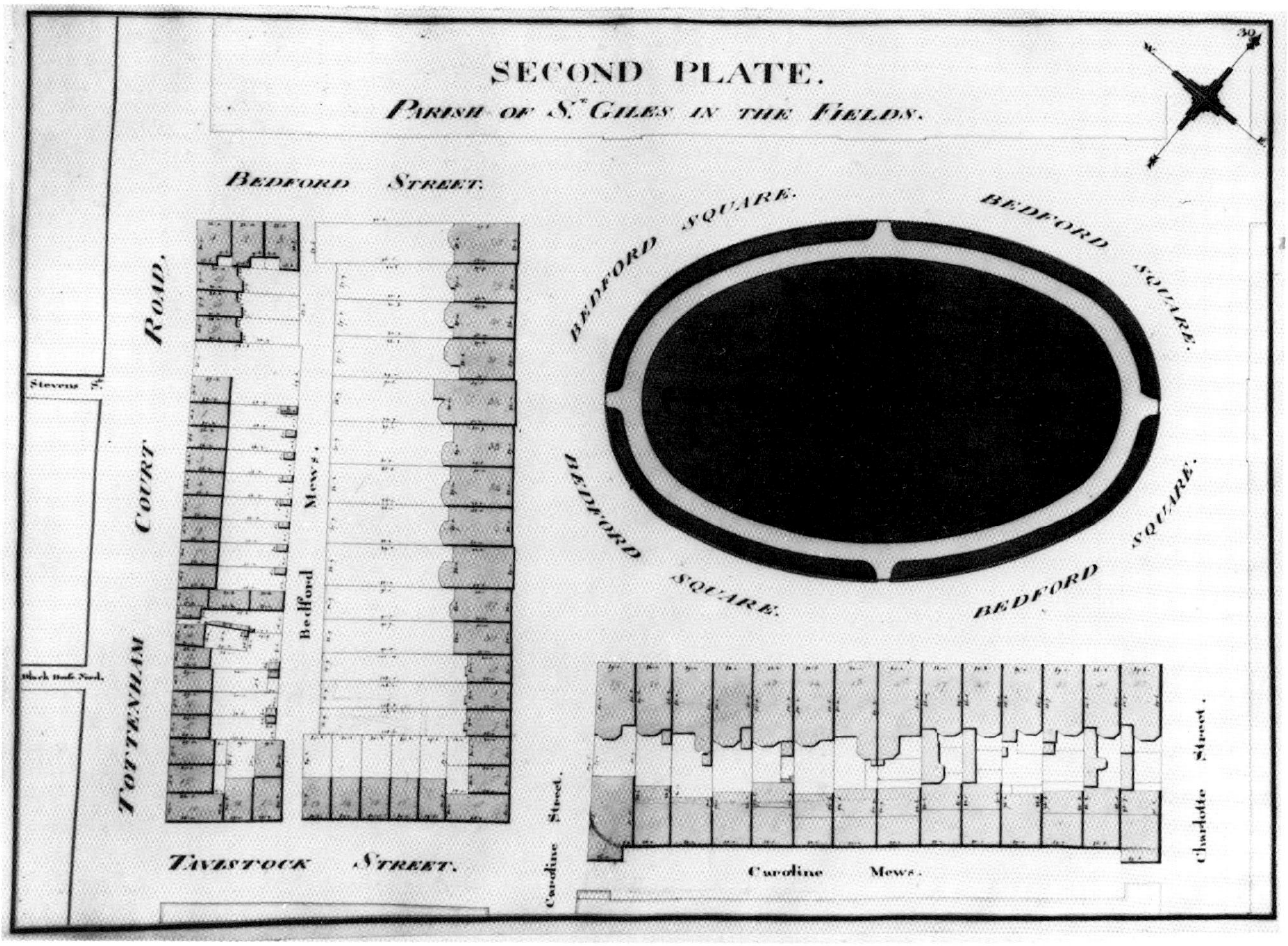

4. Bedford Square, west and south sides, survey of 1795.

in length. It was a very modest attempt at town planning and, of course, a miniature essay on the Woods' Queen Square, Circus and Royal Crescent at Bath (the latter and final part of that triumvirate then nearing completion); so miniature was it, in fact, that Dance's scheme could have just snuggled into the ellipse of the Royal Crescent.

This was Dance's first venture in town planning and indeed amongst his earliest works; he had just turned twenty-seven when he presented the scheme. It was the first appearance of the circus and crescent in London, and their use became an admirable obsession not just in many of Dance's subsequent commissions but also in those of the many architects and speculators who were following behind. It is tragic that in London he got so few commissions in the West End, tied as he was in his role as Surveyor to the City Corporation, a role that continued until his retirement from the post in 1815. He was one of the most talented architects ever produced by Britain: a pioneer of the abstraction and the chiselling away of the components of the architectural orders that produced effects based on the arrangement of geometry rather than ornament. He shared with his pupil Soane a mutually beneficial relationship that formed one of the most important threads of Neo-classicism.

A new taste in the domestic architecture of the capital was long overdue in 1768. The 1740s and 1750s had seen little domestic building activity and strict Palladian design had by now fallen out of favour. The successor to Palladian could so easily have been Greek, but the early promise of James Stuart's Grecian garden buildings at Shugborough and Hagley Hall in the late 1750s and early 1760s and 15 St James's Square, the London town house he designed for Thomas Anson of Shugborough (1763-6), was not followed up. If the publication in 1762 of the first volume of Stuart's and Nicholas Revett's *Antiquities of Athens* is also taken into account, one wonders just how he could have failed when the time was so ripe for change. Health problems, an unpredictable and complex personality, and hostility to the new style from the architectural hierarchy of Chambers, Paine and Adam seem to have combined in his inept handling of its promotion so that in the 1760s 'the present state of British architecture rested firmly in the hands of Robert Adam, the man who forestalled the Greek Revival'.[3]

By 1768, Adam had done little work in London. His handsome Doric Admiralty screen of 1760 served to obscure most views from Whitehall of Thomas Ripley's absurd portico, and was his first important work in the capital after setting up practice two years before at Lower Grosvenor Street at the age of twenty-nine. Apart from small alteration and redecoration works in the West End, and the building, between 1762 and 1768, of Lansdowne House on the south side of Berkeley Square, all of Adam's works in the first eight years of the 1760s were country houses. In 1768, however, Robert, along with his three brothers, principally James, returned his attentions to London. There followed in the next ten years, those great ten years for English domestic architecture, four individual houses of the utmost magnificence, the Adelphi and some grand speculations in the West End.

5 The Adelphi, like the Minories, was started in 1768. Its story is frequently told – the opposition from the City, the Parliamentary assents, near bankruptcy, the disposal of many of the unfinished houses by lottery – and need not be repeated here. As a domestic enterprise it was astonishing; a vast building and engineering undertaking, a veritable Spalato embanked high on the Thames. Its location was perfect, its sheer scale was unprecedented, so many of its architectural qualities were novel and its completion, against all odds, says so much about the Adams' style of operation. It was a potent mixture of arrogance, self-confidence, sheer determination and unabashed enthusiasm that saw the creation of a great new residential quarter.

The houses built on the three-and-a-half acre site (an obvious criticism of the Adelphi was the placing of too many houses into the scheme) reflected the scale of the project as a whole, and it was here that the tall town house of the later Georgian and Victorian periods, if not exactly introduced, was firmly established as the new standard for London.[4] Tying the whole development together was a uniformity on a scale never before attempted in the capital. The main terrace overlooking the river was palace-fronted, with pilasters and crowning balustrades to the end and centre houses, as was its parallel block which fronted John Street. These two terraces, which formed an island block, were in a sense a London square turned inside out which, by necessity of its identity and location, looked out to the world rather than in on itself.

The Adelphi was, apart from anything else, an architectural and town-planning triumph and the first response to John Gwynn's desire for uniformity and 'magnificence and elegance [which] are so little attended to in the capital'.[5] It is virtually no more. Defaced by a ponderous Victorian stucco in the confused Classicism of the 1870s, the island block was demolished in the 1930s. Londoners have never shirked from destroying their riverside architecture.

The Adelphi scheme exemplifies the increasing involvement of 'architects' in speculative development. Summerson reminds us in *Georgian London* that 'until about half-way through the eighteenth century there was

5. The Adelphi, aquatint by Thomas Malton. The Adelphi complex was started in 1768 and inaugurated a remarkable ten-year period in London's domestic architecture.

no such thing as an "architectural profession" in the modern sense ... Architects were recruited from tradesmen, from surveyors, and from the gentry'.[6] Many who called themselves architects were actively concerned in leasing land and speculative building, and a great many 'architects' at some stage in their careers worked as builders. By the 1770s, travel or study abroad, knowledge of theory or treatises, and drawing skills distinguished an architect from a builder, who was most likely to be a specialist craftsman such as a carpenter or bricklayer.

The Adam brothers were undoubtedly professional architects heading an office of assistants and pupils. Their work ranged from private commissions for individual houses, to the riskier business of speculative development. In the ten years following the commencement of the Adelphi, many first-rate architects were also involved in both private commissions and speculative development. Sir Robert Taylor was at work on fourteen very large and magnificently austere houses for the Duke of Grafton at Grafton Street. James Paine was working on a personal speculation on land leased from the Earl of Salisbury at Salisbury Street, an immediate neighbour for the Adelphi. Sir William Chambers was involved in the building of about two dozen houses in Berners Street in one of which,

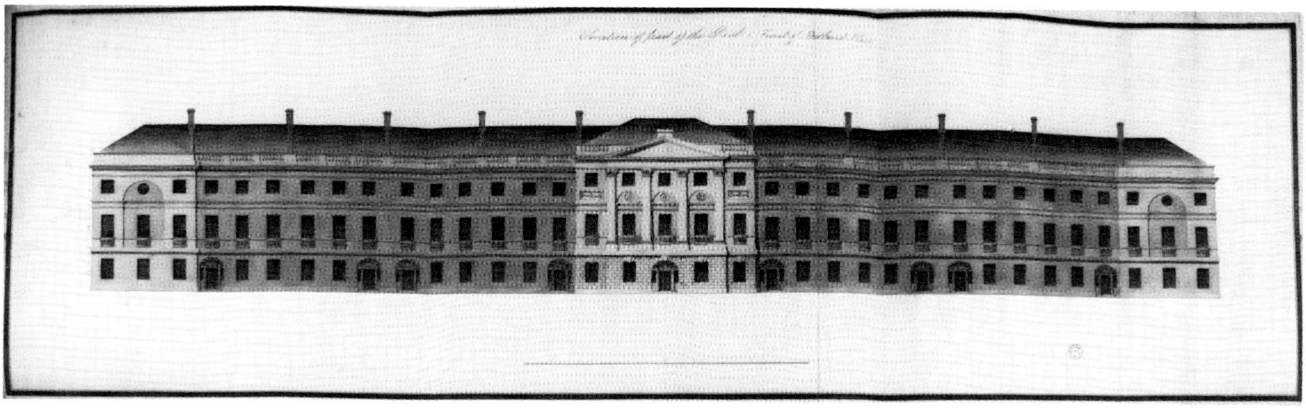

6. Portland Place, drawing by James Adam. A contemporary of Bedford Square.

7 OPPOSITE. St Giles-in-the-Fields, Morgan's Map, 1682.

like Paine at Salisbury Street, he was to take up residence. Henry Holland was speculating at Hertford Street in the late 1760s, and in 1777 started work on Hans Town, Chelsea (Sloane Street and Sloane Place, Hans Place and Cadogan Place) on land leased from Lord Cadogan, though the houses were plain and narrower than the typical three-bay houses in the West End. James Wyatt was speculating with a handful of houses on the north side of Portman Square; George Dance had, by 1777, drawn up elevations for his brilliantly eccentric terrace of nine houses on the west side of Finsbury Square, tragically destroyed in the Second World War.[7] The young John Nash, appointed district surveyor for three parishes in Southwark under the 1774 Building Act, was at Great Russell Street in 1777 building half a dozen houses with good Greek Ionic doorcases; and the Adam brothers, in addition to the Adelphi, were busying themselves on the Duke of Portland's Estate
6 in Marylebone at Portland Place, Mansfield Street and neighbouring streets and in 1776 were even speculating in the City at Frederick's Place.

Of lesser architects, Richard Edwin was working on the Corporation of London's land at Stratford Place, a most impressive symmetrical closed avenue that opens out into a small square with a large stone mansion terminating the view from Oxford Street; John Johnson was involved with the building of a fine pair of houses in New Cavendish Street cutting across the axis at the north end of Mansfield Street; and finally the work of an unknown architect on the north side of Queen Anne's Gate (Nos.14-24), six large and impressive houses all with top-lit centrally placed staircases whose full-height bowed rear elevations look out onto St James's Park.

Of the individual town houses built in Georgian London, this ten-year period produced an abundance of foremost quality. Chambers designed Melbourne House for Lord Melbourne just off the north side of Piccadilly (and from 1776 was to spend his last twenty years engrossed in Somerset House); Taylor was working for Edmund Keen, Bishop of Ely, at Dover Street (No.37) with its powerful stone façade; Stuart was at Portman Square frustrating his client Mrs Montagu with his lackadaisical approach but nevertheless giving London a fine freestanding house, placed diagonally across the north-west corner, with an austere brick façade but some magnificent entertaining rooms within. Robert Adam was involved with a series of grand commissions: Chandos House in Queen Anne Street for the Duke of Buckingham, with a fine porch and some of the most exquisite wrought-iron railings and lampholders in all of London; 20 St James's Square for Sir Watkin Williams-Wynn, with its gracious pilastered Portland stone façade; Derby House for Lord Stanley, just twenty-one when he commissioned Adam in 1773, a remodelling of a late 1720s house at 23 Grosvenor Square, demolished; 20 Portman Square for the Countess of Home which, with its austere (and altered) brick façade and astonishingly grand interior, continued the Georgian tradition of external modesty and internal grandeur for individual terrace houses. For Summerson, these four Adam houses 'represent, perhaps, the highest point of imagination and artistry in the handling of the London house'.[8]

Thus the type of building supervised by architects ranged from splendid costly 'one-offs' to the terraced houses built on the estates of wealthy landowners. The quality of these houses varied wildly and contemporary observers were often appalled at the shoddiness of construction and lack of overall planning. John Gwynn wrote in *London and Westminster Improved* in 1766:

> ... the rage of building has been carried to so great a height for several years past, as to have increased this metropolis in an astonishing manner. For want of such a publick direction, those very buildings which might have been easily rendered its greatest ornament, are a melancholy proof of the necessity there was of adopting a well-regulated plan.[9]

And concerning the new developments in the West End there was great indignation:

> Why so wretched an use has been made of so valuable and desirable an opportunity of displaying taste and elegance in this

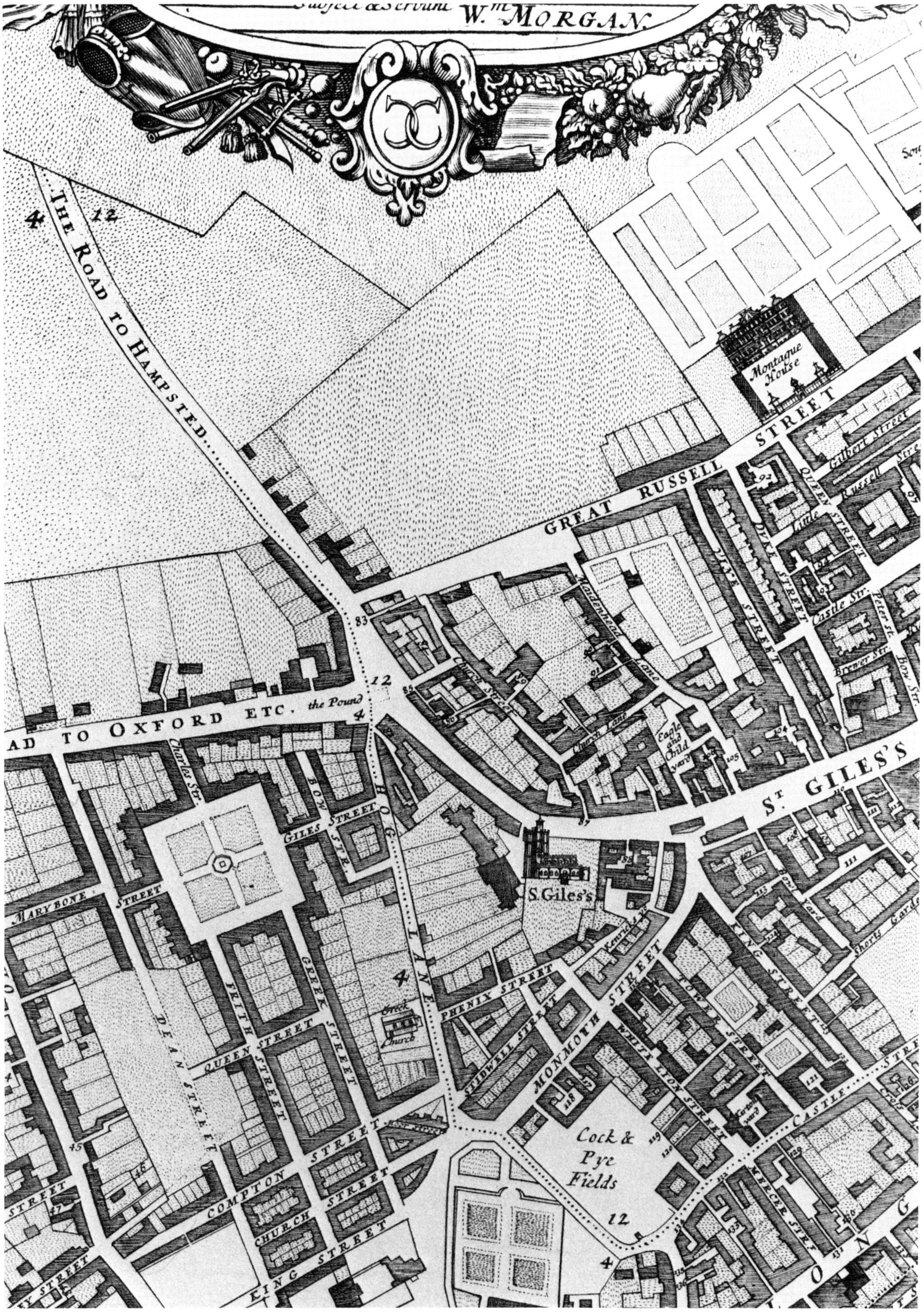
W.m MORGAN
THE ROAD TO HAMPSTED
GREAT RUSSELL STREET
Montague House
AD TO OXFORD ETC.
the Pound
ST GILES'S
S.Giles's
HOG LANE
Charles Str.
BOW STREET
GILES STREET
MARYBONE STREET
GREEK STREET
FRITH STREET
DEAN STREET
QUEEN STREET
COMPTON STREET
CHURCH STREET
KING STREET
PHENIX STREET
MONMOUTH STREET
STIDWELL STREET
WHITE LYON STREET
TOWER STREET
Cock & Pye Fields
CASTLE STREET
MERCER STREET
Greek Church
Church Street
Church Lane
Eagle and Child yard
Maidenhead Lane
Castle Str.
Brewer Str.
Peter Str.
Little Russell
Gilbert Street

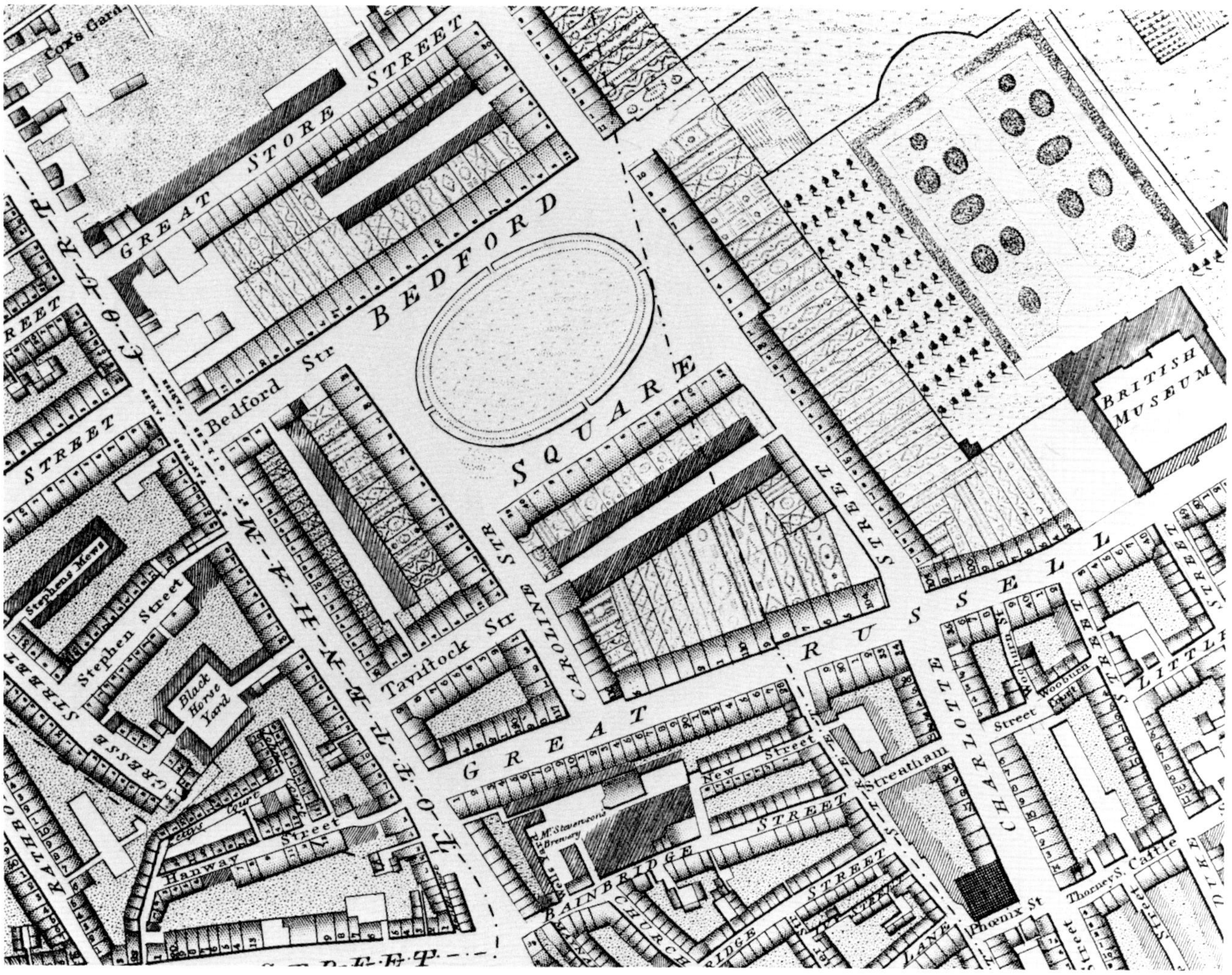

8. Bedford Square, Horwood's Map, 1799.

part of the town is a question that very probably would puzzle the builders themselves to answer.

Not all the landowners were as uncaring. The Bedford Estate had a tradition of being associated with good town planning, at Covent Garden in the 1630s, and with the orderly development of Bloomsbury Square in the 1660s.[10] This was when the Southampton Estate was absorbed into the Bedford Estate by the marriage of Rachel, daughter of and heir to Lord Southampton who died in 1667, and William Russell, second son of the fifth Earl of Bedford. Development on the Southampton Estate had begun in 1616 with the erection of houses in 'brick and stone' and up to the 1770s was confined to the area south of Great Russell Street. The dominant building was Southampton House, built in the late 1650s, which was to form the north side of Bloomsbury Square. The other three sides were made up of houses of different sizes and importance, *ie* not uniform, with alleyways and courtyards behind for the lower classes, but the feel was of a respectable residential area. For Evelyn, a frequent visitor, the new suburb was 'quite a little Towne' and Samuel Pepys on a visit in 1664 proclaimed it a great and noble work.

The great surge of building that Lord Southampton had initiated on his London estate was no sooner started than it was over. Except for the odd rebuilding when leases fell in there was now very little building activity and Great Russell Street was to form the boundary between town and country for over a century.

In the revitalised market for good houses in the 1760s, the fourth Duke of Bedford, great-grandson of William Russell, began seriously to consider resuming development of the Bloomsbury part of the Estate. By the 1750s houses were running up both its flanks in Southampton Row and Tottenham Court Road and in the latter half of that decade the New Road was mooted, approved by the Commons and driven through from Paddington to Islington, passing on its way over the Duke of Grafton's land immediately beyond the top end of the Bedford Estate. The northern limit of the West End in the seventeenth century – the line of Great Russell Street and Oxford Street – was gradually breaking down from the

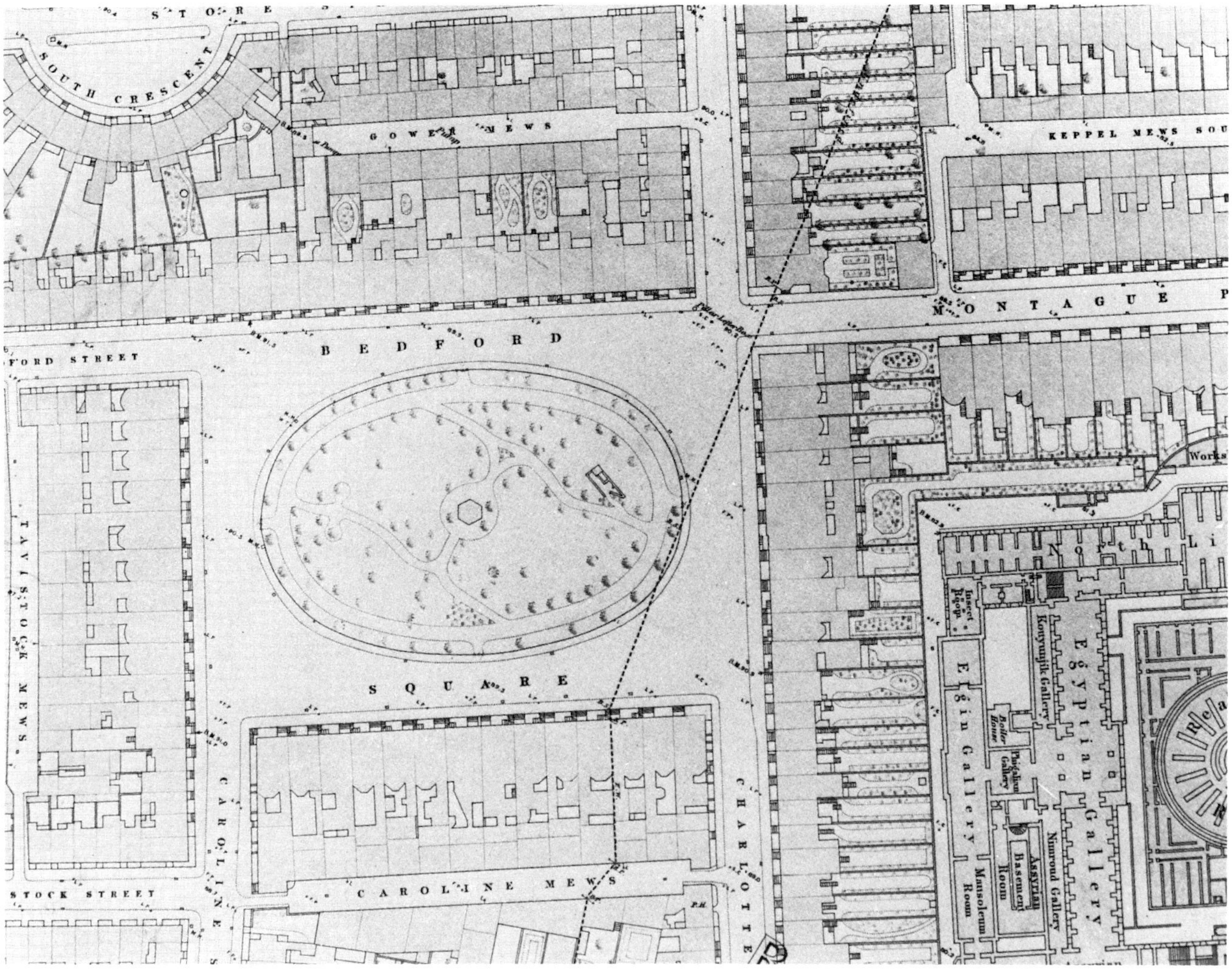

9. Bedford Square, Ordnance Survey Map, 1874.

10. No.51 Bedford Square, shoescraper at entrance. There are several surviving examples in the Square.

west to the east and with the completion of the New Road there was now a new northern boundary acting as a magnet to attract an ever-expanding city. 7, 8

Soon, a new street would emerge from Great Russell Street, a little west of the British Museum, and head north; at the same time another new street would emerge from Tottenham Court Road just south of Store Street and head east. They were never to meet because a new square was to interrupt their march. It was not an unplanned interruption though, because something grand had been envisaged there for several years.

That square – Bedford Square – had its genesis in the early 1760s following the Peace of Paris. The Duke, ever mindful of the building activities in Marylebone where 'the riches which flowed into the country, after the peace ... had excited a rage for building, and houses rose like exhaltations',[11] was toying with ideas of improvement that would further the reputation of the family that had given London Covent Garden and (indirectly through marriage) Bloomsbury Square. Although advancing in years and suffering from the gout, the Duke, ever

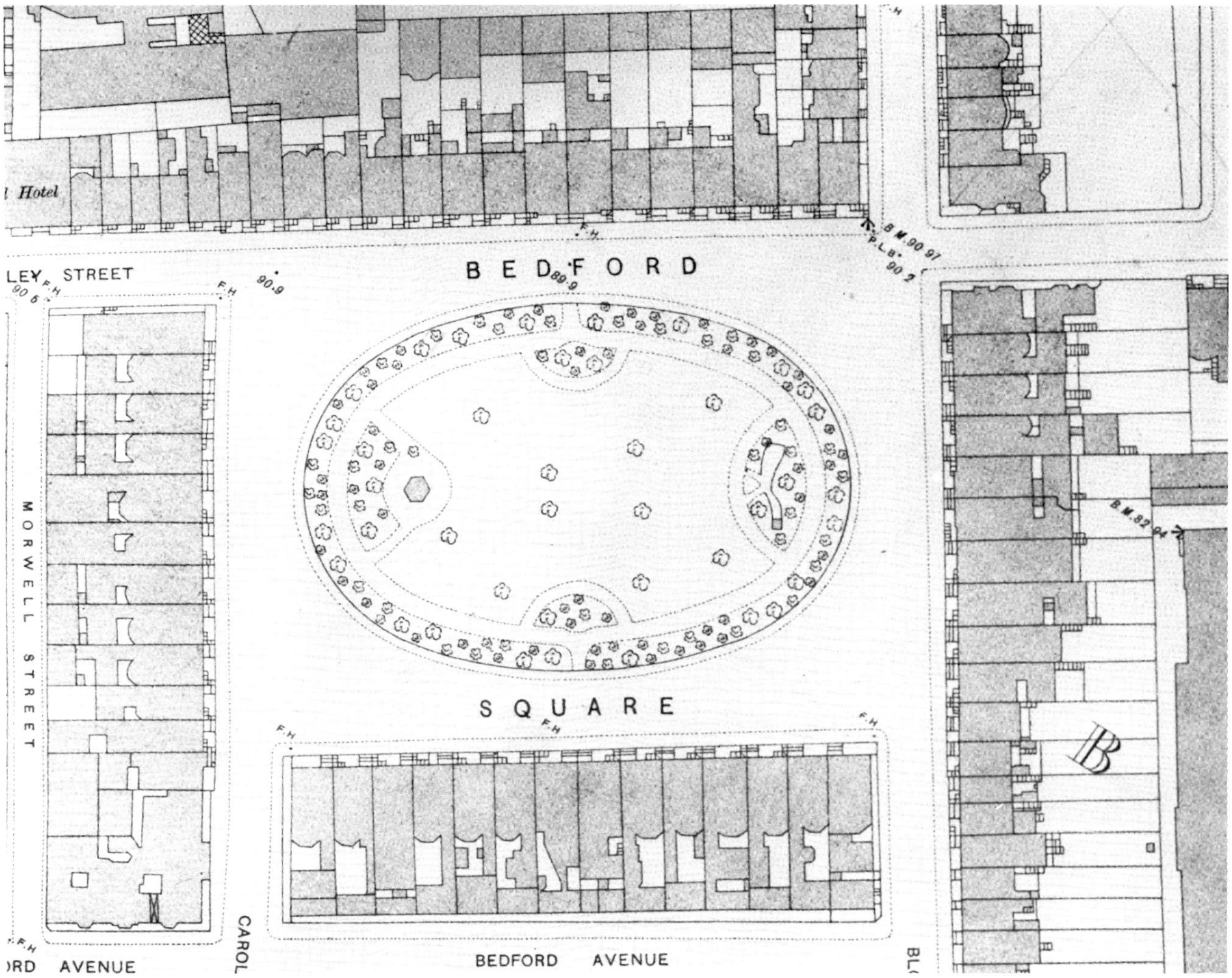

11. Bedford Square, Ordnance Survey Map, 1911.

businesslike, followed the architectural cause with enthusiasm. As a frequent visitor to Bath he always had much to keep abreast of. In particular it was that city's Circus inspired by the Colosseum in Rome, which was in course of building between 1754 and 1766, that caught his eye. So much so that he envisaged a Bedford Circus for Bloomsbury. This remained but an idea on the Duke's death in 1771 at the age of sixty-eight.

The heir was a minor and the Duke, in his will of 1767, had devised the Estate to three trustees until 1789. These three – Gertrude Leveson-Gower, the Duchess of Marlborough, and Robert Palmer, the estate steward – did not allow the initiative to slacken. The circus was built on the Duke's land at Exeter, as two opposing crescents rather than the prototype at Bath. In London, the idea of a circus metamorphosed into a square, with building agreements for it and surrounding streets agreed and signed by the trustees and the builders in 1776.

I

The Builders of Bedford Square

The four sides of Bedford Square, when glimpsed as one approaches Bloomsbury Street from Gower Street or when viewed at just slightly more leisure as one crosses from Montague Place *en route* for the Tottenham Court Road, are seemingly the embodiment of all that is so highly valued in the late twentieth century – an intact, uniform and perfect Georgian square. But it is not what it seems, for Georgian architecture, in spite of its simplicity, reveals its secrets very slowly. It is only after a more lengthy acquaintance that the Square shows itself to be far from perfect, and clumsy in several respects. Not that this should necessarily be regarded as criticism, for it is the imperfections that humanise Bedford Square and make it so endearing.

Appreciation of Bedford Square, an intact, uniform Georgian square, may be great in these days of awareness of the architectural and historic value of buildings and an interest in their conservation, but it is not new. In his lively and illuminating *Critical Review*, James Ralph described Bedford Square as

> ... a proof of the improvement of our taste. It is without exception the most perfect square in town ... the regularity and symmetry of the sides ... the great breadth of the pavements, and the neatness of the iron rails ... render it superior in everything but magnitude to any square in Europe.[12]

Bedford Square was seen by Ralph as an example of how a speculative building operation could be successful. Sir John Soane in his lectures to students at the Royal Academy in the early nineteenth century also spent time analysing what had happened in London during the preceding decades as a result of speculative building, and attempted to distinguish good from bad:

> Grosvenor Square, and the Streets surrounding and leading thereto, were among the first grand essays of the Speculative System of building ... The general appearance of the Houses in Cavendish Square is not inferior to those in Grosvenor Square ... Thus far the new system of building seems to have done no mischief. Portman Square has some Houses that would have done honour to Grosvenor Square, but the general mass of them are of a kind not much superior to those in Bedford Square. Here the Spirit of Speculation begins to show itself more decidedly: the Buildings appear less important and less substantial. The Houses in Portland Place, and in Mansfield Street held out some prospect of a return to a better style of building, and those on the south and east sides of Fitzroy Square, in the Architectural appearance, promised still more; so did those on the West side of Finsbury Square and Chiswell Street. All these appearances, however, quickly faded and our hopes of better Architecture were destroyed by the monotonous Houses forming many of the Streets and Squares, which have been built since that time.[13]

Elsewhere in his lectures, Soane made absolutely clear what he meant by the 'Spirit of Speculation':

> London is now so overgrown and crowded, and the best situations are already so occupied by slight buildings raised on speculation for a term of years, that it has become scarcely possible at any price to obtain ... ground ... sufficient to erect a magnificent mansion for himself and his family ... The leasehold system becomes abominable and fatal to the advancement of Architectural taste.[14]

The system was not only bad, according to Soane, for 'Architecture', it was also bad for the people:

> From short-sighted views of immediate gain many of our streets are miserably narrow and confined, with cramped and crippled houses. Monotony in the exterior elevations and a far too general system of bad construction has been thus made familiar to the student, while the public mind is vitiated, and ultimately becomes reconciled to these miserable productions.

It was the very system of speculative building that Soane felt led to the poor quality of construction by builders eager for early financial profit, who were not sufficiently supervised or made responsible to an 'Architect' with his superior aesthetic sensibility.

Speculative building goes back several centuries and was refined in the seventeenth century with the rebuilding of the City of London after the Great Fire of 1666 and in the eighteenth century with the new developments in the West End. It worked like this: the ground landlord would sign an agreement with a builder or craftsman to build on a particular site. The builder put up the carcass of the house – roofed over and floored, with the windows glazed and the external doors fitted so that the building was weathertight. At this point the builder was granted a lease. The property would revert to the ownership of the landlord when the lease fell in after a certain term. The building leases granted in the 1630s in Covent Garden had been of thirty-one years duration; by the time Bedford Square was being developed the usual term was eighty or ninety-nine years.

Having acquired his building lease, the builder aimed to sell on before ground rent was payable to the landlord. Until such a time, he paid only a token amount or 'peppercorn rent' to enable his capital to be spent on materials and labour for building. The building industry in the eighteenth century consisted of different trades: bricklayers, masons, carpenters, plasterers, etc. The usual procedure was for the master builder, who would be granted the building lease, to carry out his part of the work and subcontract the work in other trades to other craftsmen.

12. Bedford Square, west side.

13 OPPOSITE. Nos.11 to 18 Bedford Square, front elevations.

This system was well established by the mid-eighteenth century; as Isaac Ware writes in his *Complete Body of Architecture* (1756): 'The builders ... work jointly, one doing his share of business in the other's house, according to their several subordinate professions.'[15]

A client would then buy the shell and have it finished to his own taste, spending as much or as little as he wanted. Thus in theory all would be happy: the landowner developed his estate at little cost to himself, ensuring a small amount of income from the ground rent, and an investment for the future in the houses. The builder made a profit from the sale of the carcass, and the client, often but not invariably the first occupant, got a house decorated as he wished.

Such was the intention in speculative development, but then as now the rewards to be gained spurred people into ventures that sometimes turned out to be not so smooth running. Lack of investment often left speculators with huge debts, and shells they were unable to sell: the Adam brothers' inability to let the Adelphi development is a well-known example. Botch-ups were common; speculators cared little for who was building on the next site or estate, and paid scant regard to the alignment of façades or the relating of building height to that of neighbouring houses.

The Bedford Estate was determined to exercise a degree of control over the Bedford Square development by way of clauses in the building agreements, but precisely how this control was maintained during building is still a matter of speculation. Confusion as to the roles and identities of the people involved in the scheme goes back to the 1790s, only a few years after the Square was completed. Thomas Malton wrote in his *Picturesque Tour:*

> In Bedford Square ... we have an example of the beauty resulting from uniform design, carried into execution under individual direction; and an instance of the deformities, which are too frequently occasioned by the shackles of interested speculation. Each of the four sides of this square has a pediment in the centre, supported by pilasters; but on two of the sides the pediments extend over two houses, and have a pilaster in the middle; destroying that appearance of unity which is the characteristic of a pediment. It is scarcely to be imagined that such a fault could be committed, at a time when architecture has been so much studied and improved; yet justice requires it to be told, that the gentleman who made the design, felt this impropriety, and would have removed it; but the builder, who held the ground under the Duke of Bedford, having limited the number of houses, and determined to have a pediment on everyside, could not be prevailed upon to alter his arrangement.[16]

Here Malton poses tantalising questions: who was the

14. Nos.5 and 6 Bloomsbury Square, Henry Flitcroft, about 1745. Typical Palladian houses on the Bedford Estate which influenced the elevation designs of Bedford Square.

15. Southampton Place, east side, Henry Flitcroft, 1759-63. Flitcroft's elevation designs had an influence on those of Bedford Square.

gentleman responsible for the 'uniform design' which was carried out 'under individual direction'? Is it true that the builders, in limiting the number of houses, ignored the correctness of the pedimented centre, and would this explain the solecism of the pilaster under the apex? What was the role of the Bedford Office?

The name of the architect most closely associated with the design of Bedford Square is Thomas Leverton; other suggestions have been the Adam brothers[17] and Sir William Chambers.[18] In order to ascertain the identities of the people involved, we have to consider the development as having two distinct phases. First, there was the laying out of the Square and the building of the houses around it; and second, there came the finishing of those houses. What is certain is that Leverton 'had a principal concern in promoting the finishing of Bedford Square'.[19] This clearly shows Leverton's late involvement, and will be discussed at length, as will his career, in Chapter 6.

The elevations of the four sides of the Square need some analysis. Following the return of Palladian architecture to the capital in the early 1720s, a typical house front emerged: 'three storeys above ground sufficed for Georgian wants, with a further one in the attic, usually with dormers perching over the cornice and set within a roof of double pitch, or more rarely, treated as a fourth full storey flush with the front'.[20]

The plain brick houses in Bedford Square follow the former pattern (*ie* with dormers), and their design could be seen as somewhat conservative. Indeed, with their deep stone or stuccoed first-floor string courses, flat window arches and stone cornices, and the proportioning of their windows, they bear a striking resemblance to certain Palladian houses of the 1720s and 1730s, and in particular to those of Henry Flitcroft at Sackville Street (No.36) and St James's Square (Nos.9 and 10) of the early 1730s (though all three have probably had attic storeys added since), and, more pertinent to us, to his houses in Bloomsbury for the Duke of Bedford. 20, 24

On the south-west corner of Bloomsbury Square, for example, there are two houses by Flitcroft with a deep stone band at first-floor level and a block cornice with blocking course above doing its best to shield the dormered mansard from view. They date from the middle of the 1740s. Just across the way, many houses survive in Southampton Place, one of the most gracious survivors of mid-Georgian London and sadly one of its least-researched streets. Set at a very slight and intriguing cant to Bloomsbury Square, Southampton Place was originally 14 15 developed in the latter half of the seventeenth century as the southern approach from High Holborn to the square. It was redeveloped between 1759 and 1763 when 62- and 79-year leases were granted by the Bedford Estate. These houses are almost certainly by Flitcroft. A receipted invoice of July 1764[21] from him to the Duke for services at Woburn and Bloomsbury between 1755 and 1758 includes an item in 1758 for 'Viewing the Ground in Bloomsbury which was to be rebuilt, and making a General Plan for the same, and some particular Designs of Houses for part of the said Ground'. These houses in Southampton Place are very similar to the two in Bloomsbury Square but have a more pronounced vertical emphasis because they are taller and were built on narrower plots.

20, 24 The plain brick houses of Bedford Square show great similarities to those in Southampton Place: the same disposition of windows in relation to string course and cornice; flat arched ground-floor windows; dormered mansard (which would have been a full attic storey as at the Adelphi or Mansfield Street if Bedford Square had been more up to date). Just three changes were made. The heavy Palladian doorcases had to be dispensed with: the substitutes were off-the-shelf 'units' from the Coade arti-
51, 52 ficial stone manufactory at Lambeth. The Roman block cornice also had to go and was exchanged for a pleasing
16 dentil type. And lastly, the spacing of the windows is greater in the Square quite simply because the plots granted to the builders were wider than those available in Southampton Place.

There is little or no genius in the design of the plain brick houses in Bedford Square. They are plagiarised from designs that were first seen about forty or fifty years before, and their main ornament – the door surrounds – was collected from a manufacturer's catalogue. However, there are also the centre houses, and these show a little more inspiration in some respects together with the most astonishing details.

All the centre houses were stuccoed, probably with
18 'Adam's New Invented Patent Stucco' as it became known when the brothers acquired the patent for the facing material from Liardet, a Swiss clergyman, in the early 1770s (see p.68). On each of the long north and south sides there are two centre houses (Nos.18 and 19, Nos.46
19 and 47 respectively) and on the east and west sides just one (Nos.6 and 32 respectively). The centre house on the
43 west side is the most interesting of the six because of its clear affinity to Robert Adam's Royal Society of Arts building in John Adam Street, 1772-4. The two buildings share Ionic capitals and the wide spacing of the centre pilasters (attached three-quarter-columns at the Royal Society of Arts), the guilloche band beneath the second-floor windows, the paterae ornament in the frieze, the dentilled cornice and the swagged ornament in the

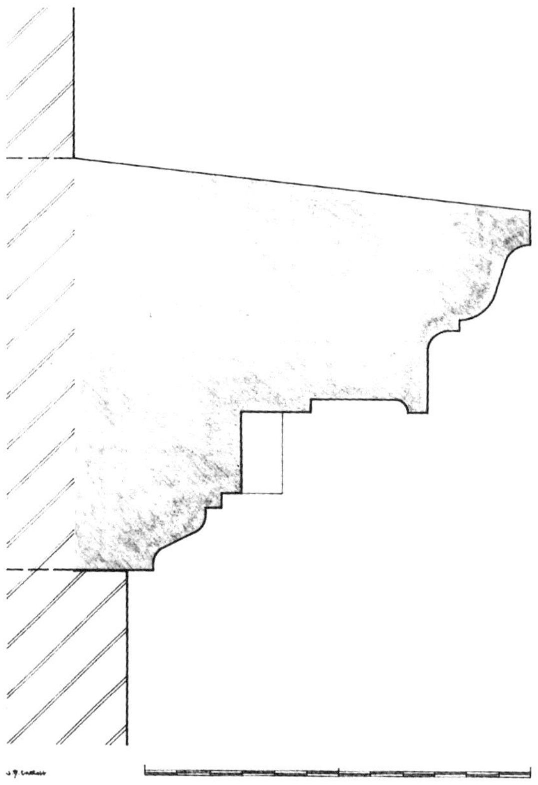

16. No.24 Bedford Square, section through main cornice.

tympanum of the pediment. In spite of the affinity, No.32 Bedford Square lacks the sophistication of the earlier building. The wide space between the centre pilasters is allocated a standard window whereas the Society's building is given a magnificent Venetian window above the tripartite entrance; the entrance at the house in the Square is set to one side because the standard London house plan was adopted, with the staircase placed against the party wall beyond the entrance hallway. Nonetheless, No.32 Bedford
Square is a particularly fine house with excellent interior 110-
details. The centre house on the east side is the largest 118
in the Square, five bays wide compared to the standard three. The entrance is in the centre, typical for such houses of the period. There is nothing out of the ordinary in the case of the four Ionic pilasters, evenly spaced over a rusticated ground floor.

The centre pair on the north and south sides are those 42
referred to by Malton above (see p.20) with their centre 19
pilasters. To the late twentieth-century eye these do not appear too bad, but at the time, as Malton asserts, it was 'scarcely to be imagined that such a fault could be committed'. The centre pilasters, I suggest, were a mistake, probably caused by a lack of anticipation. The result of achieving a true symmetry in a block of an even number of three-bay houses is a pediment whose apex occurs at the party-wall line of the centre two houses and therefore over a solid rather than a void (window). The fault could have been rectified, even at a late stage, by adding a sixth pilaster and shifting the pediment half a bay in the direc-

17. No.31 Bedford Square, front elevation.

18. No.32 Bedford Square, Ionic capital and pediment detail. It seems likely that the Ionic capitals were cast in stucco rather than being made of artificial stone.

19 OPPOSITE. No.47 Bedford Square, front elevation.

tion of that pilaster, thus allowing the apex to sit above the window line between the central pilasters. True, this would have upset an *exact* symmetry, but a shift of just half a bay in a block forty-two bays long would have been undetectable to the human eye.

The picture painted thus far of the external architecture of the Square is perhaps a little harsh, but it has been necessary to show that it is not the work of a major architect and that the façades, as Summerson pointed out, 'may be said to have been "collated" as well as designed'.[22] If the plain brick houses are based on a design some forty or fifty years old, and the overall scheme lacks the skilful handling of the Adelphi or Stratford Place, there are compensations. The use of stucco for the centre houses – in spite of the solecism of the centre pilasters – was a very early example of the renewed take up of the material and was contemporary with its employment by James Adam
6 for the centre houses of the blocks at Portland Place.[23]
The sum of the far-from-perfect parts that make up the four blocks works surprisingly well. The plain brick houses are better than their 'predecessors' in Southampton Place because they have the advantage of greater width, gaining a far better proportion along the way. The centre and end houses are pushed forward for emphasis in true Palladian tradition and the end houses
are topped with excellent balustraded parapets, as at the 20
Royal Terrace, Adelphi.

The external architecture of Bedford Square is, I believe, the work of a lower or middling surveyor or a competent master-builder. The myth can finally be laid to rest that Thomas Leverton was involved in its design. It is quite simply not good enough to be attributed to him. Leverton was a very able late eighteenth-century architect, as will be seen when the doors are opened to beckon us inside certain houses with which he was involved, and where we can analyse his work in more detail.

To support my conclusion that Leverton was not involved in the external design of the Square, I offer the following: Leverton was an unflagging exhibitor at the Royal Academy in the 1770s and 1780s. One of his two designs shown in 1778 was almost certainly for the individual house in the Square (No.1) and yet there are none 60,
for any of the four blocks. It is reasonable to assume that 61
if he had been responsible for what was obviously going to be an important addition to domestic architecture, with almost certain spin-offs for similar commissions, then he would have sent that design along to the Academy.

Let us return for a moment to Thomas Malton and his *Picturesque Tour*. Malton's meticulous plates are matched by his ability to guide us around London with

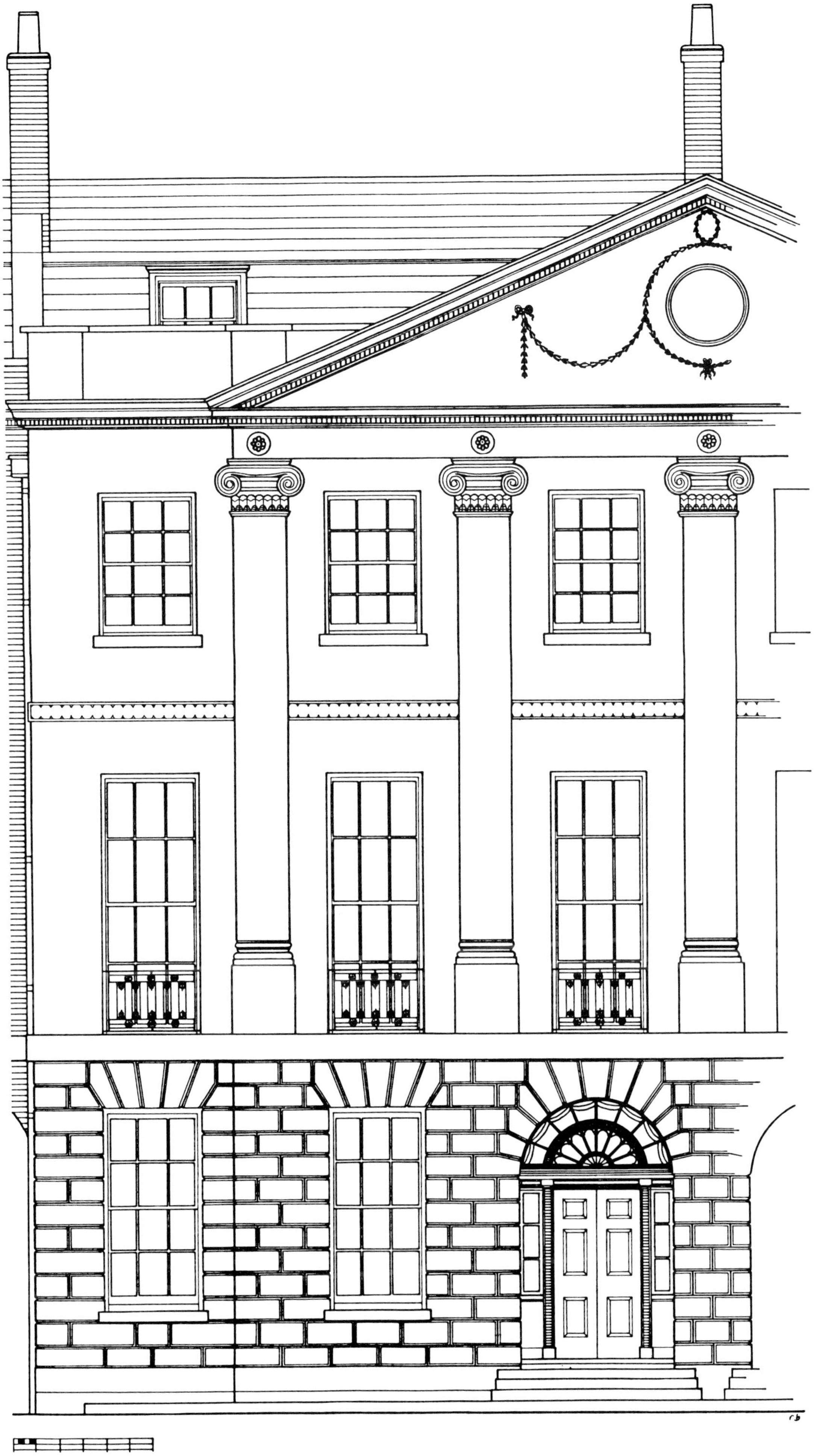

20. No.53 Bedford Square, front elevation.

an uncommonly accurate and perceptive text. We pass the new Engine House of the Phoenix Fire Office and learn that it is by Leverton.[24] We then arrive at Bedford Square and are told only that a 'gentleman made the design'. If it was Leverton, this would have been common knowledge in the London building world and Malton would have undoubtedly recorded the fact.

There are four candidates left for designer of the façades of Bedford Square: there is Robert Palmer, surveyor; there are its main builders, William Scott and Robert Grews; and there is also John Mecluer, an architect. Robert Palmer, unrelated to the Duke's steward, was a surveyor about whom we know very little. He was based in Orchard Street, Westminster, just across from the Abbey and Dean's Yard. In 1772 he was employed by the local justices to survey James Adam's Shire Hall at Hertford. On 13 January of that year he was able to report that 'On a Survey made this day of the New Shire House do find that Mr. Adam hath effectually made good the complaints and defects in the said building, and that the said works are now done in a good substantial workmanlike manner'.[25] In 1774-6 he supervised the building of a new County Gaol in the same town. Far more important was his employment by the Bedford Estate for various surveying duties in the 1760s and 1770s. There survives a letter dated 25 July 1769 from him to Palmer, the steward, regarding the proposed demolition works at Stratton Park, the Duke's house in Hampshire, together with some business in the New Forest. He carried out surveying and design work for the Crescent/Circus at Exeter. There are records of payments to him for his journey to Exeter, for surveying the old buildings at Bedford House and making plans for new buildings and estimates, and also a letter from a builder regarding drainage and pavement works and enlarging the approaches to the Crescent: 'I hope soon to receive from you or Mr. Palmer your Surveyor a sketch of the intended alteration'.[26]

Palmer died in September 1776, just two months before the first leases were granted in Bedford Square, those for the entire west side. There is no conclusive evidence that he designed the elevations but he was mentioned in the building agreement for the west side in connection with the central gardens:

> ... and the Inside thereof the said Square to be first made and inclosed with Iron Rails at the Expence of the said Duchess of Bedford Duchess of Marlborough and Robert Palmer and the pavement on the outside of the said Iron Rails to be compleated at their Expence from the End of Sixty feet to be measured from the fronts of the houses on each side of the Square but the said William Scott and Robert Grews are to do the work under the Direction of Mr. Robert Palmer Surveyor who it is hereby agreed shall settle the Bills for the same and the amount thereof to be paid to the said William Scott and Robert Grews.

Palmer probably never rose above the rank of jobbing surveyor, but that would by no means have precluded him from designing the Square. He would have been only too aware of the latest architecture in the capital and had also surveyed the Adam building at Hertford. And as the elevations of Bedford Square are a gathering of details from elsewhere, he is just the sort of person within the building world one would expect to be responsible for the design.

If Palmer was not the designer, then we must consider the other candidates. First of all, the two builders. Robert Grews was a carpenter living in the parish of St Marylebone during most of the development of Bedford Square but towards the end, as noted on the lease for No.46 dated 20 May 1782, was described as late of that parish and 'now of the parish of St Giles in the Fields'. His address was Store Street, and this was probably one of the eight houses there for which he was granted leases by the Bedford Estate in the early 1780s. William Scott was a brickmaker, a partner in a long-established family business based in Fulham. In the late 1760s he had lent money to a builder called John Spencer. Spencer was later declared bankrupt and his estate was assigned to Scott and Thomas Bond, a Lambeth timber merchant. Along with three other speculators, Scott and Bond laid out houses in Grosvenor Place which they leased to Issac Eeles of Lambeth in 1772.[27] Scott was also involved in speculating on land on the Chelsea Road that ran south-west from Buckingham Gate.

It is not known how Scott and Grews met but it seems they did work together in Marylebone. On the Bedford Estate they signed building agreements for all the houses in Bedford Square and many of the surrounding streets. Grews took leases in Bloomsbury Street, Store Street, Chenies Mews and Gower Street. Scott took leases in Bloomsbury Street, Bayley Street, Caroline Mews, Store Street and Gower Street. And they were joint lessees in Tavistock Street, Caroline Street and Bayley Street.[28] Several of these houses survive. They must have struck up a solid working relationship in order to have tackled such a large scheme. Scott died in 1786 and directed in his will that all his 'leasehold freehold and other Estates' were to be valued by Robert Grews.[29] He also left money to one, William Grews.[30]

As successful builders Scott and Grews would have been quite capable of coming up with the designs for Bedford Square. This is exactly what Grews stated in his letter of 1784 to Robert Palmer, the Duke's agent: '... in the year 1776 I, in conjunction with Mr William Scott, engaged to build the West and North sides of Bedford Square, and formed and prepared Plans and Elevations of the whole Square'.[31] Thomas Malton, however, disputed this. Writing in 1792, he distinguished between 'the gentleman who made the design' and the 'builder'.[32]

The last candidate for the elevation designs of the Square is very much a long shot. He is John Mecluer, an architect who was granted the lease of No.6 on 20 Novem-

21. Nos.47 to 53 and 1 to 6 Bedford Square, front elevations.

ber 1778. Other than his association with Bedford Square, only one thing is known of Mecluer. Under the 1774 Building Act he was appointed District Surveyor of four parishes in and around the Strand and Covent Garden.[33] It might of course be that Mecluer was merely speculating, but was it mere coincidence that he was granted a lease on the biggest house in the Square, one that took up two full plots? It was, after all, typical for those who took part in a large building scheme to be paid by way of a lease from the principal undertakers; thus the lease of No.50 was granted to Philip Woodham, a sawyer from Marylebone. Perhaps Scott and Grews used Mecluer to carry out plans and elevations for the development and paid him with the lease of No.6.

The mystery remains. We have looked at various options concerning the authorship of the Square; unfortunately, research has so far failed to provide the definitive answer.

2

The Building of Bedford Square

1. Leases and agreements

One of the most disappointing features of Bedford Square is the way in which the main blocks run on into adjacent
22 streets on three sides with houses that present a meagre quality of design. They come a long way down in the
23 speculative league, lacking a good proportion and possessing a height that clashes with the handsome balustraded end houses that they abut. There is something unhealthily parasitic about the way they cling to their larger and illustrious neighbours and one wonders why and how they were allowed to be built in such a way. Only the south side escapes as it stands self-contained between two
25 parallel streets.

What is worse, some of these houses are within the bounds of the Square. If the eye is trained directly along the face of the west side, looking north, there are three such houses; along the face of the south side, looking west, there are also three and along the same side, looking east, there are two. One of these (No.1) is, of course, not
59 a disappointment, but as we shall see later (see p.76) this house would have been just like its southern neighbour in Bloomsbury Street had it not been for a particularly enlightened patron of the arts.

The whole problem goes back to the conception of the Square and the building agreements that governed its construction. The Square was just part of a larger scheme that took in the surrounding area. For some reason it was
8 decided that five streets would enter the Square instead of a grid of eight which would have given four self-contained blocks and far more unity. Few London squares had managed this before the 1770s; there was a tendency for streets to enter at the centre of each side as at Covent Garden, St James's Square and Soho Square, but Grosvenor and Portman Squares did achieve the grid of eight.

The problem with Bedford Square may have been due to the fact that in two spots very close by there were plots of land not available to the Duke where it may have proved difficult to negotiate the extension of streets. On
3 the north side was land belonging to the City of London, where Alfred Place and its terminating crescents were laid out some thirty years after the Square (the shortening of the plots for Nos.24 and 25 to 73 feet from the 121 feet of No.23 was caused by this division of ownership, and this is why Gower Mews finishes at the rear of No.23).
2 And behind the east side were the gardens of the British Museum, granted on a long lease by the Duke of Bedford to the trustees. In addition, behind the west side, houses were already built on Tottenham Court Road, and so 4
Tavistock Street was forced south to where an opening onto the main road was available.

The four building agreements[34] or contracts – one for each side – were signed in 1776 between the Duchess of Bedford, the Duchess of Marlborough and Robert Palmer, the devisees in trust to the late Duke of Bedford, on the one part and William Scott and Robert Grews, the builders, on the other. The agreements for the north and west sides were dated 18 January 1776, and those for the south and east sides were dated 6 July 1776. According to a letter Grews wrote to Robert Palmer in 1784, Scott and himself subsequently took on the south and east sides because 'the Business might have been impeded, or the Plan deviated from had more persons been concerned'.[35] Allowing for those details that relate exclusively to any particular side, the agreements were roughly similar in format and content.

For the east side, Scott and Grews were to build on 'all that piece or parcel of Ground situate partly on the East side of a new Square intended to be made and to be called Bedford Square partly on the East side of a new Street intended to be made from Great Russell Street northwards and to be called Charlotte Street [Bloomsbury Street] and partly on the north side of Great Russell Street ... and partly upon Ground (intended to be inclosed for a Stable Yard thirty feet wide) now let to Mary Baker ... abutting upon a Street or opening intended to be made in the same Direction and width as Bedford Street [Bayley Street] ... upon part of which said piece of Ground four houses now stand fronting Great Russell Street in the occupation of Margaret Snell Mrs Van Hoeck Mary Wynne and Elizabeth Blake'. In addition to these four, two further houses had to be demolished to open up Charlotte Street. These were occupied by George Foyle and Mary Jurin who both took up occupation in the earliest houses to be completed in the Square, perhaps as part of a compensation deal struck up between the parties.[36] Grews and Scott were to be allowed the building materials from these six houses.

The agreement for the south side dealt only with the self-contained block, a rectangular plot 397 feet wide by 130 feet deep 'in the parishes of Saint Giles in the Fields and Saint George Bloomsbury in the said County of Middlesex abutting East on a new street intended to be made and to be called Charlotte Street West on another new Street intended to be made and to be called Caroline Street and South on an intended Stable Yard ...'.

22. Nos.36 and 37 Bedford Square, front elevations, showing the difference in scale between houses inside and outside the palace-fronted blocks.

23. No.37 Bedford Square, front elevation.

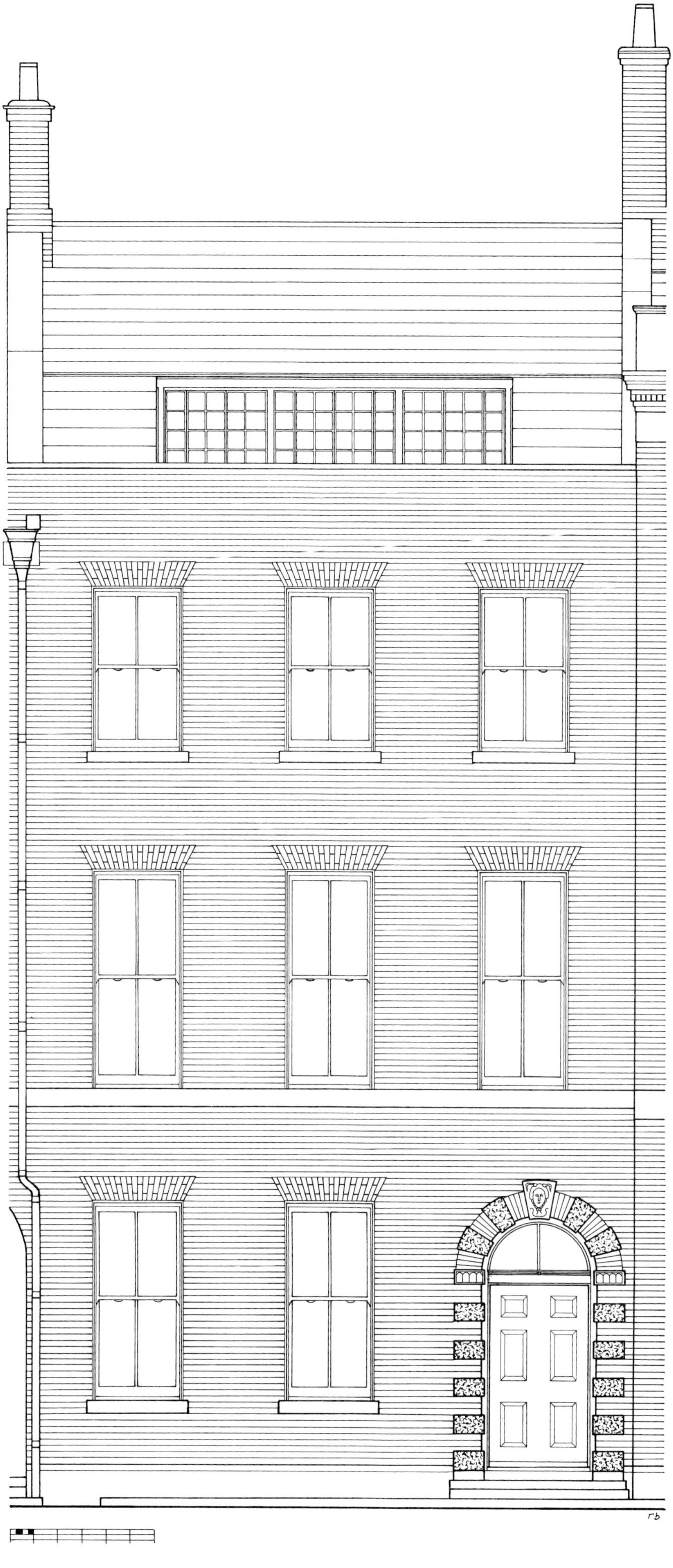

24. No. 30 Bedford Square, front elevation.

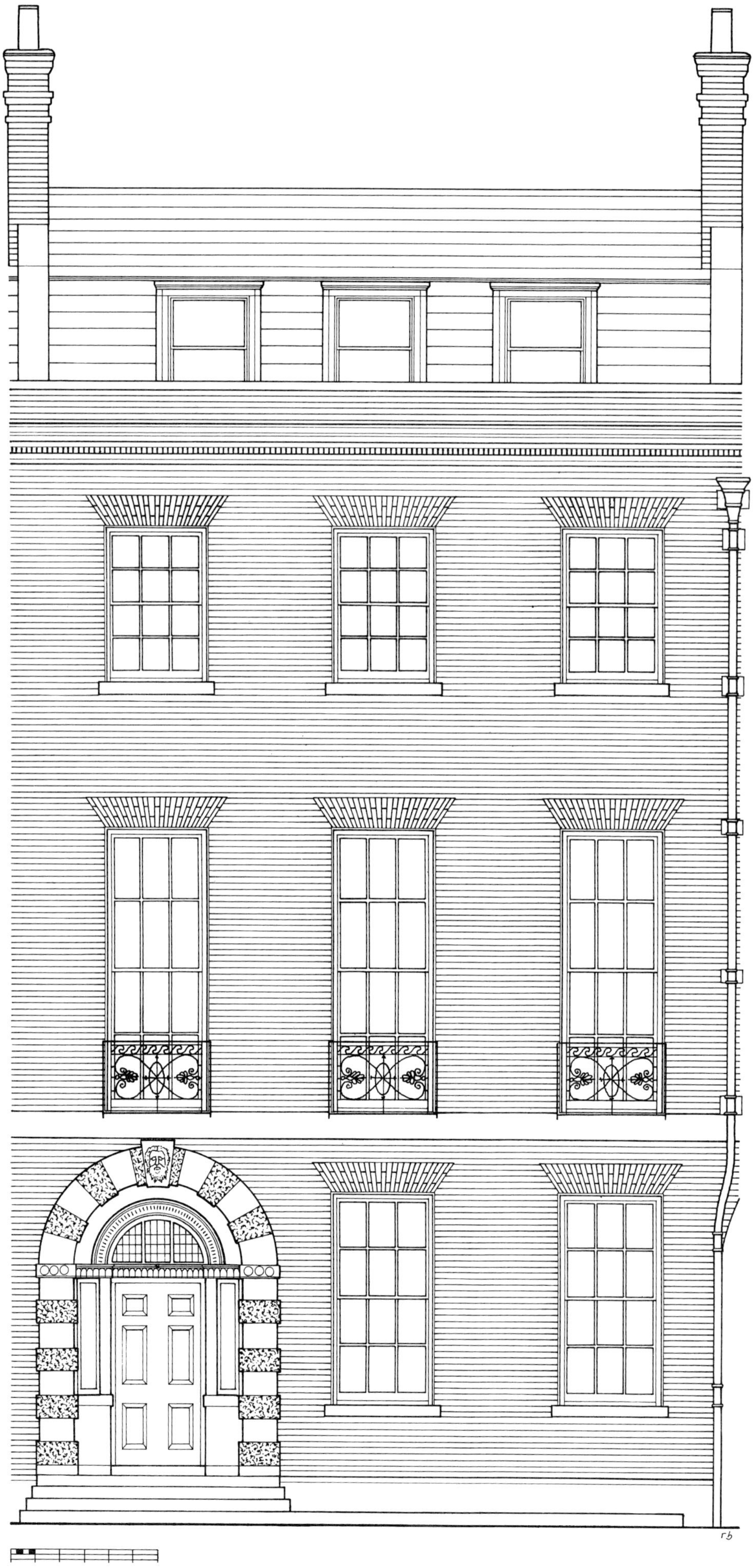

25. Bedford Square, south side.

The agreement for the west side comprised the complete block bounded by Bedford Street to the north, Tottenham Court Road, Tavistock Street and Caroline Street and Bedford Square, excepting a long strip in Tottenham Court Road some 70 feet deep where houses were already finished. The agreement for the north side took in the complete block bounded by Gower Street (in the plan drawn on the agreement it is referred to as Charlotte Street, though it was not long before it took up the name it retains today), Store Street, Tottenham Court Road and Bedford Street and Bedford Square, excepting that portion in the north-west corner belonging to the Corporation of the City of London. The only house
26 missing from the four agreements was No.11, on the junc-
83 tion of Gower Street and Montague Street. An agreement here was signed on 6 March 1781 between the devisees in trust and Scott and Grews.

Looking first at the agreement for the north side, we see that it is headed 'Articles of Agreement made indented concluded and fully agreed upon this eighteenth day of January in the year of our Lord One thousand seven hundred and seventy six Between The Most Noble Gertrude Duchess of Bedford The Most Noble Caroline Duchess of Marlborough and Robert Palmer of the parish of Saint George Bloomsbury in the County of Middlesex Esquire Devisees in Trust of the real Estate of the late Most Noble John Duke of Bedford deceased of the one part and William Scott of Grosvenor Place in the Parish of Saint George Hanover Square in the said County of Middlesex Brickmaker and Robert Grews of Westmoreland Street in the Parish of Saint Mary le Bone in the said County of Middlesex Carpenter of the other part'.

All four agreements tell us that the building plots they contain were 'late on lease to Robert Bramley'. He was presumably farming the fields, since Rowland Dobie, writing in 1829, tells us that 'as the buildings progressed, Bedford Square arose, from a cow yard, to its present magnificent form'.[37] One exception was parts of the rear of the plots where Nos.1 to 6 were built; these were the kitchen gardens let to the trustees of the British Museum.

On completion of the houses Scott and Grews (or whoever they might nominate) were to be granted 99-year indentures of leases from the feast of St Michael the Archangel prior to the date of the agreement (*ie* 29 September 1775). The houses were to be built within five years of that date, such period to be covered by a peppercorn rent. For the remainder of the term the yearly rents for the north side were to amount all together to 'One hundred and sixty eight pounds of lawful money of Great Britain'.

There followed a convenant for the fronts of the houses to remain in a line and without any projections so as to conform with the 1774 Building Act, and for 'the Premises

26. No.11 Bedford Square, elevation, looking north into Gower Street.

with the appurtenances and all the brick walls and fences pavements sewers and drains belonging to the same' to be kept in good repair. At the end of the term the lessee was 'to surrender and yield up the same premises with the Doors Wainscotts Locks Keys Bolts Bars Staples Hinges Hearths Marble and other Chimney Pieces Mantle Pieces and Chimney Jambs Foot Pieces and Slabs Covings Glazed Windows and Sashed Windows Window Sashes and Window Shutters Partitions Pumps Pipes Posts Pails Rails Bailes Racks and Hangers' plus other items fixed or fastened during the term. The lessee was also to pay a reasonable share both for 'Making Supporting Repairing and Amending Party Walls Party Gutters Common Sewers Public Sewers and Drains' belonging to the premises and for 'maintaining supporting repairing lighting cleansing paving and keeping in good order and condition the said Square intended to be called Bedford Square and the Iron Rails thereof and the inside thereof'.

The Bedford Estate was to survey the houses for defects twice a year; any such found were to be repaired within three months of notification to the lessee in writing. This was of course to apply after the houses had been finished. More frequent surveys would probably have been made during construction.

The clauses contained in the agreements were typical of the period. The Bedford Estate, however, was particularly concerned to promote and maintain an enviable reputation, both social and environmental, in the development of the Bloomsbury land. A covenant was therefore inserted for the lessee not to cause anything to be done 'in or upon the said premises or any part thereof which may be or grow to the Annoyance Grievance Damage or Disturbance of the said Duchess of Bedford Duchess of Marlborough and Robert Palmer ... or their heirs or any of their other Tenants in the said Parish of Saint Giles in the Fields'. In addition there was a clause for 'Re-entry in Case of Nonpayment of the Rent or if any person or persons who dwell in any houses fronting the square who shall therein use or follow any trade or business whatsoever without a licence first obtained from the Estate'. Thus the Bedford Estate could exercise control on the 'character' of the area.

The agreement also dealt with the constructional details of the houses. Scott and Grews were to build one uniform row of houses to front south on the Square 'agreeable to an elevation for the same signed by the said Robert Palmer William Scott and Robert Grews and deposited in the Stewards Office at Bedford House'. The houses were to be built 'the Cellar Stories Ten feet high The Ground floors Twelve feet Six Inches high The One pair of Stairs floors Fourteen feet Six Inches high The Two pair of Stairs floors Ten feet high and the Garrett floors Seven feet Two Inches high all in the Clear'. These are typical dimensions for good First Rate houses of the period but not as generous, for example, as the houses in Stratford Place (1773-4) where the floor-to-ceiling height on the first floor is fifteen feet four inches.[38] The more modest houses on the remainder of the ground (*ie* not fronting the Square) were also to be uniform, with the following floor-to-ceiling heights – cellar nine feet, ground floor ten feet, first floor ten feet six inches, second floor eight feet six inches and the garret seven feet.

The agreement went on to define the materials to be used. All houses were to be built with 'hard Place Bricks faced with good Grey Stocks of Uniform Colour The Walls of all the said houses to be flushed solid with good Mortar and to be carried up and continue in every respect agreeable to the Act of Parliament lately passed for Building houses in the Cities of London and Westminster All the windows of every Story of the houses fronting the intended Square And also of every Story of the houses fronting Bedford Street and Tottenham Court Road to be continued and remain during the continuance of the said term of Ninetey nine Years agreed to be demised in a line with each other but liberty to be given to cut down any of the windows of the houses in the Square or Bedford Street so low as the floors of the Rooms in the said houses if the same should be required by the Owner thereof'.

This last clause is an unusual one. Although the builder/owner was at liberty to cut down any of the windows, the target here was really the first floor where the design would probably have shown these windows several courses above the deep string course – an arrangement that only a minority of the houses in the Square exhibit today. The freedom to cut down to floor level meant a window rising from the string course that roughly defined the internal level of the first floor. We tend to think of lowered first-floor windows as being a later alteration to early and mid-Georgian houses, a result of the *piano nobile* becoming more and more pronounced, reaching a peak in the early years of the nineteenth century. Quite how many houses were built from the outset with the first-floor windows rising from the string course and how many were subsequently cut down it is impossible to say. What is likely is that the clause was anticipating the insertion of balconies at this level, following the lead set by the Adam brothers at the Adelphi, where all the first-floor windows of the Royal Terrace were designed to be formed 5
from the string course with the insertion of balconies. Of the 46 houses contained in the four palace-fronted blocks at Bedford Square, 33 have windows cut down to the string course, and all but one of these have balconies, 27
many of which are Victorian or later.[39]

Garret windows (dormers) were to be inserted in the roof, and the parapet wall that would attempt to conceal as much of it as possible was to be of the same height in each of the four blocks and coped with Portland stone. The window cills to the front were also to be in Portland stone, though no mention was made of those at the rear. Before all those houses fronting the Square, the areas were to be seven feet six inches 'in the clear' (reduced to five feet in front of the others) and fenced with iron railings set into a Portland kerb. Houses in the Square were to be roofed with slate, with a choice of plain tile or slates elsewhere. The roof gutters were to be in lead not less than (a very heavy) seven pounds to the square foot with lead rainwater pipes 'as low as the upper part of the 28
parlour storys to convey the water into the drains'. The best Memel or Riga timber was to be used in the principal timbers, and the floors laid with good yellow seasoned deals free from sap.

In front of the houses a footway was to be formed, paved with Yorkshire paving stone, to a width of nine feet six inches which would include the area kerb. Beyond, the carriageway was to be paved to the extent of sixty feet from the fronts of the houses. There was also a requirement for the west side of Charlotte Street and the north side of Bedford Street to have footways six-feet

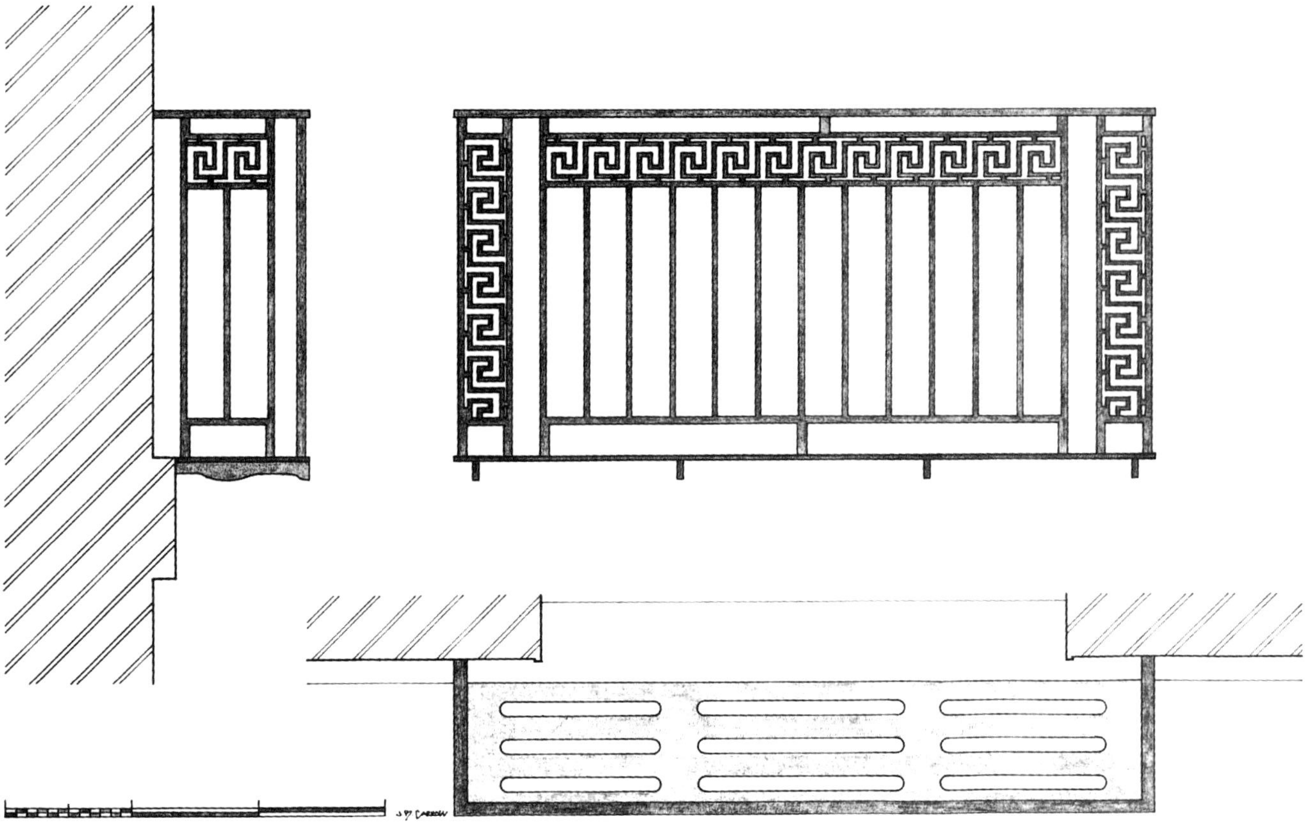

27. No.40 Bedford Square, balcony, elevation, plan and side elevation.

wide with their carriageways paved to the middle of those streets. A 'proper Common Sewer' was to be laid under Bedford Street and the north side of the Square. Finally, there was a requirement for 'good and substantial Coach-houses and Stables with proper Offices behind the said Houses to be Erected on the North Side of the Square'. The agreement allowed for any disputes arising during the building works to be settled by a surveyor who would be appointed by the Estate – another indication of the strength of control exerted by the Bedford Office.

There is a strange amendment to the agreement for the east side. It reads 'be it remembered that the within named William Scott and Robert Grews have requested that the Leases of the Houses to be erected on the within mentioned piece of Ground marked with the Letter A should commence at Michaelmas One thousand seven hundred and seventy five and be for the first five years at a peppercorn Rent instead of Commencing at Michaelmas One thousand seven hundred and seventy six and the first four years at a pepper corn rent as expressed in the within written Contract'. It is dated 19 November 1777. The only clue that might explain this bizarre amendment is that it was made the day before the first leases were granted on the east side, for five of the houses. I cannot, however, explain it at all.

Having signed the building agreements, Scott and Grews had entered into a contract to build Bedford Square. When the shell of each house was completed they were granted a lease which they could mortgage, sell on or assign to a fellow builder as payment for his part in the development.

The leases for the houses in Bedford Square were granted over a period of six and a half years with the first ones coming late in 1776. They differ little one from another. The following is an abstract of the lease for No.7: 'A new Messuage or Tenement on the East side of Bedford Square being the 4th Southward from the opening opposite Bedford Street'. It was granted on 20 November 1777, running for 99 years from Michaelmas 1775, with the first five years at a peppercorn and a ground rent set at an astonishingly low £2 per annum. The average rent was nearer ten times that amount.

The three trustees of the Duke of Bedford granted the lease of No.7 to William Grindall 'in consideration of the great Expense and charges which the said William Grindall hath already been at in erecting a Messuage or Tenement on the piece of Ground hereinafter demised And of the further Expense and charges he will be at finishing the same as hereinafter mentioned (which said Messuage or Tenement is built upon part of a piece of Ground contracted for by the said William Scott and Robert Grews by Articles of Agreement bearing date the sixth day of July One thousand seven hundred and seventy six ...) ... (at the request and by the direction of the said William Scott and Robert Grews testified by their being parties to and executing these presents) ... Do demise lease sett and to farm lett unto the said William Grindall and his Executors Administrators and Assigns

28. No.10 Bedford Square, rainwater hopper and cornice, side elevation. The rainwater hopper and downpipes are in lead.

All that piece or parcel of Ground with the Messuage or Tenement thereon erected and built ... Together with all Rooms Chambers Cellars Sollars Vaults Areas Yards Gardens Lights Ways Paths Passages Easements Drains Watercourses Sewers Profits Commodities and Advantages whatsoever to the said Messuage or Tenement ...'.

The dimensions and descriptions were contained on a plan of the ground plot located in the margin. To the nearest foot the plot measured 29 feet wide by 133 feet deep, and the house itself is 49 feet deep with a bow to part of the rear elevation projecting further. The owners of the two neighbouring plots (south, Scott and Grews, north, Stephen Mear and Thomas Dalston) are also given.

After allowing for five years 'grace' by way of peppercorn rent, the ground rent was to be paid 'yearly and every year during so many years of the remaining ninety four years ... at the Steward's Office near Bedford House on the North side of Bloomsbury Square in the said County of Middlesex the yearly Rent or Sum of Two Pounds ... at or upon the four most usual Feasts or Days of payment of Rent in the Year that is to say the Feasts of the Birth of our Lord Christ the Annunciation of the Blessed Virgin Mary The Nativity of Saint John the Baptist and Saint Michael the Archangel by four even and equal portions'.

The lease, granted after a certain stage in the development of the plot, went on to deal with the method of finishing both the house and the mews and the land in front of the house towards the Square: '... and that he the said William Grindall his Executors Administrators and Assigns or some or one of them shall and will at his their or some or one of their own proper Costs and Charges within two years from the Date hereof compleat and finish the said Messuage or Tenement hereby demised in a good substantial and workmanlike manner and ... within the said Spare of two years from the Date hereof erect and build good and substantial Coach houses and Stables behind the said House The Top of the Roof of the said Coach houses and Stables not to exceed the Height of Thirty feet from the Surface of the intended Mews and the said Roof to be slated And also shall and will pave the whole of the said Mews before the front of the said Coach houses and Stables and inclose the said Mews (which is to be the breadth of thirty feet) with a Brickwall of nine feet in height to divide the same from the adjoining Ground'. As it turns out, the coach house and stables for this house were built and then almost immediately demolished on the order of the Bedford Office (see p.41).

The lease repeated the requirements for forming and finishing the land in front of the house included in the building agreement, that is the area, the pavement and the carriageway, but went into more detail. The builders were to: '... make an Area of Seven feet six Inches wide in the clear before the front of the said House and inclose the said Area with Portland Kirb and Iron Rails and also shall and will make a footway Nine feet six Inches wide (including the Kirb of the Area) before the said House and pave the said footway with Yorkshire paving and also shall and will pave the Carriage Way in the said Square to the extent of Sixty feet from the front of the said House with Scotch Granite or Square Jersey Pebbles And ... bear pay and discharge a reasonable Share and Proportion of the Expence of maintaining and supporting repairing cleansing paving and keeping in good Order and Condition the said Square when made and the Iron Rails which are to inclose the Oval within the said Square and the Inside thereof and also of lighting the Lamps which are to be placed around the said Oval'.

The lease concluded by reiterating many of the items in the building agreement: to maintain the building, surrender the lease on completion with all fixtures, fittings etc., share the maintenance cost of shared amenities such as party walls, drainage and sewers, twice yearly (or more frequent) inspections for dilapidations, annoyance and disturbance to landlord and fellow tenants, restrictions on trades, repossessions for non-payment of rent or flouting of clauses in the lease. These, then, were the Bedford Estate restrictions, the clearly defined parameters within which the builders of Bedford Square were obliged to operate.

The building programme

The building agreements for Bedford Square, as we have seen, were signed in 1776; in January for the north and west sides and July for the south and east sides. The first leases were granted in November of the same year for
12 the entire west side (Nos.28-39). Now clearly something is wrong here. These dozen houses would almost certainly not have been covered in within ten months. Either the agreements were signed after the building had started or leases were granted prior to completion of the shells. I suspect the former, as there was little benefit to the ground landlord in granting a lease before completion. Perhaps building work started in 1775 or even 1774; either way, the sequence of building activity, judging by subsequent leases, was anti-clockwise. The south side was leased in 1777 (though 1782 was the year for No.46), the east side in 1777 and 1778 (except Nos.1 and 10, probably both in 1781), and finally the north side, most affected by the shortage of money during the American War of Independence, where leases were granted by the trustees in 1781 and 1782 (except Nos.24-27, granted in 1777). The last leases came in August 1782 and, accepting the 'seven years constant and unwearied attention' that Grews reported to Palmer in his letter of 1784 (see Appendix 1, p.155), the start would have been made in the summer of 1775.

In 1774, John Hele was appointed the first District Surveyor for the parishes of St Giles in the Fields and St George Bloomsbury under the great Building Act of that year. Little is known about Hele but he remained in this role until 1810. He was a local man and the previous year had taken up residence in a house at the southern end of Charlotte Street, west of Tottenham Court Road, just up from Percy Street.[40] He certainly had more illustrious colleagues – John Nash, John Crunden, George Gwilt Senior and S P Cockerell were all appointed District Surveyors in 1774 – to whom the Surveyorship was perhaps less important.[41] Bedford Square would have been the most prestigious 'patch' to Hele in his first ten or so years and his 'signings-off' of the houses are in the volumes of Building Affidavits held at the Greater London Record Office. The first of these are dated 9 April 1777 for six houses on the west side and one each on the south and the north. These affidavits are useful because they give the name of the builder and while these names should not be taken as definitive, builder being a broad term in the eighteenth century, they are in certain cases, perhaps, a more accurate guide than the names that crop up as original lessees. William Scott and Robert Grews, together or singly, appear on just six of the forty-five houses in the Square listed in the first volume of affidavits and yet they were original lessees of twenty-six of the fifty-three houses built. How many of the houses the pair actually *built* it is impossible to say but it is perhaps fewer than Grews implies in his letter to Palmer. It is anyway a fairly fruitless path to follow as so many unrecorded agreements and deals were made, sealed only by the shake of hands for which no documentary evidence exists.

What happened on the south side hints at such unwritten agreements. All of the original leases for the fourteen houses were granted to Scott and Grews, seven to each, and all but one in three batches in 1777. Within days they were subleased to a second party, all building craftsmen, except in four cases where the pair subleased to each other. What they were able to do, though, was to sublease at a greatly increased ground rent with a shorter peppercorn period. In the case of No.49 for example, Scott subleased to James Tomes, a bricklayer; within the month Tomes had 'bargained sold assigned transferred and set over' the lease to the Reverend Richard Walter of Portsmouth.[42]

No.40 tells a similar story of assignments but with an interesting twist. On 20 November 1777 a lease was granted to Grews with the usual requirement to build a coach house and stables at the rear of the plot within two years. Eleven days later, Grews subleased to Scott. Six months after that came the twist. On 8 June 1778, Grews surrendered the leasehold interest of the whole plot to the trustees for five shillings. After five days he was granted a new lease identical in every respect except that the plot had been slightly reduced at the south-eastern corner backing onto Caroline Mews. A chunk of land, some seven feet wide by ten feet deep, had been taken away and the whole plot was reduced by a few inches in length. The only explanation I can offer is that the Estate, which had originally required 'the said coach house and stables to open into Caroline Mews aforesaid and not into Caroline Street', had second thoughts and required the entrance to be put completely out of sight from Caroline Street by containing it within the recessed south-east corner.

When Britain went to war in North America in 1775, the great prosperity of the building trade in London came to a halt. By the end of 1777, nonetheless, thirty-four houses had been leased in Bedford Square. The following year only three more were added to the list and over the next two and half years not a single lease was granted. Then, all of a sudden, with the building world still in a slump, fifteen houses were leased in as many months. That left just one house – No.11 – which had a separate agreement of 1781 and lease in June 1783. Grews later admitted that 'The great scarcity of Money, occasioned by the unhappy American War, so severely affected many of the persons concerned under us, that some were compelled to stop, and we found ourselves under the unfortunate necessity of taking back the Ground, and completing the Houses thereon.[43] A similar story was told in 1787 when William Adam attributed the financial problems of

William Adam and Company 'above all ... [to] ... the diminution of the value of buildings from the fatal American War'. As for his brothers Robert and James, William thought the war 'proved as destructive to their business of architecture as it had been to the building business'.[44]

How was it then that Bedford Square was completed so quickly when the slump was at its worst? The answer appears to lie with the Bedford Estate and in particular the steward Robert Palmer. He made a great fortune in the property market. Some time before the laying-out of the Square he had purchased the reversion of the manor of Otes in Essex from Lord Masham. On his death early in 1787, at his house in Great Russell Street, Palmer is said 'to have died possessed of £4,000 a year freehold, and at least £60,000 in mortgages and in the stocks'.[45] Palmer appears to have lent money on the Estate's developments. In 1775, Giles Painter, one of the speculators working on the Duke's land at Exeter wrote to Palmer of the '... great and heavy expense in building the Circus, having eight houses almost finished, others to the Parlour floor, stables and coach houses garden walls all neat finished ... have advanced our last shillings should be sorry to make a stop here ... lend £1,000 to finish and pay £300 borrowed from Turner'.[46] Whether the money was lent we do not know, but we can be more certain that Palmer lent on the building of Bedford Square. Grews hinted at this, 'I am bound ... to express my sincere Thanks to you, for the attention and ready assistance which you have from time to time offered me'.[47] And John Holliday of Lincoln's Inn wrote in 1788, 'Were not the lessees of the Portland and Bedford Estates enabled to build upon, and give large prices for the ground, not only from the concurrent circumstances of the ground being accessible to the East, West and South, and in many instances to the North, but also from the builders being supplied with large savings during long minorities? ... witness the immense sums lent by the late Mr Palmer to those who built Bedford Square and Gower Street – without which (as he frequently owned) the Buildings would never have been finished'.[48]

The large savings referred to by Holliday bring us to the ground rents charged on the leases. In most cases these were set at or slightly above the limit expressed in the building agreements of 'ten shillings per foot on the fronts of the large houses towards the intended Square'; No.32, therefore, with a frontage of thirty-two feet, was rented at £18. Those houses that were granted to Grews and/or Scott, however, had greatly reduced ground rents. Nos.21-23 were rented at less than eleven pence per foot and Nos.37-39 at under sixpence per foot. The same 'subsidy', though far less pronounced, was given to the pair on the south side. When these houses were immediately subleased the annual ground rent was increased by up to three and a half times.

The best side of Bedford Square was always going to be the east, for the simple reason that it backed onto land belonging to the Estate, and the British Museum Gardens. 2
These stretched east to the grounds of Bedford House and north to the fields and must have given this side in particular a lovely character. Paradoxically, it was this open land that was later to threaten these houses for so long after 1860. Two of the Square's three individual houses were built here (Nos.1 and 6) and the third (No.11) on the north-east corner. In an early bid by the Estate to retain this benefit, against what would eventually prove to be increasingly difficult odds, came the most bizarre twist in the development: the first demolition occurred before the last lease was granted. It was not one of the houses, but the story is nonetheless well worth telling.

In the agreement for the east side, provision was made for a stable yard behind the rear gardens of the four northernmost houses (Nos.7-10). Shortly after being granted a lease for No.7 in November 1777, William Grindall assigned to Samuel Hartley who 'in pursuance of the Covenant ... did erect a Coach house and Stable at the East end of the piece of Ground'. This building would probably have been completed by November 1779, because two years was the timetable period set out in the covenant. Judging by the 'specification' given for this outbuilding in the lease, it would have been fairly intrusive (see p.39). Shortly after its completion, Hartley 'hath since at the request of the said Duchess of Bedford Duchess of Marlborough and Robert Palmer and of the occupiers of the adjoining houses taken down the same and it hath been since agreed that there shall not be any Stable Coach house or other Building whatsoever erected on the Ground'. The other three plots were caught in time, and the lessees made to enter into covenants restraining them from erecting any building whatsoever. In all cases the land was added to the respective gardens and leased at two shillings per annum for 91 years from Michaelmas 1783.

On that date, 29 September 1783, some two acres and twenty perches of enclosed pasture ground at the rear of Nos.6-10 were leased to Alexander Wedderburn, the 'Right honourable Alexander Lord Loughborough Baron of Loughborough in the County of Leicester for 21 years from Michaelmas 1783 at £28 per annum determinable by either part at 12 months notice'.[49] Wedderburn was acquainted with Palmer[50] and had far more of a benefit to lose than Hartley's other neighbours and I suspect that it was chiefly he who prevailed upon the trustees to have Hartley take down his outbuilding.

The first occupancy in the Square took place in the first three months of 1779 when Mr Serjeant Glynn moved into No.41 (albeit for less than a year). The last house to take an owner was, inevitably, on the north side, No.23, when Thomas Burn moved in during the last quarter of 1784.

On average it took two and a half years between the grant of lease and initial occupation. This was the stage when the house would be finished and decorated, but even allowing for the high standard that was achieved in these houses, this seems an excessive time and perhaps reflects the difficulties the lessees had in selling them.

Finally, what sort of deal would have been struck between the builder and the purchaser of a house in Bedford Square? Fortunately, an agreement survives for the sale of No.17, which gives us a good insight.[51] The house was leased to John Utterton, a plasterer, on 20 August 1782. On 17 October he signed an agreement with Samuel Gardiner, a merchant from Bishopsgate Street in the City. The house was 'not yet compleatly finished but a plan or particular of what is intended to be done and fixed thereto respectively hath been Drawn and agreed upon by the said John Utterton and Samuel Gardiner which plan they have Deposited in the hands of James Poultney of Fore Street London Builder'. Gardiner agreed to buy the premises provided it was completely finished before 24 June 1783. The price was £2,200. He paid a deposit of £1,000 with a further £500 due on 25 December 1783 and the balance due on the signing of the lease. Gardiner moved in during the first quarter of 1784 and stayed until some time in 1786.

Gardiner was typical of the class of person that occupied Bedford Square until at least the beginning of this century. The next chapter will discuss the strata of Georgian society for which Bedford Square was the setting.

3

Georgian Society and Bedford Square

Why was Bedford Square built, what sort of house purchaser might have been in the minds of the Duke of Bedford's trustees and the builders and, when the Square was built, what sort of person took a house? Quite simply, what were the forces that produced Bedford Square?

To start with, in order that our view of the Square be given as sharp a focus as possible, we must take a 'global' view of London. In the eighteenth century the capital was made up of two distinct parts – the City and the West End – linked by the Strand, then the main shopping street, and High Holborn. The two 'cities' were as chalk and cheese: in architecture, in social habit and in day-to-day business. A fascinating portrayal is given by Johann Wilhelm von Archenholz in *A Picture of England* published in 1789:

> The shops are open by eight o'clock every morning in the city; all is then in motion, everybody is at work; while on the other hand, at the *court end* of the town, the streets are empty, the houses shut, and even the very domestics are asleep; the sound of coaches is not heard, and one seems to walk about in a place that has been deserted. This difference, which extends to drinking and eating, amusements, dress, and manner of expression, occasions a kind of hatred between the inhabitants of each. Those in the city charge the people who live at the west end of the town with luxury, idleness, effeminacy, and an attachment to French fashions; while the others speak of a citizen as a dull, fat animal, who places all his merit in his strong box.[52]

And of the architecture:

> The city, especially the houses along the banks of the Thames, is composed of old ruins: the streets are narrow, obscure, and badly paved: it is the residence of the seamen, of the workmen employed in ship-building, and of a great part of the Jews who reside in London. The contrast betwixt that and the western parts of the metropolis is astonishing: the houses there are almost all new, and of an excellent construction; the squares are magnificent; the streets are built in straight lines, and perfectly well lighted: no city in Europe is better paved. If London were equally well built, no place in the whole world would be comparable to it.[53]

Much of what Archenholz saw in the West End was under thirty years old and most under seventy. Back in 1760, Marylebone still awaited its development to the north of Cavendish Square and similarly, in Bloomsbury, to the north of Great Russell Street. After two decades of very little building, there was a pent-up demand for new housing as the 1760s dawned. Between 1762 and 1779, boom years for the speculators, some 43,000 houses were reckoned to have been built in London[54] and they made up a large proportion of the 118,448 dwellings recorded in the first official census of 1801.

Society was changing and an ever-increasing range of social levels was able to take on the purchase and rental of housing. The *British Magazine* noted in 1762 that 'the present rage of imitating the manners of high life hath spread itself so far among the gentlefolks of lower life, that in a few years we shall probably have no common folk at all'.[55] London had also greatly increased in importance to the upper classes and a London townhouse was considered essential now that they were spending up to six months, November to April, in its grasp.

Those areas that could be developed were restricted by ownership of land and by geographical and man-made obstacles. St James's Park, Green Park and the King's Garden at Buckingham House screened Westminster from Mayfair and St James's, Hyde Park formed a boundary to the west, and the New Road provided a similar function to the north. The City provided a buffer to the east, and the river always proved a stumbling-block to a flow of fashion southward. The prime development areas were Marylebone, Bloomsbury, Belgravia and Pimlico. These last two would be built up much later and it was Marylebone and Bloomsbury that became the most fashionable new residential locations after the 1760s. Both were equidistant from Westminster, but of the two, Marylebone, further west, had the best location and ended up with houses of a better standard, although Bloomsbury achieved more in terms of town planning. Marylebone stole the initial march on its rival and by the time building started in Bloomsbury – at Bedford Square in 1775 – it must have become clear, if it was not already so, which was the appropriate type of housing to be built on the Bedford and Foundling Estates.

That was as may be, but there were great conflicts of interest in speculative house-building in Georgian London. What was seen as appropriate by the freeholder may not have been considered so by the builder. The aim of the ground landlord, as freeholder, was to have large well-built houses put up in the hope of attracting a good class of tenant and so maintain the financial and social standing of the estate until the reversion of the leases. The builder, on the other hand, was investing his money in the houses he was building and naturally aimed to 'shoehorn' as many houses as possible onto the ground he had taken and build them as quickly as possible.

The conflicts of interest between the two parties were often resolved by compromises in the ideal type of house each would like to see built. Building agreements signed by both parties set out the size of the houses, the standards of building and the materials to be used, and this attempt at the enforcement of sound construction was often backed up, especially on the larger estates, by estate surveyors who oversaw the building works. In spite of the attempts by the ground landlord at enforcement, it sometimes proved impossible to police. One example illustrates this and, by coincidence, it occurred on the Bedford Estate just a few yards from Bedford Square, in Keppel Street, in 1807. The builder, Thomas Lewis, had built contrary to the agreement and justified his non-compliance to the Duke's stewards by stating that he had told his fellow-builders in the street to build smaller houses than intended 'knowing that in these times many genteel families will give more for a small house in a good situation than for a large one'.[56]

There are no outward signs, albeit after more than 200 years, of such difficulties in the building of Bedford Square and certainly no signs of compromise in the overall design while finishing off the scheme during the harsh years of the American War.

As for the cost of a house in the Square, there are two aspects to be looked at. First, the cost of building. Although I have found no record that actually relates directly to Bedford Square, Isaac Ware, writing in 1756, reckoned that the 'common' five-storey London terrace house with two rooms and a closet room per floor could be 'built for six or seven hundred pounds, or it will cost upwards, according to a little more extent of ground, and a little more than usual ornament. The common builders ... are generally ready to sell them for fourteen years purchase, exclusive of ground rents'.[57] Thirty years before, the rectory of Christ Church in Spitalfields, four bays wide – a similar width (31 feet) to some of the houses in Bedford Square – and over five floors, cost £1,456 to build.[58]

Second, there is the question of the sale price that could be achieved, and here we know that No.17 was sold for £2,200 in a finished state in 1783 (see p.42). That would compare with the rectory in Spitalfields in a century during which inflation was uncommon and after allowing the builder a good profit on his building costs. As a comparison, the value put on some of the houses at the Adelphi, for the purpose of the 1774 lottery to dispose of the
5 houses there, was £3,700 for houses on the Royal Terrace, £2,230 for those in John Street, and £1,370 to £1,800 for those in Adam Street.[59] And in 1730 the Earl of Thanet had paid Edward Shepherd £7,500 for No.19 Grosvenor Square, the highest price then paid for a house in the square.[60]

The finishing of Bedford Square brought a respectability to Bloomsbury that continued as wide streets and large squares spread across the estate up to the New Road and over to Southampton Row. Although the estate was never aimed at the upper classes – if it had been there would have been more individual houses like No.1 Bedford Square, and the lesser houses in the streets away from the squares would have taken on the size and appearance of their larger neighbours – it became an upper middle- 29,
class suburb. 30

Bedford Square was one of the best addresses in Bloomsbury, if not *the* best, and succeeded in attracting upper middle-class residents; occasionally it even managed to pull in an upper-class tenant. It failed, however, to match the better parts of Marylebone, the areas around Portland Place and Harley Street, for example, and never got near to matching the attractions of Mayfair and St James's. In 1792, for example, the 20 entries in *Boyles Court Guide* for Berkeley Square produced ... six Lords, five Earls and one Duchess, Dowager Duchess, Marquis, Viscount and Lady apiece, while the 47 entries for Bedford Square produced merely a Lord and a Lady. Four years later, *Boyles Court and Country Guide* shows a similar picture when the two areas are again compared. Of the 35 residents listed for Berkeley Square only eight are without country residences, still the true home of the upper-class Englishman, whereas the comparable figure for Bedford Square is 22 out of the 52 entries.

Rather than being the London address of an indolent aristocracy, Bedford Square established itself as a prime London address for 'the aristocracy of the City and the 31
Inns of Court'.[61] The Right Honourable Sir Nicholas 32
Conyngham Tindal, Lord Chief Justice of the Common 33
Pleas, lived at No.44 between 1827 and 1846, Sir William Best, a predecessor of Tindal at the Court of Common Pleas, lived at No.29 from 1819 until 1830. Sir Soulden Lawrence, resident at No.16 between 1795 and 1814, was replaced at the King's Bench by Sir John Bayley (No.42, 1811-35). The list is long. Examples from the City include Sir Lionel Lyde (see p.76) and Benjamin Boddington, 'an eminent West India merchant, a director of the South-sea Company and of the Million Bank; treasurer and a governor of the City of London Lying-in-hospital, City-road; a governor of the Small-pox hospitals, and of almost every other charitable institution'.[62]

Towards the end of the Georgian era, Bloomsbury began to experience problems in retaining its reputation as a well-to-do district. Houses were remaining empty in the lesser streets and there was 'the disposition which exists to move westwardly'; the very thing that had helped establish the area was now bringing a slow decline, as fashion moved into Belgravia, Pimlico, Bayswater and Kensington. The more important squares, however, retained a healthy immunity to decline and in 1880 W S Gilbert had Mr Foggerty, a day-dreaming bank clerk in one of his short stories, 'desire only a brougham and pair to drive me home to a good house in Bedford Square'.[63]

The decline of Bedford Square from residential haven

29 TOP. Bedford Square, east side, looking north, watercolour by T H Shepherd, 1851.

30 BOTTOM. Bedford Square, east side, looking south, watercolour by T H Shepherd, 1851. Note the tented verandah at No.2, since taken down.

31. No.25 Bedford Square, ground-floor, front room. Photograph by Bedford Lemere, taken in 1902.

32 OPPOSITE. No.25 Bedford Square, first-floor, rear room. Photograph by Bedford Lemere, taken in 1902.

to commercial quarter was a long drawn-out affair that had its initial stirrings in the 1890s and its completion in the 1940s. In 1890, the London County Council was authorised by Parliament to remove three of the five gates on the Duke of Bedford's Bloomsbury Estate. These gates with their small lodge houses had been erected at the northern end of the estate by Thomas Cubitt in the 1820s; they permitted the passage of 'gentlemen's carriages of every description, cabs with fares, and persons on horseback' but prohibited the passage of 'omnibuses, empty hackney carriages, empty cabs, carts, drays, wagons, trucks, cattle and horses at exercise, or funerals' and were closed to all traffic from eleven in the evening until seven in the morning.[64] In 1893, the London County Council removed Bloomsbury's two surviving gates as well as the remaining gates elsewhere in London. The effect of their removal must not be understated, for it changed Bloomsbury from a secluded, almost private, neighbourhood into a busy thoroughfare for all West End traffic on its way to and from much of north London and the three great railway termini of Euston, St Pancras and King's Cross.

It was in the first decade of this century that Bedford Square experienced its first incursion of non-residential users.[65] On 22 June 1901, Mary Hodgkinson wrote to the Bedford Office from No.11 complaining of a notice that had appeared on the railings of No.6a announcing 'The Physical Therapeutic Institute'. In 1904, No.43 had become offices as had No.46 a couple of years later. By 1909 the Associated Board of the Royal Academy of

33. No.25 Bedford Square, first-floor, front room. Photograph by Bedford Lemere, taken in 1902.

Music were at No.15 and the Royal Agricultural Society of England were next door at No.16.[66] If the changes were slow in the first years of the century they were to quicken in the years of the First World War. In 1913 about eight houses were being used as offices but by 1919 the figure was twenty-six. Nine years later a further fourteen houses had become offices and in 1938 there were just six private houses left. After the Second World War, the Square was given over completely to offices, although a few residents remained, sharing the houses with office users.

Today there are no residents in Bedford Square, although the odd house has a company flat on the top floor and a caretaker's flat in the basement. Many of the houses have sympathetic users but there are far too many fluorescent lights fixed to fine decorative ceilings. But the saddest feature of all is that Bedford Square only functions for nine hours a day, Monday to Friday.

PLATE I. No. 1 Bedford Square, elevation.

PLATE II. 25 Bedford Square, first-floor front room or drawing room, *c.*1830. A watercolour dating from the residency (1815-36) of Basil Montagu, writer and philanthropist, when this house was a meeting place for much of London's literary society. Montagu's son-in-law, Bryan Waller Procter, the writer and lawyer, lived at this house with his wife and Montagu. Procter wrote under the nom de plume of Barry Cornwall and this watercolour is entitled 'Barry Cornwall's Drawing Room in Bedford Square'.

The room is interesting for many of its decorative details. The walls are plain papered with a border empanelling each wall from the dado rail to the cornice, an arrangement popular from *c.*1820 to the middle of the century. The joinery is painted in an off-white, usually known as stone colour. The neo-classical decoration of the dado rail, door architraves and overdoors is original and either carved or made from 'composition'; this was a mixture of glue-size and whiting which could be pressed into moulds and applied to joinery. It was a type of decoration much favoured by the Adam brothers and popular in the mid- and late-Georgian eras. The decorative plaster ceiling is painted plain white and a six-light chandelier hangs from the feathered centrepiece.

The patterned carpet is not fitted or planned to the room – often in this important room the carpet echoed the design of the ceiling; instead, the carpet appears to be sewn together in strips with a border of dry-rubbed floorboards between it and the skirting boards. The splendid green continuous drapery curtains are hung in a style popular from about 1815. The fabric complements that used for the furniture, window seats and table covering.

The furniture reflects a wide time span. The set of two pedestals and tables are in a Rococo style and appear to be made of wrought iron; they date from the 1750s or 1760s. In the far left-hand corner there is a miniature organ and stand of *c.*1780. In the foreground, on the left, is a teapoy of *c.*1810. Typically the box contained two caddies for green and black tea and a cut-glass bowl for sugar. The set of six single chairs are of similar date to the teapoy and are in the style of the classical Greek Klismos chair.

There are not as many pictures in this room as one would expect and in a somewhat ungainly way they are all hung low down. The two figures mounted above the doors are most striking and probably made of bronze or of plaster painted in imitation.

The far door of this room is the entrance from the staircase; the near door leads to the rear room. Behind us is the fireplace.

PLATE III. No.8 Bedford Square, ceiling design for rear room, first-floor, from the office of the Adam brothers. This design was probably not carried out.

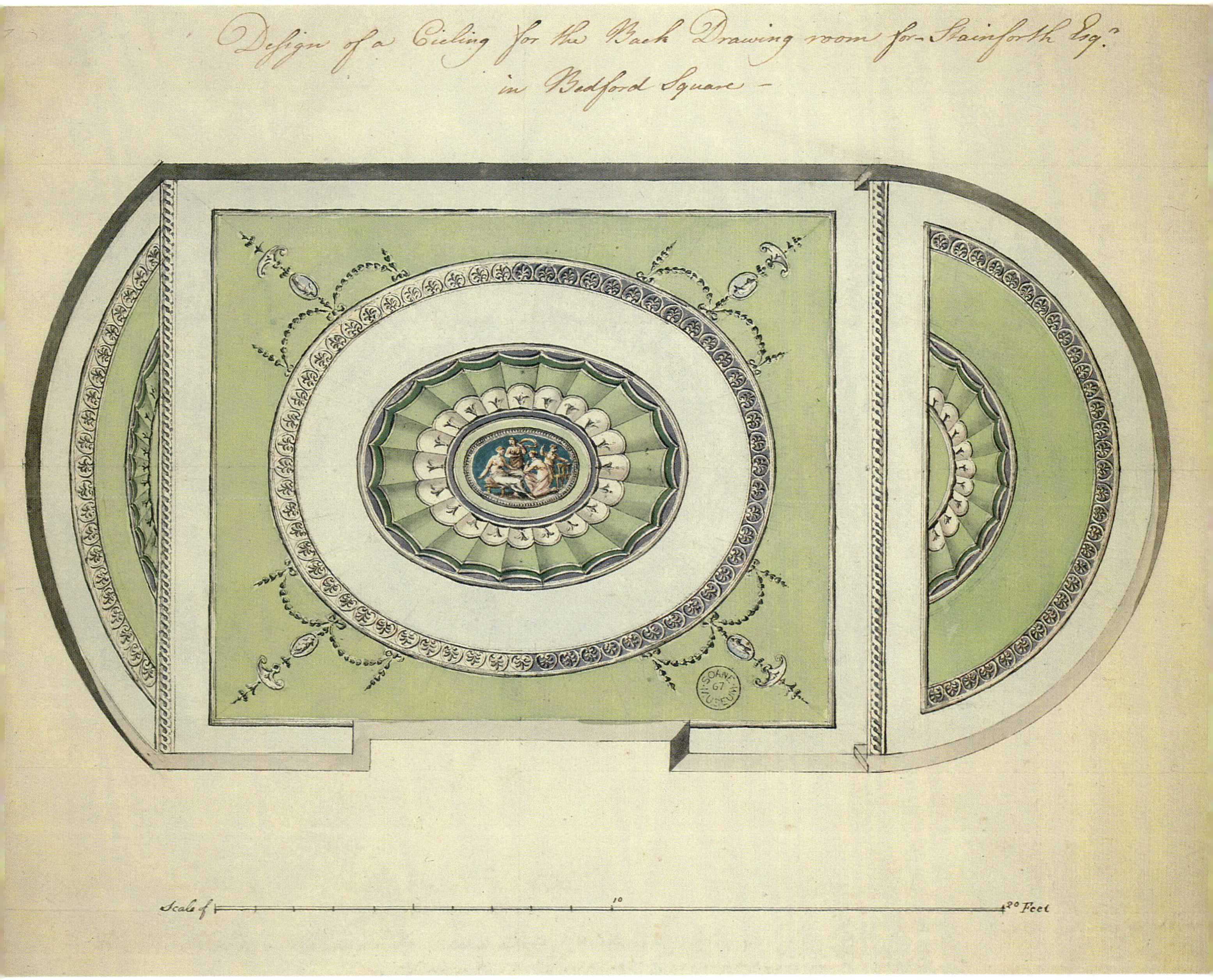

PLATE IV. No. 13 Bedford Square, ceiling, front room, first-floor.

PLATE V. No.40 Bedford Square, ceiling, front room, first-floor.

PLATE VI. No. 51 Bedford Square, staircase lantern.

PLATE VII. No.1 Bedford Square, ceiling, rear room, first-floor.

PLATE VIII. Bedford Square, south side from the gardens.

4

The Gardens

The individual rear gardens

One of the features of the better type of Georgian terrace town house was the concept of the complete self-sufficient unit. The house was just a part of the whole ensemble that started underneath the pavement in the form of storage vaults and ran through to the lane that served the 3 coach-house and stable at the rear. In between was the front area, the house itself and the rear garden or courtyard. In London, this form of arranging the long narrow plots was especially common in the Georgian development of districts such as Mayfair, Marylebone, Bloomsbury and, later on, Belgravia.

In Bedford Square the average plot length was 130 feet which produced front areas about 8 feet deep, a house perhaps 50 feet deep, a rear garden some 30 feet deep, and a coach-house perhaps 40 feet deep. On the north side of the Square the coach-houses and stables were not so large, which allowed a longer rear garden, and on the east there was neither a back lane nor coach-houses.

2 On the east side, the land behind the houses served as true rear gardens running down, initially at least, to the gardens of the British Museum. On the other three sides, however, the term courtyard would be far more appropriate. This was a gloomy area surrounded by the towering rear elevation of the house, tall brick garden walls and the rear wall of the coach-house; the space was very much restricted in its ability to support flora and was typically paved with flagstones or gravel, which was cheaper and more common. Isaac Ware confirms as much in his *Complete Body of Architecture* as part of his description of the typical London terrace house:

> ... if there be any little opening behind, to pave it. Some attempt to make flower-gardens of these little spots, but this is very idle; plants require a purer air than animals, and however we breathe in London, they cannot live where there is so much smoak and confinement; nor will even gravel continue clean many days from the turning. In this respect, therefore, instead of borders under the walls, the best method is to lay the whole with a good sound stone pavement.[67]

The outbuildings – mainly stables and coach-houses – that once lined the 'mews lanes' behind the main houses have suffered badly over the years. Often annexed early on as a separate plot from the house and altered or demolished, they are a building type that has become extremely rare; and it is a very sad loss because of the vital and prominent role they played in the pre-railway era of urban Georgian London.

In several cases these outbuildings had a fine and highly architectural rear wall, that is the wall that faced the rear of the main house. They can be seen, for example, in Sutton Nicholls's famous bird's-eye view of Grosvenor Square; that to No.19 had a particularly handsome pedimented Roman Doric façade.[68] There are survivors at the rear of No.71 South Audley Street (actually an elaborate chimney and screen to the flank wall of No.28 South Street), at No.45 Upper Grosvenor Street and some of the more important Adam houses.

Two examples survive on the north side of Bedford Square. Behind No.19 is a stuccoed elevation over three 34 floors with Coade stone details and behind No.21 is a 35 remarkably well-detailed pedimented brick elevation whose facing work is frankly better than much of that of the main houses. Both appear to be contemporary pieces and were placed in front of a separate building attached to the rear wall of the coach-houses. The rooms would probably have served as offices or servant accommodation. In addition, the flank wall of the coach-house that terminates Gower Mews has a decorative façade which, although rebuilt, incorporates two Coade stone rosette panels, presumably retained from the original walls.

The central gardens

The increasing number of squares that were laid out in London as the eighteenth century progressed was quite simply due to a fundamental desire for improvement. John Gwynn, the great influence in the drive for improvement in the 1760s, when speaking of parts of Marylebone, believed that 'if a range of squares had been formed ... instead of that heap of absurdity and confusion ... it would certainly have been more profitable, as well as more elegant and convenient'.[69] Gwynn argued that the builders were deceiving themselves by contriving a narrow street for 'whenever a more spacious venue is built, those ill-contrived things will be deserted, and the inhabitants flock to places where they can breathe freely and better enjoy the conveniences of life'.[70]

Such was the improvement in town planning in the twenty-odd years after Gwynn made his observations, that a visitor was able to announce that[71] 'No city is adorned with such fine squares as London. They are all composed of noble and handsome houses ... in the centre there is usually a piece of ground laid out in a beautiful manner, which serves as an agreeable walk ... those who reside there have the advantage of breathing a pure air, and are never disturbed by any noise'. The same writer

34 TOP. No.19 Bedford Square, outbuilding facing rear elevation of main house, ground-floor window detail. The impost, tympanum decoration, keystone and string course are all in Coade stone.

35 BOTTOM. No.21 Bedford Square, elevation of outbuilding facing rear elevation of main house. A beautiful example of a building type now very rare in Georgian London.

36 OPPOSITE. Nos.1 to 3 Bedford Square, from the gardens.

37. South and east sides of Bedford Square, from the gardens.

38 OPPOSITE. The garden house and the west side of Bedford Square, from the gardens.

noted that 'people of distinction' were spending a greater amount of the year in London because it had 'lately acquired more attractions' and 'the nation already begins to be less attached to hunting, and to feel a greater passion for the fine arts, and everything that can add to the pleasures of a sensual life ... This new inclination, by which the wealthy are induced to live in London, has given to projectors the idea of building large streets and extensive squares, adorned with excellent houses'.

36-42 At quite what stage the gardens and railings in Bedford Square were completed we do not know, but a clause in the lease for No.45, granted on 20 November 1777, has key words crossed out, implying that its future construction was by then a reality: '... the said Square when made and the Iron Rails which are to inclose the said Oval ... the Lamps which are to be placed round the said Oval'.[71a]

The building agreement for the west side deals with the formation of the gardens. The works involved in forming the gardens, the enclosing railings and the pavement between the carriageway and the railing were to be carried out by William Scott and Robert Grews under the direction of Robert Palmer, surveyor to the Bedford Estate. Palmer was also to agree the costs involved and recommend to the Estate trustees the payments due to the pair.

One anomaly remains. The building agreements call for a footway to be made in front of the area railings beyond which a carriageway was to be laid out and paved to the extent of sixty feet from the fronts of the houses. The central gardens were therefore to be oblong in shape like those at Berkeley Square. The leases repeat these requirements in similar terms but a later clause contradicts the earlier one by referring to the 'Oval within the said Square'.

James Ralph, writing in 1783 in fulsome praise of the Square, was able to comment on 'the neatness of the iron-rails which encloses an oval grass-plat, environed by a gravel-walk',[72] and this is how Horwood recorded the gardens in his map of London published in 1799. The first 8
Ordnance Survey map of 1874 recorded the central 9
gardens in a state resembling that in which we can see them today, well-established with trees and a six-sided garden-house in the centre. The same year, that in which the 99-year leases lapsed on all the houses, the Duke of Bedford commissioned a Mr Meston to rearrange and, in part, replant Bedford Square.

On 19 December 1874, the journal *The Garden* reported:

As we write, Bedford Square is undergoing a thorough overhaul. The fine old Pines stand out grandly as the dwindling, mean, under-shrub vegetation, common to Bedford, as to the other west-central squares, is being swept away, root and branch, from beneath the trees that are to remain.[73]

39 TOP. Central gardens and enclosing railings.

40 BOTTOM. East and north sides of Bedford Square and the Senate House, from the gardens.

41 OPPOSITE. Garden house, No.40 and Centre Point, from the gardens. The garden house appears to date from before 1866.

42. Centre houses on the south side of Bedford Square, from the gardens.

At the same time the garden-house, which appears to date from before 1866, was moved to its present position towards the western end of the gardens. Other than the major changes carried out in 1874 little has changed to the central gardens since they were laid out. The enclosing railings are original as are the entrance gates at the north and south sides with wrought-iron overthrows.

An ilanthus was lost in the great storm of October 1987 and more recently a plane tree opposite No.20 was taken down because of a fungal disease. The gardens are dominated by the towering planes which take so much of the light away from the competing trees and shrubs. Nonetheless, weeping elm, holly, variegated laurel, privet, forbea, juniper, mahonia, lilac and periwinkle manage to compete in one of the most beautiful gardens of all of London's garden squares. VIII

5

Structure and Fabric

The building agreements and leases give a certain amount of information about the construction of the houses, basic measurements, for example, and materials to be used, but they do not specify precisely how the houses were to be built. To understand the structure and layout of the build-
43 ings, we must look at their physical fabric.

There are several common threads tying together the terraced houses of Georgian London, be they early or late,
46 large or small. A common floor-plan predominates – a
48 room at the front and a room at the rear with the staircase
to one side adjacent to the rear room and possibly a closet room tacked on behind. About a dozen houses in Bedford Square were built with a closet wing, and the great majority of these were on the north side where there were few full-height bows or canted bays. A basement was universal, except in the most humble dwellings, and almost invariably required an area in front to light and ventilate it, with protective iron railings run along at
45 pavement level. Sliding sash windows were also universal
and a stone-coped parapet became ubiquitous early on after the 1707 Building Act was passed. There would always be the exception, and fashion would change the superficial make-up, but the speculative houses were bound into a uniformity by constraints of finance, the ready acceptance of standardisation and the physical restrictions set on the size of plot by the sheer necessity of building as many houses as possible on any given parcel of land.

The consistent good quality of the facing brickwork of the Georgian houses in London belies the often poor construction of the core of the buildings, particularly those parts that were to be covered up. Shoddy construction has long been associated with speculative building in general, mostly due to greed and limits on time, and Bedford Square was no exception. This may come as a surprise to certain admirers of Georgian architecture because on purely aesthetic grounds the Georgian house sets a very high standard, perhaps unrivalled. Structurally, though, the story is very different.

It is, perhaps, an unfair criticism, given that Georgian houses were built to last the length of their lease and now, in their present esteemed status, are expected to have a permanent place in the future life of the capital. Many early Georgian houses, leased for 60 years, are now in their fifth life; perhaps we expect too much when they are stripped back during renovations and reveal their dark secrets. There have been, nonetheless, some horrific discoveries of poor building practice over the years; tales of internal walls built of turf blocks in Dublin,[74] for example, and I have seen houses on the Tredegar Estate in Bow, East London, of *c*.1825, with a timber frame covered by a meagre half-brick facing skin. There was an awareness of the poor standards and certain efforts were made to combat them. These included the Building Acts and the use of surveyors by the ground landlord to oversee the building works, but a tendency for the problems to be seen as an inevitable consequence of the way the majority of houses came to be built militated against any improvements.

When, for example, in the seventeenth century brick became the established building material to form the shell of the structure, certain methods were quickly established to construct the walls and incorporate the timber framing that they contained. These became traditional building practices, handed down from generation to generation, which can be seen in all houses through to the first half of this century, at which point there was a move away from certain traditional materials (for example, softwood lintels were replaced by concrete lintels). These methods were used across the complete range of house types and we shall look at them now in detail in relation to the houses in Bedford Square.

The first task to be performed was the excavation for the basement, the area immediately in front of the house over which a 'bridge' would be placed leading to the ground-floor entrance, and the vaulted cellars under the pavement. In London's streets, the excavated material from the basements on either side was generally used to build up the roadway, so that a full excavation was unnecessary. The original ground level can usually be seen at the rear where the garden is approached by a few steps up from the level of the basement floor. In Bedford Square the picture appears to have been similar but excavation work took in the entire plot, rather than just the section on which the house would stand, which on all four sides of the Square had an average length of 130 feet. The spoil would probably have been used to raise the height of the streets and the future gardens in the centre because that was the most convenient place for disposal.

The vaulted cellars under the pavement, generally three per house, were constructed of brick. Those belonging to No.12, for example, are 10 feet deep by 10 feet wide and 6 feet 3 inches high to the centre of the arched vault. They served as storage spaces, mainly for coal and the ashes removed from fireplaces. The coal was poured into the vault through a hole in the pavement sealed by a

43. No.32 Bedford Square, axonometric.

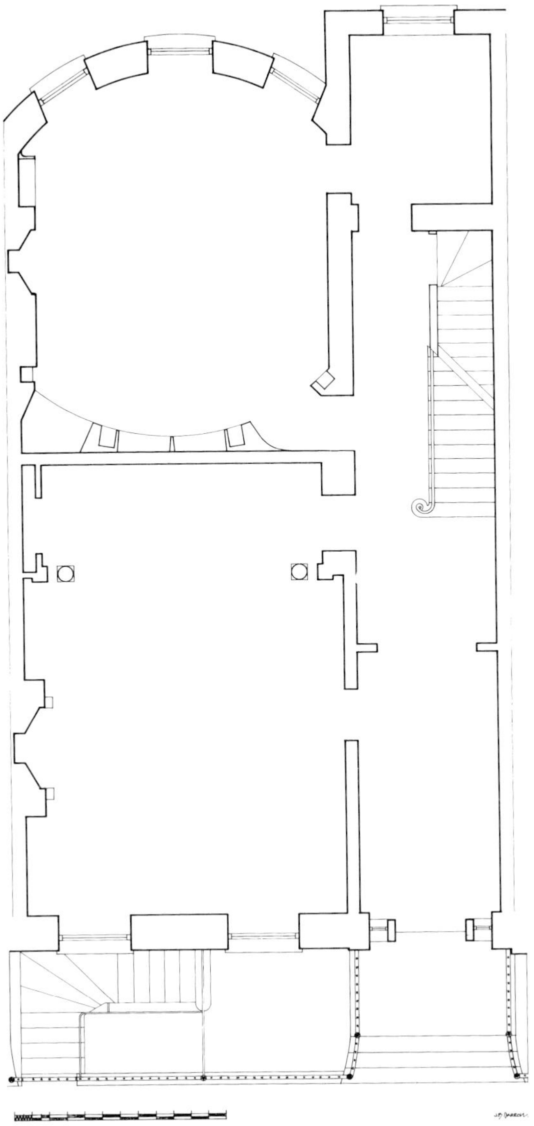

44. No.33 Bedford Square, ground-floor plan.

45. No.29 Bedford Square, front basement area, with original stone steps and flagged floor and later tuck-pointing to the brickwork.

circular cast-iron cover. None of the 100 or so cover plates that survive appear to be original.

Excavation for the foundations was taken down between two and three feet below the level of the basement floor. The first four or so courses laid were corbelled on both sides of the wall in order to spread the thrust and load of the structure above.

The typical basement plan in the Square consisted of a full-width room at the front, a vaulted room behind
94 running parallel to the front and rear walls, but not taking up the full width because of the space taken by the staircase leading up to the ground floor. This staircase was of stone and ran down from a point near to the rear wall against the party wall on which the entrance door and main staircase were positioned. The rear room of the same width was located behind the vault with perhaps a closet room positioned behind the staircase. The vault served for storage, generally wine, and some houses contain a second vault which was used to store the family silver. A good example of both survives at No.18.

The important factor is that all walls in the basement are in brick. The front and rear walls and the party walls are $22\frac{1}{2}$ or 27 inches thick, that dividing the staircase area from the rooms is 18 inches thick and the walls of the
vault are $13\frac{1}{2}$ inches thick. On cross-section the vault is 49
h-shaped, the upstand rising to the ground floor to support the spine wall that divides the front and rear rooms on the floors above. As the brickwork rises it is reduced still further; the parapets at roof level are either 9 or $13\frac{1}{2}$ inches thick.

Many of the foundations in Bedford Square have failed, it would appear, because of the inadequate nature of the soil on which they were placed. In spite of the deep excavation necessary for the basement and foundations, it is doubtful if an adequate base was ever encountered by the builders, because Bedford Square appears to have been built on an area of made-up ground. I have seen photos of underpinning works that show a hopelessly inadequate soil structure. To overcome this dilemma, great baulks of timber were placed within (not under) the stepped brickwork footings to act as stiffening beams. Over the years these beams, measuring around 15 inches thick by 12 inches deep, have been prone to rot. In 1889, for example, Mr Holmes Spicer, who the previous year had taken a lease on No.6a, wrote to the Estate outlining the failure of his foundations:

It was discovered in May of this year that the party wall between this house and No.7 Bedford Square was sinking, and by order of the County Council the failure had to be made good. In digging out the foundations it was discovered that the house had been built on timbers which were not resting on any solid ground at all; in course of time the superincumbent weight of the house had caused these to yield, and the wall had consequently sunk ... It was necessary to underpin the house, and to dig out the earth until solid ground was reached, about 8ft below ... The pier of the next house had sunk so much that it was necessary to rebuild it entirely.[75]

Similarly, in 1910 the flank and rear walls of No.28 were taken down and rebuilt 'on account of settlement due, as was discovered when the ground was opened up, to the footings having been laid upon irregular baulks of timber'.[76] And the major renovation works at No.1 in 1983 included underpinning the front and rear walls to remedy the problems caused by the collapse of the original fill and the rotten timbers built in below ground level.[77]

The basement floor was laid in stone flags, now widely replaced by concrete, and the upper floors in timber, except for the entrance and staircase halls which were finished with stone slabs laid on a base of ash or sand over a timber boarding fixed to timber joists.

Because the rooms on the ground floor were wide, the joists were insufficient to span between the walls and so a large main beam, about 12 inches by 12 inches, was introduced, running from front to back roughly down the middle of both rooms. Notched into the beam were the floor joists, about 9 inches deep by 3 inches thick, running on one side to the party wall and on the other side to the wall that divided these rooms from the staircase and entrance halls. These halls were joisted separately, running across to the opposing party wall, a distance of some seven to ten feet, dependent on the floor plan. There was generally a downstand of the main beam visible in the basement because of its greater depth compared with the joists it carried. The beam ran from the pier slightly above the two basement windows parallel to the party walls to the similar pier of the rear wall in two lengths, supported also by the spine wall in the centre of the house. Where the rear wall was bowed or canted, and probably divided into three bays, the beam was run at a slightly oblique angle to avoid bearing on the lintel spanning the head of a basement window.

From the ground floor up, all the internal walls were built in timber *except* for those forming the main staircase compartment where the walls continued in brickwork. This is because the main staircase, which was in stone, was cantilevered and relied for some of its support on the weight imposed upon it by the brickwork. Each tread 96
and riser was one individual unit housed into the unit beneath and in turn back to the main landing or half-

46. No.14 Bedford Square, ground- and first-floor plans.

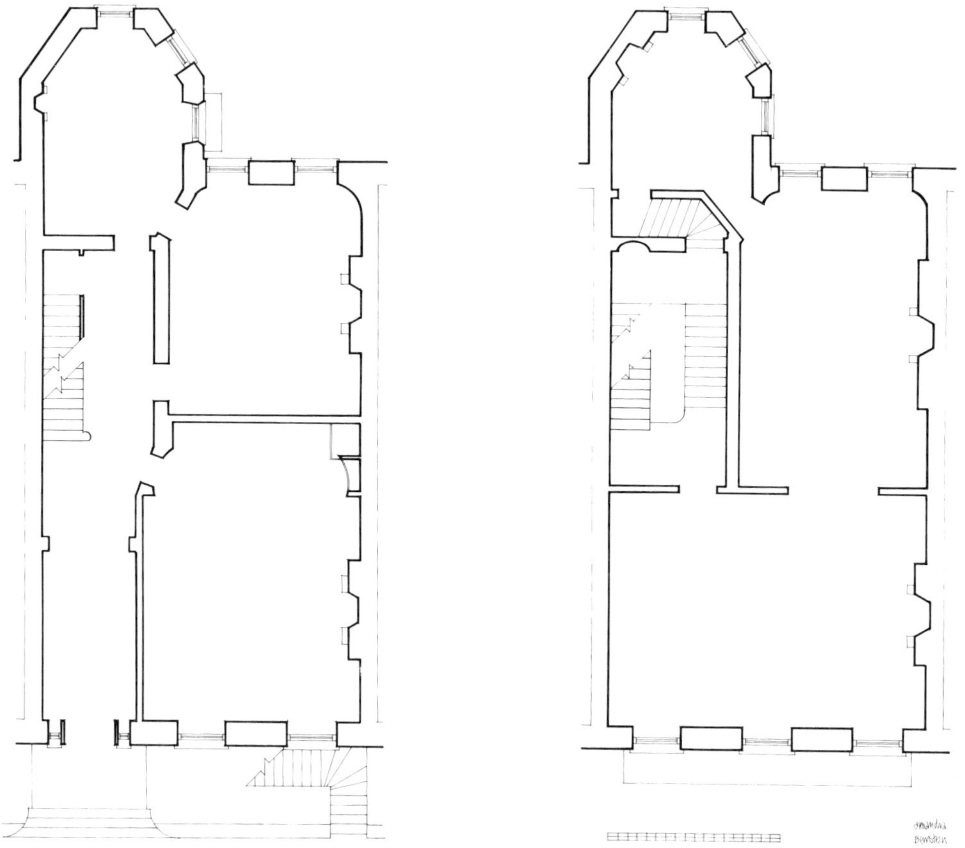

landing where additional support was provided. The balustrading was always in iron, occasionally cast but more often wrought, topped with a moulded mahogany handrail.

The first-floor plan typically comprised a large room in the front running the complete width of the house and a room behind sharing the rear half with the staircase compartment and possibly a closet at the rear. The typical floor structure here followed the principles set by the floor below but with definite differences arising from the plan. In the front room two large main beams, of similar section size to that found below, were positioned at points equidistant from, and running parallel with, the party walls. They gained their support from bearing on the brick piers between the three windows on the front wall. At the other end, one of these was supported by the brickwork of the staircase compartment where this met the spine wall and the other was borne by the spine wall itself and also on a deep timber lintol over the doorway through to the rear room. This last beam either continued through to the rear wall of the house or a separate beam was introduced running in a similar direction. Alternatively in this rear room, one or two main beams were run from either or both sides of the chimney breast across to the brickwork of the staircase compartment.

In all cases on this floor, the main beams served as bearing points for the floor joists which were notched into the beams. But whereas on the ground floor there were just floor joists of lesser depth than the beams, resulting in a downstand in the basement ceiling, here on the first floor there were separate floor joists, perhaps 6 inches deep by 3 inches thick, to take the floor boarding, and separate ceiling joists, perhaps 3 inches deep by 2 inches thick, to take the ceiling. The undersides of the latter were kept level with the underside of the beam and the ground-floor ceiling was carried across in one plane. Alternatively, every fourth or fifth joist was the full depth of the main beam and carried the ceiling joists which ran in the opposite direction.

Occasionally, the ground-floor ceilings were finished with decorative plasterwork but more often this type of ceiling was installed in the first-floor rooms, particularly the main one in the front of the house, because these were the entertaining rooms, the rooms on which a large portion of the finishings budget was spent. The plain ceilings were formed in two plaster coats; a thick first coat was applied to thin, spaced strips of wood known as laths which were nailed to the ceiling joists, with a key obtained by the wet plaster being forced between the gaps in the laths over which it folded and held when dry; this was followed by a much thinner finishing coat floated over the base coat. The decorative ceiling was formed by applying pre-cast mouldings and motifs set onto wet plaster. There was no free-hand plasterwork in Bedford

47. No.51 Bedford Square, frieze and cornice details to second-floor staircase landing soffit. The cantilevered staircase leads to the closet wing.

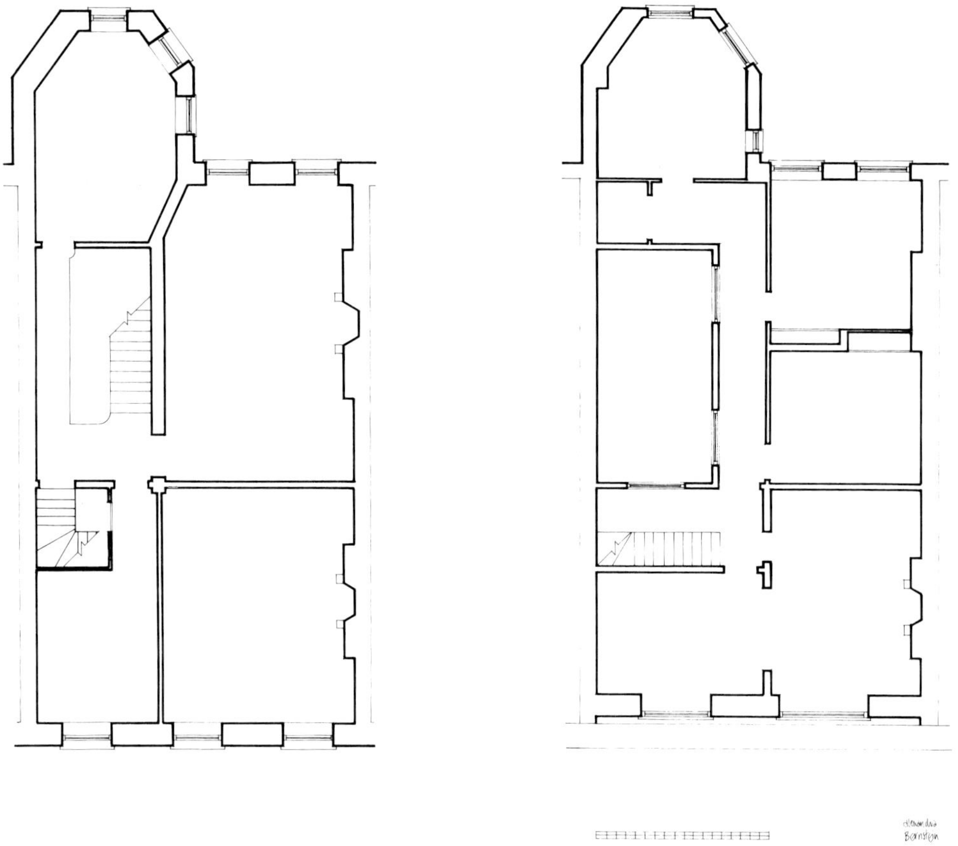

48. No.14 Bedford Square, second- and third-floor plans.

Square of the type associated with the earlier Georgian period, in particular that seen in Ireland.

48 On the second floor, the main staircase terminated, and a separate, simple wooden right-angle or dog-leg flight rose to the third floor usually against the same party wall as the main staircase and positioned in the middle part of the house; it was lit by a very simple top light.

The structure and plan of the second floor was usually an exact duplicate of the floor below, except for the front room which was often divided by a partition two-thirds back from the party wall that contained the chimney breasts (*ie* that opposite the entrance hall/staircase party wall). The smaller of these two rooms was often rendered smaller still because of the space taken by the staircase flight to the floor above. An angle chimney breast at the junction of the front wall and party wall contained the fireplace in this room.

On the third floor, the perimeter walls were taken up in brickwork except the front wall which was formed as a mansard containing two dormer windows. These dormers were always the same width as the windows in the remainder of the front face but many have been substantially widened over the years. The parapet at the front was coped with Portland stone. The rear wall continued flush, and finished as a parapet above the third-floor ceiling level; this was also coped with Portland stone.

The typical roof in Bedford Square had five slopes, all of them parallel to the front and rear walls. It was double pitched (four slopes), all set above the third-floor ceiling and containing no accommodation, with the fifth slope visible from the front, containing the two dormer windows of the third-floor front room(s). Thus from the pavement the roof appears to be of the mansard type. Under the building agreements, the roofs were to be covered with slates. This remains the covering today on all houses in the Square, although few, if any, roofs will have their original slates.

Brickwork

The bricks used in Bedford Square were generally the yellow and brown stock variety that became the fashionable colour for the fronts of houses in the 1730s, when the softer red bricks became increasingly unpopular under the architectural austerity of the Palladians. The fine gauged brickwork employed at the head of the windows and in between the vermiculated blocks of the rounded arch over the doors was also formed in yellow bricks of the finer rubbing variety.

Occasionally red brick can be seen, especially in front basement walls; the red dressings to the façade of No.1 are painted yellow bricks. The bricks were laid in Flemish
bond – alternate headers and stretchers in each course 50
– the usual manner of laying bricks throughout the entire Georgian era.

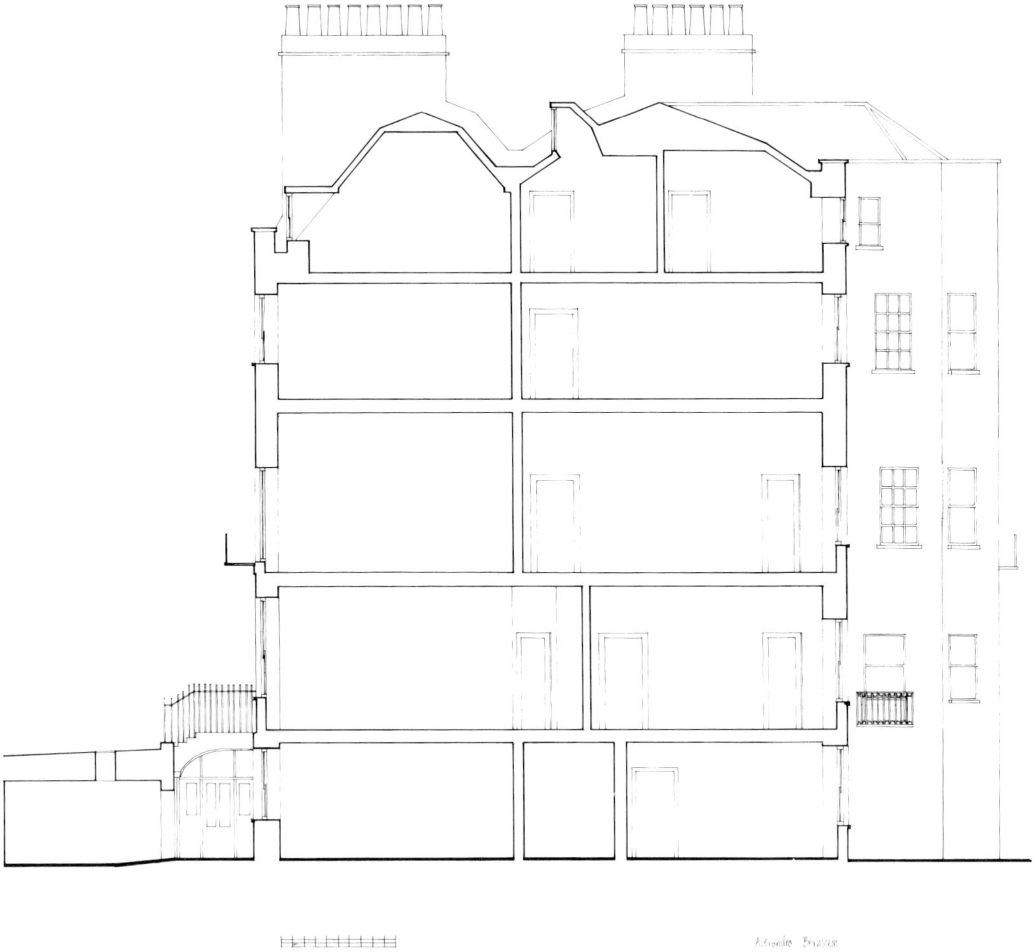

49. No.14 Bedford Square, section through house.

50. Nos.12 and 13 Bedford Square, parapet and brickwork detail showing later tuck-pointing to No.13.

Over the years, rebuilding, repointing, settlement, staining and constant exposure to the weather and grime of the capital have cast a heavy veil over the virgin brickwork of the 1770s, but it still looks good and was doubtless of the very high quality that was so characteristic of Georgian facing brickwork in London. From the larger houses in the West End through to the humble terraces of the East End runs the same thread of quality. But behind the facing skin the quality ends, particularly so in a structural sense.

The walls were made up of two skins. The outer skin was the facework, good quality regular bricks laid four courses to eleven inches with flush pointing, sometimes scored. The facework was half a brick thick – four and a half inches – and fronted the inner bulk of place brickwork, generally irregular and of poor quality, which could be anything up to 22½ inches thick. It was this inner hidden brickwork that bore the structural loads imposed by floor and roof timbers. The problems encountered by the bricklayers when building a wall made up of two separate parts was dealt with by a contemporary observer:

> When the Fronts are faced with unrubbed Bricks, 'tis customary to work up their Insides with Place Bricks, which, to make good Work, their Courses should be laid in no greater a Thickness of Mortar, than the Stock Bricks, that thereby every Course may be kept Level, and strongly bonded together ...[78]

and yet as we soon learn:

> ... Bricklayers will often carry up the Face of a Building of a Brick's Breadth only, for 8, 10, nay even 12 courses together, before they bond in upon the Place-Bricks; so that, in fact, the whole Wall, though of a Brick and half in Thickness is very little stronger than a 1 Brick Wall; because, between the Grey-Stocks and the Place-Bricks, there is an almost continued upright Joint. Which is not only a very great Deceit, but, in lofty Buildings, is dangerous.[79]

Dangerous indeed, yet universally adopted: in Bedford Square, in the Mile End Road and right across London. The problems encountered in 1889 by Mr Holmes Spicer with his foundations (see p.59) were further compounded by this lack of bonding:

> The pier of the next house had sunk so much that it was necessary to rebuild it entirely; while this was being done the District Surveyor discovered that the front of this house was made by a 4½ inch course of brickwork standing in front of the main wall, but not bound down to it in any way. He thought this unsafe and ordered it to be secured.[80]

The lack of bonding between the two skins was not, as implied by Holmes Spicer, complete. On average, I have been told, bonding in Bedford Square took place on every tenth course, which is better than on other brickwork I have seen in London.

To compound further still the subsequent failure of walls associated with poor bonding, the Georgian speculative builder would insert softwood timbers into the brickwork as it was carried up. Unlike the lack of bonding, which quite clearly would have been avoidable given a little more time and expense, these timbers performed several essential purposes, from carrying the immediate load of beams and joists and spreading it evenly throughout the structure, to reinforcing lime-mortar brickwork that cracks vertically under load, thus allowing a faster rate of construction, to providing fixing for internal joinery such as skirting boards and dado rails. Given the anticipated limited life of these houses and the advantage afforded by the heavy use of slaked lime in the mortar (and the internal plaster in houses built after the 1730s) which preserves timber, the practice was understandable and was standard to every Georgian, and indeed Victorian, house. But in their extended old age, with at least one period of poor maintenance which every survivor will have endured – involving poor pointing, a leaking downpipe or failed parapet gutter – these wall plates and bonding timbers have decayed under the burden of wet and dry rot. The decay causes the inner part of the place brickwork, in which the timbers were used, to compress, forcing the outer face to bulge. And this compounds the problems of poorly bonded brickwork where differential movement between the place brickwork and facing brickwork, caused by moisture, extremes of temperature and settlement, will have been at work for several decades already.

If you could strip the original internal plasterwork from any wall in any house in Bedford Square, the wall plates and bonding timbers would be there. Nowadays they are taken out and the voids are bricked up. Bulges in brickwork are removed by rebuilding if considered dangerously excessive or else restrained, in many cases invisibly, by the steel ties and straps conjured up by ingenious structural engineers.

Coade stone

The most striking embellishment of the plain brick houses 51-
in the Square is their conspicuous doorways. The semi- 53
circular openings are framed with large vermiculated 74
blocks and voussoirs, imposts and keystones all of which 108
are artificial stone. This is Coade stone that came from the Coade Lithodipyra, Terra-cotta or Artificial Stone Manufactory, established on the Thames-side at Narrow Wall, Lambeth in 1769.

Coade stone proved itself to be one of the great building materials of the Georgian era after its introduction in the 1760s. Far from being seen as an inferior substitute for more expensive natural stone, it was taken up by virtually all the leading architects. Sir William Chambers used it for the parapet vases at Somerset House, Robert Adam used it at No.20 Portman Square, James Wyatt decorated

51. No.40 Bedford Square, entrance doorway in Coade stone. This type, one of two versions in the Square, was illustrated in the Coade catalogue and is seen in the earlier houses in the Square – on the west and south sides (see figs.52 and 74).

the front of his house in Foley Place with it and, just around the corner, some forty years later John Nash used it for the Ionic capitals of the portico, and the Corinthian capitals of the drum tower, of his church of All Souls, Langham Place,[81] which was otherwise constructed of Bath stone. Its repetitive use at Bedford Square typifies the healthy attitude towards standardisation and mass production in an age obsessed with good taste.

It is difficult to pinpoint the reason why this type of doorway was produced by Coade and used so extensively at Bedford Square and then in so many parts of London, but the 1774 Building Act certainly had a lot to do with its subsequent popularity. The bulky Palladian doorcase was already long since out of fashion by the year the Act was drafted, ousted by the more delicate doorways of the Adam school. The Act firmly reinforced the demand for this type of doorway although it did not, as is commonly thought, completely ban woodwork from the fronts of houses. While it decreed that there should be no external wooden decoration, it made exceptions, one of which was for frontispieces to doorways of houses of the Second, Third and Fourth Rates. The houses in the Square, all of the First Rate, therefore required something other than wood, and what better than the successful new artificial stone from Lambeth.

The Coade stone doorways in Bedford Square are prob-
106 ably the earliest surviving examples of their type in London, a type that was promoted by Coade and used all over the country, but particularly in the capital. There are good examples, all later than Bedford Square, at Thurston House in Rectory Grove, Clapham and at No.7 Nightingale Lane on the west side of Clapham Common, in Baker Street, Harley Street, New Cavendish Street and Clarges Street in the West End, and more modest examples in Kennington Park Road and New Road, Whitechapel. There is an example on the side doorway of a house at Camberwell Green and also in Charterhouse Square, Clerkenwell. In Exeter they can be seen decorating the fine houses at Southernhay. All these examples date to within about forty years of their appearance in Bloomsbury.

While Portland stone has weathered, Coade stone
136 remains as intact as the day it left Lambeth. This was something certainly not lost on the proprietors, as they pointed out in their 1784 catalogue;[82] 'The property which this *artificial*, has above *natural* Stone, of resisting the frost, and consequently on retaining that *sharpness* in which it excells every kind of Stone Sculpture, renders it peculiarly fit for statues in parks and gardens, also for tombs and monuments in the church-yards of this, or a severer climate'.

The Coade stone used at Bedford Square is listed in *Coade's Gallery*, a catalogue published in 1799. Given as a joint entry with Gower Street, it reads 'Rustic Frontis-

52. Coade stone doorway, from *Etchings of Coade's Artificial Stone* (1777-9). This doorway was used for all the plain brick houses in Bedford Square (see figs.51 and 74).

pieces for Doorways, Guilloche Fascia, etc'.[83] The Rustic 124
Frontipieces are made up of several components whose cost is given in the company's 1784 catalogue; I have calculated this to be between £11 and £12. The Guilloche Fascia is the string course on the stucco-fronted houses in the Square. The 'etcetera' is more difficult to identify. The balustrade parapets could be in Coade stone as could the tympana decoration of the centre houses; but the Ionic capitals of these houses are probably not, as we shall see now.

Stucco

In his *London and Westminster Improved* John Gywnn railed hard against the plain brick houses in London. The new houses in Marylebone did, he said, 'give no better idea to the spectator than that of a plain brick wall of prodigious length'. At the time of writing, 1766, there was no reliable stucco available to the speculative builders for covering brickwork. A version had been used in the seventeenth century for important buildings such as the Queen's House at Greenwich but had never become a desired requirement for the capital's terraced houses.

Gwynn recognised the potential of stucco: '... as the building with stone is so very expensive in this metropolis,

53. No.52 Bedford Square, Coade stone detail to doorway. The keystone depicts a barbarous bearded head, perhaps emblematic of a race not destroyed by the Greeks and thus a free man.

54. Nos.46 and 47 Bedford Square, entrance doorways to the centre houses on the south side.

it is to be lamented that encouragement is not given to some ingenious person to find out a stucco or composition resembling stone, more durable than the common sort, and in which exterior ornaments might be easily wrought at a very easy expense'.[84]

The previous year, Dr David Wark of Haddington in Scotland obtained a patent for an Oil Mastic Stucco and eight years later, in 1773, John Liardet, a Swiss clergyman based in Great Suffolk Street, patented a similar material. Both patents were purchased by the Adam brothers in 1774.[85] For the next fourteen years the brothers had the sole rights to produce and apply stucco, though such an advantage was to prove a great burden on their finances.

In 1776 the patent was re-assigned to Liardet so that he could petition Parliament for an extended term of exclusive rights to manufacture and apply what he claimed was an improved stucco. The specification called for two coats, the first of whiting (lime), white or red lead, oil and sand and a second coat of the same materials but a greater proportion of oil.[86] The extension was granted, allowing Liardet a term of eighteen years on the proviso that he should 'not demand or take any greater price than Six Pence per Foot Square, on the Surface of all plain Buildings, and Two Pence per Foot, running Measure, for Arrises (being external Angles)'.[87]

In Bedford Square, Liardet's stucco was probably used 18
for all the centre houses. It was certainly used at No.6 for which Lord Loughborough paid £155 in 1784. Because of failures he was further obliged to pay for repair works which were carried out in 1788.[88] In 1778, or perhaps a little earlier, an Ionic capital that had been pre-cast in a mould fell from a house in the Square. Apparently it was fixed with nails and came away during a storm.[89] Going by the date of the leases this could only have been either No.32 on the west side or No.47 on the south.

Away from the Square, the Adam brothers used Liardet's stucco for the remodelling of David Garrick's villa at Hampton in 1775, at No.11 St James's Square in the same year, for which Sir Roland Winn paid over £500, and probably on some of the houses they built on the Portland Estate. I say probably, because although they continued to manufacture and sell the material, they stopped using it on their own buildings in 1779.

The trouble with the composition was the use of oil as an ingredient. Although it was thought this would give good weather protection, it actually encouraged failure because of poor adhesion. The problem was further exacerbated by lining the surface with a trowel to imitate the joints of stonework. The stucco failed at Kenwood, Lord Chief Justice Mansfield's great house at Highgate, and also at Hampton where Mrs Garrick, compelled by a clause in her late husband's will to maintain the house, was advised by Sir William Chambers to cover the stucco with mathematical tiles to prevent further failure. Worst of all, in 1784 the brothers were successfully sued for £1,500 by Lord Stanhope after failure of the stucco at Chevening.[90]

The important feature to note about Georgian stucco
54 work is that it was not painted in the way we see it today. Rather it was colour washed and frescoed so as to imitate as closely as possible the real stone that the London speculative builder could not afford to use. Peter Nicholson wrote in his *New and Improved Practical Builder* in 1823:

> When the works are finished, they should be frescoed, or coloured, with washes, composed in proportions of five ounces of copperas to every gallon of water, and as much fresh lime and cement as will produce the colours required. Where these sorts of works are executed with judgement and finished with taste, so as to produce picturesque effects, they are drawn and jointed to imitate well-bonded masonry, and the divisions promiscuously touched with rich tints of umber, and occasionally with vitriol; and, upon these colours mellowing, they will produce the most pleasing and harmonious effects.

In Bedford Square this illusion was enough to trick Ralph, who enthused: 'The regularity and symmetry of the sides, each of which is adorned with a central building faced with stone and enriched with pilasters and a pediment'.[91]

Judging by its earlier failure at Lord Loughborough's house and elsewhere, it is almost certain that none of the original stucco survives in Bedford Square. Early replacement may have been Bryan Higgins's water-based cement, patented in 1779, or James Parker's Roman Cement, patented in 1796, and used by John Nash at Park Crescent in 1812 as the prelude to the great age of stucco of the Regency.

Hartley's fire-plates

No detailed account of Bedford Square would be complete without a mention of Hartley's fire-plates. In 1981, a remarkable discovery was made in No.7 during restoration works. Thin overlapping sheets of iron nailed to the joists were found at the first- and second-floor levels. These were Hartley's fire-plates, the invention of David Hartley, and an important part of the many attempts devised in the Georgian period to prevent fire.

David Hartley was born in 1731 and studied science at Corpus Christi and medicine at Merton. He entered Parliament in 1774 and spent the bulk of his time there in opposition to the American War; in 1783 he signed the Treaty of Paris which ended the war.[92]

Hartley was as well known for his fire-plates as his political life. In 1773 he had obtained a patent for his invention, and the year after was granted a sum not exceeding £2,500 by the Commons to defray further costs in his experiments. With this money he was able to build a house on Putney Common which became known as the Fireproof House and which played host to some spectacular experiments.

The installation of the fire-plates was described by Hartley in 1776:

> In common dwelling Houses it will be sufficient to lay the Plates under each Floor; it would be a needless expence, additionally, to apply them to the Ceilings ... The manner of laying down the Plates is most simple and plain. The sheets are folded together to a sufficient length, and then laid upon the joists and nailed on. The Plates are painted to secure them from accidental rust.[93]

The plates worked by 'preventing the immediate access of the fire itself to the timbers of the house, and partly upon their preventing that excessive draught of air, without which no house can be set on fire'. As to the cost, Hartley reckoned on two or three per cent, or around £50 to £60, of the total building cost of a London house with 'three windows in a front of 24 feet, with two rooms and a closet upon one floor'.[94] In Bedford Square they were installed at No.7 in the 1780s for Samuel Hartley, almost certainly related to David Hartley, who took up residence early in 1781 and stayed for eight years. Hartley also had his plates installed at Mrs Montagu's house in Portman Square and at his own house in Golden Square (No.20); Sir William Chambers used them at Windsor in 1777, Henry Holland at Carlton House and Woburn, and James Wyatt at the Pantheon where, however, they could not prevent the fire of 1792.[95]

Hartley was, by all accounts, a great eccentric. His dress was more seventeenth- than eighteenth-century and he restricted his diet to bread and butter and tea. He would always celebrate His Majesty's birthday 'in the midst of flames' although Sir William Chambers, seemingly resigned to such patriotism, sympathetically suggested he 'give his feast on the Queen's birthday, when the weather is not so hot, and rather in town than in the country, as fire-engines are there more easily obtained, to extinguish his guests should the fire prove rebellious'.[96]

George III took a great interest in Hartley and made many a visit to the Fireproof House at Putney, both to test the fire-plates and discuss politics. On one occasion, the King visited with the Queen, the Prince of Wales, the Princess Royal, Princess Augusta and others. They were treated to a wonderfully bizarre series of experiments specially arranged by Hartley to demonstrate the effectiveness of his invention. A kettle was boiled on the floor of an upstairs room where the guests later saw a four-poster in flames. A horse-shoe was forged in a fire made on the floor of a downstairs room and two fires were made on the staircase and one underneath. The day ended with a large magazine of faggots, pitch and tar furiously burning in a downstairs room with their Majesties and the rest of the party retiring to the room immediately above.[97]

6

Forms and Features: The Role of Thomas Leverton

55. Nos.6 to 10 Bedford Square, rear elevations, showing full-height bows to the three middle houses.

The 1774 Building Act, 'an Act for the further and better Regulation of Building and Party Walls; and for the more effectually preventing Mischief by fire', came onto the statute book just in time to influence the design and building of Bedford Square. It dealt, for instance, with the thicknesses required for structural walls and the sound construction of party walls and parapets; it appointed parish surveyors to supervise and, in theory, ensure the quality of building works and it caused the box frames of double-hung sash windows to be set behind a facing brick nib which would serve to shield the frame from fire.

The Act also placed houses into one of four Rates, depending on their size and value. The houses in Bedford Square were all built as those of the First Rate, defined as having a value of £850 or more and exceeding nine squares on plan (a square being 100 square feet, measured on 'the Level of the principal Entrance').

The average plot width granted in the Square was between 28 and 30 feet, with a depth averaging 130 to 140 feet through to the lane at the rear. Of that depth, the house takes up between 40 to 52 feet, extending anything up to 16 feet if the rear wall takes the form of a bow or canted bay. Such rear walls became particularly fashionable in London after the 1760s and added greatly to the possibilities available for a more interesting floor plan and for admitting light into the rear rooms. They 55
are common on the east, south and west sides – sometimes canted, sometimes rounded – but not on the north side. On the front elevations of this side though, there are several windows with decorative wooden blind boxes, 13
Today, it would appear, they are redundant.

The typical floor plan of these houses is dealt with elsewhere (see p.57), but it is worth considering here the uses of the individual rooms. The following list is taken from a 'Schedule of the Lessees Fixtures now to be found in the Dwellinghouse and premises No.2 Bedford Square'. It was made in 1874 when the lease fell in, and the rooms it identifies can be taken as a reasonable guide to their use for the first 99 years and several subsequent years until the houses were eventualy given over to commercial users.

The schedule reads as follows:[98]

THIRD FLOOR: Front Dressing Room, Front Bed Room, Back Bed Room, Back Dressing Room, Housemaid's Closet and Landing

SECOND FLOOR: Landing and Water Closet, Dressing Room, Front Bed Room, Back Bed Room

FIRST FLOOR: Front and Back Drawing Rooms

GROUND FLOOR: Dining Room, Study Hall, Store closet, Water Closet and Passage

BASEMENT: Men Servant's Room, Butler's Pantry, Passage, Housekeeper's Room, Pump Room, Scullery, Kitchen, Larders, Washhouse

Before we deal with the houses in the Square individually, and in particular their interiors, we must describe in more detail the contribution made by Thomas Leverton. We encountered him briefly when examining the designs of the façades (see p.23), for which I do not believe he was involved, and we shall encounter him again when we examine No.1 which he certainly did design.

Thomas Leverton was born at Woodford, Essex, in 1743, two years after the younger George Dance and three years before James Wyatt. His father was a builder, as was his elder brother, Lancelot, described on his death as 'a builder in London'.[99] His younger brother, Andrew, was a bricklayer, based in Woodford, who for some twenty years from 1768 held long-term leases of brick- and tile-making rights on eleven acres of land at Higham Bushes, Walthamstow.[100] We know little about Leverton before 1770 other than that 'he worked and acquired a knowledge of the principles of construction'[101] under his father's tutelage.

He gained some significant commissions early on in which he was 'enabled by influential patrons, among whom was Mr Kendall, a banker, to perfect himself in architecture'.[102] Woodford Hall was the first and probably his earliest important work, doubtless gained from family connections. With the exception of 1779, he exhibited every year from 1771 to 1785 at the Royal Academy. All of his exhibits – the last made in 1803 – show him to be based in London, in either Holborn (Newton Street and Great Queen Street) or Bloomsbury (Charlotte Street and Bedford Square).

His career was a varied one. He supplemented the income he received from designing country houses with the more regular work offered by institutions. He was appointed Surveyor to the Phoenix Fire Insurance Company in 1782 and designed their offices in Lombard Street in 1787 and their Fire-Engine House in Cockspur Street in Charing Cross in *c.*1792. The latter was illustrated in Malton's *Picturesque Tour* and thought by the author to be 'bold and striking'. He was also Surveyor to the Grocers' Company (Grocers' Hall, Poultry, 1798-1802) and the Theatres Royal in London. He came second (to Dance the younger) out of a list of five for election to the Surveyorship of St Bartholomew's Hospital in 1778 and he made two approaches to the Bedford Estate for a post. On the first occasion, in 1785, he wrote speculatively to Robert Palmer from Charlotte Street, Bedford Square: 'The Period being now nearby at hand when his Grace the Duke of Bedford will enter into that Distinguished sphere of life ... the Town or Country residencies of the Family may require some repairs or alterations, I should be exceedingly happy to have the Honor of being Employed by his Grace on the occasion'.[103] In 1797 he made a more official approach, applying for the post of Surveyor, but the application was unsuccessful. For many years he was a Surveyor in the Land Revenues Office with John Marquand and, after the latter's death in 1809, he worked with Thomas Chawner, one of his pupils. In 1811 this partnership unsuccessfully submitted an alternative plan for Marylebone Park in competition with Nash and Morgan.

Like most architects of the period, Leverton was actively involved in the world of speculative housing. In Bedford Square he was granted the lease of No.13 in June 1781 and was responsible for the design of its interior. He did not take up residence until late 1795. Elsewhere on the Estate he was granted leases of the more modest houses on the west side of Gower Street that run from 56
the Square up to Store Street (No.43), all of which survive. He also took 21-year leases on two houses on the west side of Bloomsbury Square at the very end of the eighteenth century;[104] these would almost certainly have been granted after renovation works rather than redevelopment.

Although he practised until he was in his seventies, his work tails off after the first decade of the nineteenth century. He appears to have settled down to an active life as a Justice of the Peace for Surrey, Kent, Middlesex and the City of Westminster. It is surprising that in both the announcement of his death in the *Gentleman's Magazine*[105] and in the obituary that appeared in the following issue, not one mention is made of his career as an architect.

Leverton's life was long – he died in his 81st year – and doubtless successful – he left an estate of more than £60,000. His life was, however, marred by the death of his only son, Henry, who died in 1789 aged just twelve. His first wife died in 1802, after a long illness, aged fifty-five, in the thirty-sixth year of their marriage. Leverton died in September 1824. His body was interred in a vault at the family's parish church at Waltham Abbey, and a monument, for which he had left the sum of £300, was erected to his memory.

On top of more than £50,000 that he left to relatives and friends, he bequeathed some £12,000 to various charities. We find an illuminating description of the man in

56. No.1 Gower Street, stucco entrance doorway. Leverton took the lease on this house and probably designed the doorway which is a toned-down version of that at No.1 Bedford Square. The stucco to the remainder of the ground floor is late Victorian.

his obituary in the *Gentleman's Magazine*: 'His humility was only equalled by that benevolence which pervaded all his actions. At times he almost repented of these bequests, lest they should get into print and seem ostentatious; though they were sweet to his soul. To use his own expression, "no merit of mine; it is all the work of Providence"; which enabled him to raise a handsome fortune, of which he considered himself only a steward for the benefit of others, and gave him strength of mind and body to enjoy many comforts, in full possession of all his faculties, to an age which few attain.'

Leverton's career suffers from a combination of the lack of an accurate record of his known works, a consistently (and wrongly) aired suspicion that he was assisted by Joseph Bonomi, and extensive demolition of his buildings, particularly later on when his output appears to have declined. It is also probable that he carried out many more commissions in the City of London than are actually known, and which have disappeared in the rebuilding programmes that have occurred far more frequently in that part of the capital.[106]

It is frequently suggested that Joseph Bonomi was a drawing assistant in Leverton's office in the 1770s. The earliest and probably first reference is in Volume Five of the *Architectural Publications Society Dictionary* under the entry for Leverton. Significantly, this was written by Thomas Leverton Donaldson, the son of Leverton's niece Jane.

T L Donaldson (1795-1885) was a highly respected figure in his day as a founding father of the Royal Institute of British Architects, and as Professor of Architecture at London University. He tells us that Bonomi entered Leverton's office when he first came to England from Italy. This was in 1767 when Leverton would have been 23 or 24, at which stage it is doubtful if he had started in practice, let alone built up one sufficient to employ assistants. Nonetheless it has proved a convenient account for historians, especially if we bear in mind that Bonomi had also worked in the Adam brothers' office until 1781 and that Leverton designed in the Adam style. Bonomi's alleged association with Leverton is, however, denied (by implication) in a letter the Italian wrote to the Earl of Buchan in 1807:

> While Messrs. Adam of the Adelphi were in Rome, they saw some drawings I had made, especially those for obtaining the gold medal in Architecture, which pleased them very much, in consequence of which they offered me some salary if I would *entirely* work for them ... I arrived in London the 15th of June 1767 ... I continued with Messrs Adam 14 years, when at that time they begun to be neglected. The building of the Adelphi, and other undertakings of their own, made them neglect the work of others; besides, Mr Wyatt building the Pantheon, and more Architects starting, the works begun to be subdivided, so then I thought to try my own success, of course I left them.
> I had for some months, a great deal to do in making designs of my own to show, as during my stay with them I could do nothing, not only for other people, but even for my own use, under a penalty of paying them £200:0:0 ...'.[107]

Bonomi would have left the Adam office some time in 1781. The first known works under his account are in 1782. There was still time for design work on the later houses in Bedford Square but no documentary evidence has ever emerged linking him with Leverton or the Square.

Leverton was at the height of his architectural career during the 1770s, the decade in which his two finest works
– Woodhall Park at Watton-at-Stone, Hertfordshire
(1777-82) and No.1 Bedford Square (1778-81) – were I
designed. His private work tailed off as he took up surveyorships, and his designs became less interesting, lacking the occasional hints of genius that pepper his early works. His designs for the new Exchequer Office in Whitehall, for example, were very dull indeed and it was no misfortune for London that they were never built.

How Leverton would have fared had Robert Adam not appeared we do not know, but he was undoubtedly influenced by the revolution led by Adam and capitalised on it very successfully. The 'triumphal arch' entrance to
No.1 Bedford Square and the pavilions and link blocks 64
of the garden front at Woodhall Park, for instance, are modelled on the south front at Kedleston, and the motif
of cherubs holding the scrolling foliage of arabesques seen 71,
in the ceilings of the first-floor rear rooms at Nos.1 and 80,
10, and the tympana of the overdoors and niches on the VII
staircase at Woodhall are copies of those in the Marble Hall at Kedleston. Leverton was, however, no mere copyist. At its best his own work shows an originality and an esoteric, idiosyncratic touch, seen in interiors in Bedford Square known to be by him.

57. No.1 Bedford Square, plasterwork to wall and cornice, rear room, ground floor. The lowest member of the cornice consists of miniature Doric columns, a motif consistently used by Leverton in the 1770s and 1780s. The soffit moulding is derived from the Bacchic friezes of Palmyra.

Other than that on his own admission he designed the interiors of Nos.6 and 13 (see p.91), there is no evidence available of the other houses with which he was involved. We do know, however, that his 'principal concern in promoting the finishing' of Bedford Square involved 'several on my own account', two of which were certainly Nos.1 and 10. Other possibilities are Nos.14, 25 and 32, which are what might be called 'architect's houses' and which have some excellent interior detailing. We must also consider the possibility that while he may not have designed complete interiors, he may have executed designs, for example, for decorative ceilings, of which just over fifty original examples survive. Those in Nos.21, 30, 31, 43 and 47 either repeat his motifs or share the same stylistic niche as his known works.

It is worth looking for a moment at Leverton's works of the 1770s and 1780s and linking them together with the motifs and details he used. The most fascinating of
57 these is the miniature Doric columns that he used in his cornice designs, always suspended from an abacus. It is a charming detail that I have never seen anywhere other than in a Leverton house. This cornice appears on the staircase dome and in the little library at Woodhall Park, at the top of the staircase compartment at Boyles Court, Great Warley, Essex (*c.*1775), and at Plaistow Lodge, Bromley, Kent (1780), where a small section survives on the ground floor. It is also seen in complete rooms at
Nos.1, 6, 10 and 13 Bedford Square. One of the two alter- 75
nating staircase balusters used at Woodhall Park is
repeated at No.6 and similar examples are at Nos.1 and 68
10, though the outer uprights are vertical rather than 79
splayed. The decorative plaster band of waved anthemion seen on the staircase at Woodhall Park is repeated in the
staircase compartments at Nos.1 and 6. 69, 75

Other details include the main bedroom ceiling at Woodhall Park, which is a flat version of the barrel-vaulted example on the first-floor front room at No.10 (but without the painted panels); a groin-vaulted ceiling in the entrance hall at Plaistow Lodge with a similar example on the second floor at No.1; identical decorative overdoors and carved architraves seen at Woodhall and No.1; and decorative plasterwork on the staircase walls at Woodhall repeated in the ceilings of the first-floor rear rooms of Nos.1 and 10. Leverton also made great use of niches. There is a profusion of these both inside and outside at Woodhall and on the staircases at his houses in

the Square. Finally, a mention of decorative plaster medallions. There are several at Bedford Square but one
58 in particular is repeated in Nos.1 and 9, and in the dining-room at Woodhall. It is an off-the-peg example, but one wonders if the design could have emanated from Leverton.

Two things remain to be said prior to presenting a detailed gazetteer of the houses. First, in March 1866 a report was prepared for the Building Act and General Purposes Committee of the Metropolitan Board of Works for the purpose of distinguishing the irregularly numbered houses in the Square.[108] From its completion in the 1780s, the houses had been numbered, starting in the south-eastern corner with Sir Lionel Lyde's house, appropriately No.1, and working anti-clockwise. Up to No.38, on the west side, there was to be no change. The adjacent and final house on this side was No.39a and the south side was numbered 39-52. The motion for change was passed and No.39a became No.39 and the south side became Nos.40-53. These numbers remain today and all but No.39 survive as original houses. No.39, which was very small and insignificant judging from surviving floor plans included on the leases at the Bedford Estate Office, was demolished in the late 1890s and replaced by the present No.39, a high-Victorian building of little architectural merit. In all references to houses in this book, the present numbers are given.

Second, a word about the gazetteer. This deals primarily with interiors. For several reasons, one major feature has been excluded, however, and this is the chimney-piece. The chimney-pieces have been the subject of great attention for many years. Judging from the reeded and consoled examples surviving in many houses, these began to replace the originals in the Regency period. And records show that theft started at least as early as the turn of this century.[109] It has been a continuing problem, particularly acute in the 1980s, and especially from the vacant houses on the east side, prior to their refurbishment. Not 73
wishing to encourage this despicable practice, I have excluded chimney-pieces from the gazetteer, for which I make no apologies. Some plates of the original examples 137-
are given, however, but their location has not been 146
identified.

58. No.1 Bedford Square, plasterwork to chimney breast, rear room, ground floor. The oval plaque depicting a Roman couple embracing was an off-the-peg model also used by Leverton at Woodhall Park, Hertfordshire.

7

Number One

No.1 Bedford Square is a very special house. It stands alongside Kent's 44 Berkeley Square, Adam's 20 Portman Square and Taylor's 35 Lincoln's Inn Fields (since destroyed) as one of the great terraced houses of London. Far smaller and less richly detailed than those houses, it is, perhaps, something of an underdog, but it has an intimacy and endearing qualities that make it special. It is the ace in the pack of fifty-two houses that survive in Bedford Square.

It is the one house in the Square that is the work of Thomas Leverton – inside and out – and shows him to be an architect of outstanding ability. There is a ceiling here that matches anything that Robert and James Adam
VII were putting into their speculative London town houses, an entrance hall that anticipates the stripped Classicism of the 1790s and a most elegant staircase that fits into
66 the tightest of spaces with a wonderful sense of deport-
I ment. And outside is a façade that shows just what could be done within the sometimes intolerable confines of what was deemed correct in the application of the classical idiom to the fashionable West End terraced house front.

The house would not have been built in such a way had it not been for a gentleman who showed himself to be one of the most enlightened patrons of the arts in the years after the 1763 Peace of Paris. He was Lionel Lyde,[110] a tobacco merchant in the City and a director of the Bank of England, who was created a baronet in 1772 and knighted some time before 1779. He owned the manor at Ayot St Lawrence in Hertfordshire, the manor house serving as the country residence for him and his wife (and cousin) Rachel. In the late 1770s, Sir Lionel paid for the old church at Ayot to be taken down and for Nicholas Revett's Greek replacement. In appearance the church was more romantic garden ornament than ecclesiastical building, and had a Palladian plan with its flanking wings; but it was one of those important early Greek buildings left by the two antiquaries who fell so fast after the publication of their *Antiquities of Athens* in 1762. It was consecrated by the Bishop of Lincoln on the last Wednesday of July, 1779.

At the same time, Lyde was arranging the building of his town house in Bedford Square. I have mentioned that the house would have been a much more modest affair were it not for his intervention and the reason is this. It is outside the self-contained symmetry of the east side and was therefore destined to be like those other houses in
22, 23 a similar position – Nos.26 and 37 for example – and also its neighbours in Bloomsbury (then Charlotte) Street. So it would have been built on a narrower plot with a greatly reduced height and a general paucity of good detail. At an early stage, Lyde, who obviously wanted something more individual than the standardised façades in the Square, must have struck a deal with either Grews or Scott or even John Hakewill, who was the builder of the two adjacent houses south of No.1. The deal, I believe, involved the plots of those two houses and that of Lyde's house. Because Sir Lionel required a plot as wide as those in the Square, there had to be adjustment to the narrower ones (by an average of six feet) and this was made not on the property of Lyde's immediate neighbour but on
the next one down (No.58 Bloomsbury Street) which is 59
a two-bay house.

The lease to No.1 is missing and so in the absence of certain details the story cannot be complete, but it was granted to Lyde – one of only five leases in the Square granted to the first occupier – and his name is given as builder in the District Surveyor's building affidavit. He would not, of course, have been the builder but this paradox appears on one or two affidavits. Perhaps the builder was indeed John Hakewill whose name appears as such for three houses on the east side.

As to the architect, the whole of No.1 is almost certainly the work of Thomas Leverton. Whereas there is no conclusive documentary evidence for this, and although reliance solely on stylistic details has its pitfalls, we do know that Leverton designed the interiors of Nos. 6, 10 and 13 and the abundance of motifs in those houses that are repeated in No.1 puts the matter beyond doubt. As for the façade, there is, again, no conclusive proof of Leverton's involvement. Yet it is undoubtedly an architect's, rather than speculator's, façade. It has a gentler
proportion than the other houses; comparing it to its 60, 61
neighbour, No.2, it has the first-floor string course set slightly higher and the identical dentil cornice much lower, giving it a more horizontal emphasis which is reinforced by the reduced height of the first- and second-floor windows. The cornice is topped with a deep blocking course, the centre section composed of an ornamental
Coade stone urn and arabesque panel similar to those 62
used by Robert Adam in his remodelling of Kenwood House a decade before. This is the only original decoration on any of the plain brick houses in the Square, the doorways and balustraded parapets excepted.

But it is the central entrance that distinguishes this 64
house, not only for its decoration but also because it is central. This was the ever so rare exception for the stan-

59. Nos.56 to 60 Bloomsbury Street and 1 to 3 Bedford Square. No.58 Bloomsbury Street is a two-bay house because the plot width taken by No.1 Bedford Square was greater than that intended for houses in Bloomsbury Street.

dard three-bay terraced house in Georgian London
65 because it required an ingenious plan to accommodate the staircase. This is why, just from looking at its 'architectural make-up', I believe the complete house is by Leverton; the façade is inextricably related to the interior by its central entrance. The whole interior flows from it as one enters, it is the linchpin just as in Kent's great house on the west side of Berkeley Square.

If that is not sufficient evidence, then I offer this. One of the two exhibits Leverton showed at the Royal Academy in 1778 was for 'The front of a town house of a person of distinction now building in London'. The date is spot on, the description fits and no other town house has ever been put forward as candidate.

Because the lease is missing we do not know when the grant was made. But No.1 has a sister in No.10, the two houses having so much in common. Most importantly, the other house was leased to Sir Lionel's younger brother Samuel, who lived there during most of the 1780s. The District Surveyor's affadavits were sworn on the same day

60. No.1 Bedford Square, elevation.

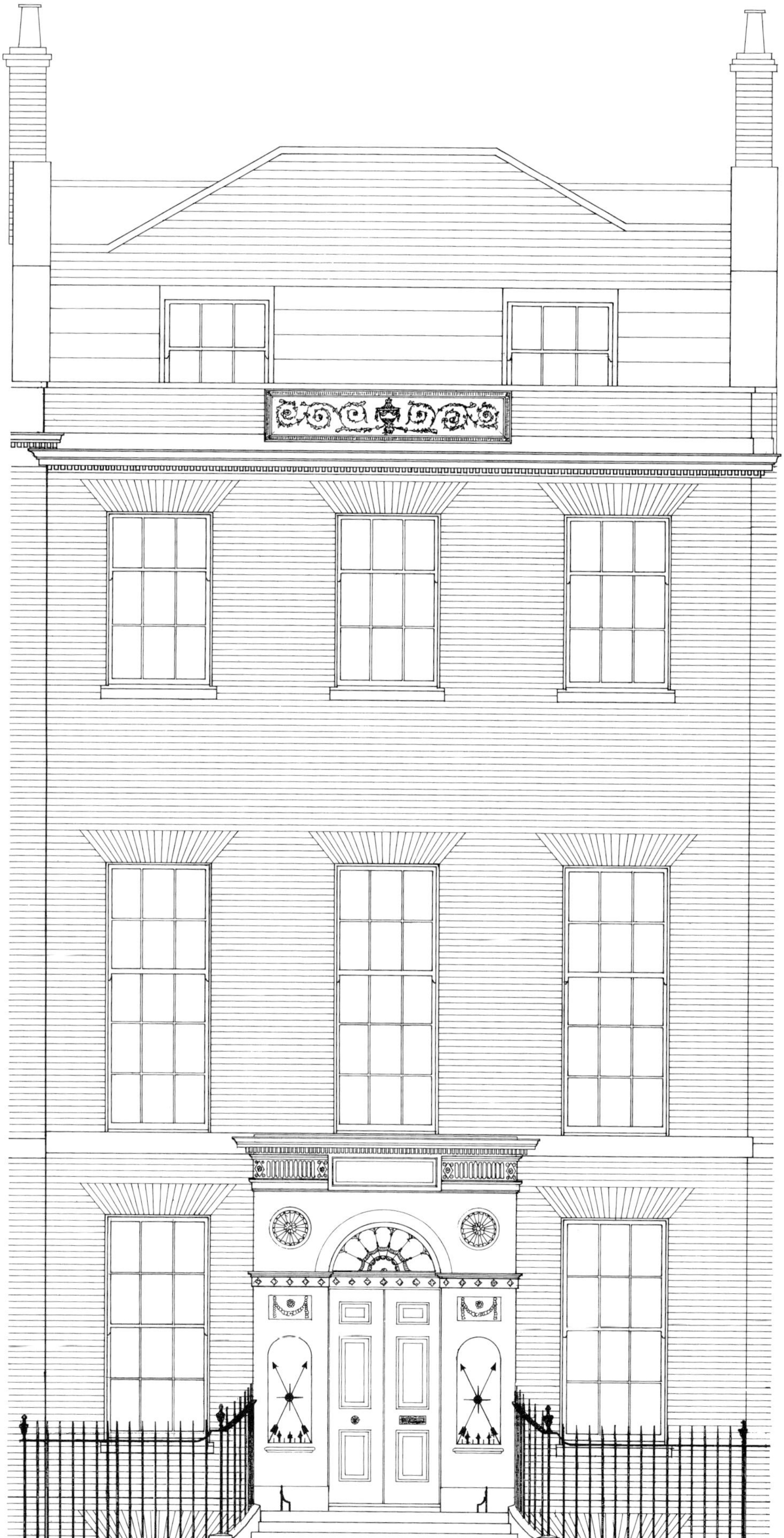

61. No.1 Bedford Square, front elevation. A remarkably accomplished elevation by Thomas Leverton. Note the contrast with the adjacent house in Bloomsbury Street.

62. No.1 Bedford Square, parapet and roof detail. The plaque in the blocking course is in Coade stone.

63 RIGHT. No.1 Bedford Square, ironwork detail to entrance.

– 2 March 1781 – and the lease granted on Samuel's house on 1 June the same year. I suspect Sir Lionel's lease was granted the same day as well; the affadavits signal this, as do the dates of occupation – the first quarter of 1782 for No.1 and the second quarter for No.10.

VII As we shall see, many of the designs and motifs in No.1
80 are repeated in No.10, but before we go inside it is worth having a second look at the front.

60, 61 It is an astonishingly good façade and one that improves as acquaintance develops. It comes, like all good Georgian house fronts, in three distinct layers, divided by the almost obligatory string course at first-floor level and the cornice above the second-floor windows. This house, however, stands way above almost all the plain brick façades of Georgian London, distinguished by exquisite proportioning and sublime detailing. It is the Neo-classical sister of the Palladian front at 44 Berkeley Square.

The proportioning is self-evident, essentially a half square to the ground floor and a square to the first and second, with good window heights, all of which would render it austere but for the stone and stucco detailing which enrich and dignify the whole composition. The
16 dentilled cornice, identical to that used for all the houses in the four palace-fronted blocks, and the decorative Coade panel in the blocking course are both excellent,
64 but it is the stuccoed entrance that is the crowning glory. The steps curve in gently to meet it, the railings likewise set on their own kerb. One is graciously ushered up to the 'triumphal arch' that contains the door. There are few doorways in London that can match this one. It shows the standards Leverton was capable of when his imagination was left to flow. It is a highly original collection of

64. No.1 Bedford Square, entrance doorway.

details; the dentil cornice crops up again, the radial fanlight is modest and the flanking niches contain a pair
63 of crossed spears – a wonderful touch of architectural melodrama.

There is one further detail to be noted. The red brick dressings given to all of the windows, and the quoins that flank the house, are painted on although they have been there a long time. It is also likely that the window arches have been painted red, although red brick arches were by no means rare in the latter half of the eighteenth century.

It is now time to enter the house and as an approach is made towards the door one begins to wonder how Leverton has arranged the interior beyond his centrally placed entrance. The doors are opened, the threshold is
crossed and one walks into the entrance hall; this divides 65
to the left and right into separate, but associated, spaces, the whole area floored with square stone slabs and black diamond inlays. The hall is rectangular, long and narrow, both ends returning in the form of piers with a semi-circular ceiling and a niche in the spine wall opposite the doorway. The middle section, being open, affords access to the adjacent areas and has an oval saucer dome sitting on semi-circular arches on the short sides and segmental

arches on the long. Both flanking spaces have apsidal ends. To the right, in what we might call the anteroom, is a decorative ceiling of three large guilloche circles, each containing a rosette, and every 'corner' has a niche. There is a much larger niche in the centre of the party wall with the house to the south. A doorway in the spine wall leads to the rear room and stands opposite one of the two windows to the front elevation. Much the same arrange-
66 ment happens to the left of the entrance hall, the space containing the staircase which we will walk up in a moment.

But first it is necessary to look in more detail at the entrance hall. It is much more than an exquisite grouping of spaces, for here Leverton shows himself to be far more than the mere competent imitator of Robert Adam that he is so often painted to be. The delicate detailing of the 'Adam style' is here reduced to an extreme attenuation and simplicity that would be interesting in a good interior of the 1790s, but is nothing less than remarkable for a design of the late 1770s. It anticipates the abstractions of Soane by many years. The essential elements are virtually absent – the columns become coupled 'pilasters' whose base is formed by a shallow skirting board moulding and headed by consoles whose projection is so slight that they are only just recognisable as such. The moulding that sits on the consoles also has the narrowest of projections and stops immediately it returns into the anteroom and staircase areas. Flat surfaces predominate; the only movement in the walls occurring where vast recessed arches happen to punctuate the wall surfaces of both party walls – answering the segmental arches of the entrance hall – and on the spine wall opposite the door, but the recesses barely exceed an inch in depth.

We now move into the rear room where the gentle welcoming effect given by the curved walls, niches and round arches of the entrance hall is repeated in an original way by having the four corners rounded; the shallowness of the projections met with before is hinted at again in the chimney-breast which protrudes just five inches into the room. The carved wooden chimney-piece is original.
There is some beautiful plasterwork on the far wall 57
between the windows and also above the chimney-piece
where an off-the-peg oval plaque is framed by floral 58
festoons. The ceiling is not exceptional[111] – concentric
circles set within a square border with square and rect- 67
angular panels at both ends – but the cornice is very special. The lowest member consists of miniature Doric columns, each suspended from a miniature abacus, a highly original treatment that is repeated in other Leverton houses (see p.73).

The staircase in this house is the second of its three glories. Because Leverton moved completely away from the standard London house-plan – entrance to one side, staircase beyond in the rear and main first-floor room at the front – we have the staircase in the front. There is a small terrace in Camberwell Grove that has this arrangement, as does Compton Terrace in Islington; the houses on the demolished east side of Tavistock Square also had it and closer to home so do many houses in Southampton Place, Bloomsbury Street and Gower Street.

In this house, and probably some of the others, the reason for the reversal was to allow the main rooms, which would take in the full width of the building, to be placed at the rear where there was a view to be had. In this case the room overlooked the gardens of the British Museum. There were three other houses on this side of the Square (Nos.4, 6 and 10) which adopted this arrangement. The staircase rises to the second floor, with a separate stair

65. No.1 Bedford Square, ground- and first-floor plans.

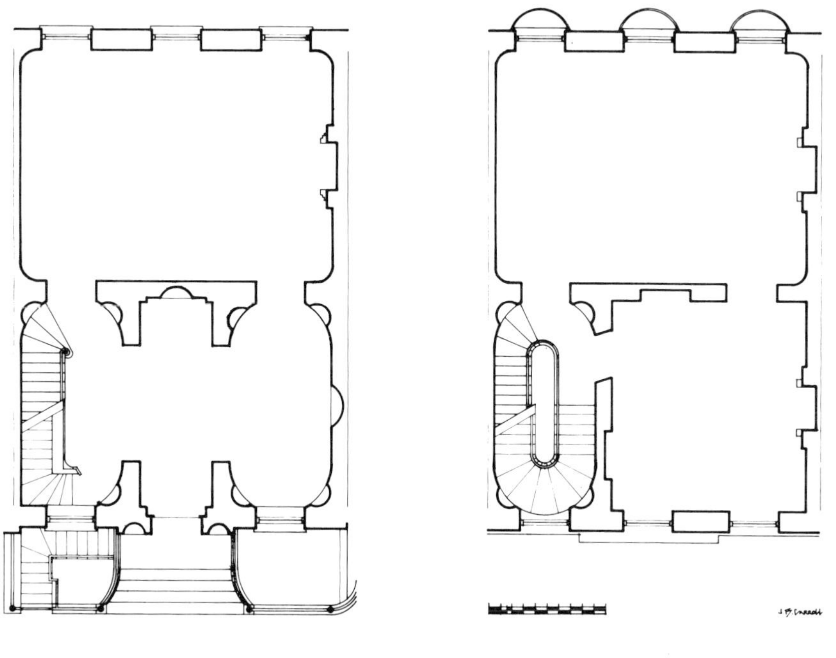

66. No.1 Bedford Square, staircase from the entrance hall.

67. No.1 Bedford Square, ceiling, rear room, ground floor. It is possible that this is an early twentieth-century reproduction (see p.82).

68 RIGHT. No.1 Bedford Square, staircase baluster.

to the third rising in a different position towards the centre of the house. There is nothing unusual in this separation of the staircases – it is standard to almost every house in the Square – but there is much that is extraordinary in the way Leverton designed the main one in this house. It fits into the smallest of spaces – 17 feet by 8 feet 6 inches – but, just like Kent's handling of Lady Isabella Finch's staircase at 44 Berkeley Square, manages to convey a far greater sense of space than is available to it. It 'steals' space on the ground floor from the entrance hall and gathers light from the ground- and first-floor windows as it passes.

69, 70 There is a magnificent grace to the whole composition: the flood of light, the curved ends with a niche at every 'corner', the beautifully-carved moulded stone soffit to each tread and riser, the abundance of winders because of the sharp turns and lack of half-landings – there are no harsh lines or details. The arrangement of the
68 balustrading is typical of the other houses, with a decorative baluster alternating with two straight uprights. Here Leverton uses another of his trademarks, an exquisite

69. No.1 Bedford Square, staircase around first-floor landing. The baluster and flowing anthemion band are standard Leverton motifs.

70. No.1 Bedford Square, staircase, looking up to the second-floor landing and ceiling from the first-floor landing.

71 TOP. No.1 Bedford Square, frieze and ceiling, rear room, first floor. An identical example was installed in the same room at No.10 Bedford Square (see fig.80 and colour plate VII).

72 BOTTOM. No.1 Bedford Square, painted panel in ceiling, rear room, first floor. Venus, the goddess of love, supported by a putto, is accompanied by Hymen, the goddess of marriage, bearing a torch, and a trio of putti celebrating marital love.

73. No.1 Bedford Square, chimney-piece, first-floor rear room. Stolen in 1982.

composition probably in wrought-iron which was also
79 used in Nos.6 (though this design has splayed sides) and 10 (and probably for the original staircase that was removed from No.13 in the Victorian era) and also at
69 Woodhall Park. There is lovely deep band of flowing anthemion ornament to the apron of the first- and second-floor landings; it is also seen at No.6 and at Woodhall Park.

At the first-floor landing we turn right into the front room. It is almost square on plan and warrants little description. It is plain with a late-Victorian chimney-piece and a strange abundance of doors. The double set we entered by are matched by a false pair and the couple that lead to the rear room also have a matching pair. The carved detail of the architraves is also seen at Woodhall Park.

The rear room on this floor is identical in plan to the one below, and shares similar details – rounded corners, a very low dado and the shallow projecting chimney-breast. It contains, however, something that makes it very
VII important. The ceiling in this room is quite magnificent, one of the most sublime pieces of decorative art contained in any London town house of the Golden Age. The frieze 71
is exquisite and the ceiling is full of the most beautiful motifs – cherubs hold the scrolling ends of foliage in outstretched arms, winged sphinxes face each other across a painted panel on which a front foot nonchalantly rests, cameos take a place where space permits, foliage scrolls almost untamed around painted panels and figures. The attention to detail is superb and the craftsmen employed to carve the moulds must have been of the very highest calibre to have achieved such a crispness of form. Within the whole composition are seven painted panels pre- 72
viously believed by some to be by Antonio Zucchi and others by Angelica Kauffmann. It now seems likely that these panels, which are repeated in the same room at No.10, were produced by a mass-production process known as 'mechanical painting' promoted by Matthew Boulton, the Birmingham metalworker. This was a form of colour printing finished off by hand. Kauffmann possibly supplied Boulton with originals but was probably never

associated in any other way with Bedford Square. It appears that she did much less decorative painting than previously thought and concentrated mainly on houses that Robert Adam was commissioned to build.[111a] The beautiful car-
73 ved marble chimney-piece in this room was stolen in 1982.

That concludes our visit to No.1, except to note a groin-vaulted ceiling just off the second-floor landing, a niche with good arabesque plasterwork in the rear room of the same floor, two original wooden chimney-pieces on the top floor and a surviving curved corner in the rear room of the basement.

Leverton had very little space to work with in this house; within the walls it measures just 27 feet across and 39 feet deep, one of the smallest houses in the Square. He avoided the cliché of contrived proportioning and debased imitation and concentrated instead on his own original detailing and a fine collection of spaces that mark this house out as one of the masterpieces of domestic English architecture.

Sir Lionel Lyde moved into the finished building early in 1782 and remained until his death, occasioned by a 'very short illness' in the summer of 1792. In his will he directed that both this house and the manor at Ayot St Lawrence be sold at auction. The purchaser of the London house was one George Gostling, whose family was to live here for the next seventy years.

The first threat to No.1 Bedford Square occurred in 1860[112] when Mr Oldfield, an employee of the Archaeological Department of the British Museum, proposed a new building for the Department of Antiquities. The plan required the purchase of 17 houses in Charlotte Street (Nos.4-20 Bloomsbury Street) and Nos.1-3 Bedford Square. The purchase cost of the houses and gardens was estimated at £65,000 and the new building cost at £145,000. The scheme was not carried out. Then in the early 1930s the Museum, now owners of the entire east side of the Square, proposed a new building for the exhibition of the Elgin Marbles. Unlike the 1860 plan, it did not require any demolition but did call for a building that would stand only twenty feet from the rear elevation of No.1. The threat produced a long article in *Country Life* that heralded the house as 'a masterpiece of English architecture' and of 'exceptional merit'. Support came from Sir Edwin Lutyens who, describing it as a 'most interesting house ... of exceptional quality',[113] saw the proposal as the death knell for the house as a private residence and suggested that if the new building had to be erected, the British Museum take over No.1 as an exhibit.

The Duveen Gallery was built shortly before the Second World War and, today, its plain brick flank wall is the view from the first-floor drawing room of No.1, rather than the gardens of its Museum – which was such an important consideration in Thomas Leverton's original designs for the house.

The Gazetteer: 2-53 Bedford Square

Number Two

This is the end house of the palace-fronted east side. The lease is missing but that for No.3, granted on 10 December 1778, tells us that it abuts 'South upon a Messe or Tenement granted on lease bearing even date herewith to John Addison'. Addison was one of only five lessees in the Square who were also first occupiers (see also Nos.1, 10, 11 and 14).

36 Because of its position within the terrace, it has the emphasis of a balustraded parapet and a slight projection from the neighbouring house to the north. There are later individual cast-iron balconies to the first-floor windows and an original radial fanlight to the doorway. Along with No.24 this is one of the narrowest houses in the Square.

Inside, it is a plain house containing the standard London ground plan – entrance to one side, staircase beyond, the front and rear rooms of the ground floor both entered from the staircase hall, with the latter room slightly narrower because of the width taken up by the staircase. The only room of note is the front room on the first floor, which has a good decorative plaster ceiling with four painted panels and an arabesque and griffin frieze. The architraves and shutter-mouldings have carved details. The ceiling in the rear room on this floor consists of one massive oval guilloche band contained in an oblong panel and a two-feet deep coving (which is possibly later).

Number Three

Leased on 10 December 1778 for 99 years from the Feast of St Michael the Archangel 1775 to James Higley, carpenter of the parish of St Clement Danes. The plot was 27 feet wide by 135 feet deep, let at an annual ground rent of £13 10s after the peppercorn period of five years.

The façade has no decoration at all and the first-floor windows are set several courses above the string course. The rear elevation has a full-height bow.

The floor plan is standard but the rear wall of the front room on the ground floor is segmental in shape. The stone staircase has an S-scroll baluster alternating with two straight balusters supporting a mahogany handrail. The main room on the first floor has a good decorative plaster ceiling.

Number Four

Leased on 20 November 1777 to William Jacques, carpenter of the parish of St George the Martyr. The plot was 30 feet wide by some 134 feet deep, with a rent of £18 p.a.

74. No.4 Bedford Square, entrance doorway in Coade stone. There are two types of Coade doorway in Bedford Square. This type has a full fanlight, the other has a concentric arch of Coade stone within the brick and block arch (see fig.51).

There is a good fanlight over the door and a surviving lampholder and link extinguisher to the left of the entrance steps. Inside, the house has little to recommend it but the floor plan is of interest: this is one of only four houses in the Square to have the staircase rise in the middle of the house between the front and rear rooms and parallel with the façade; the staircase compartment is lit by an oval lantern. This deviation from the usual London floor plan was criticised by Sir John Soane, who believed that convenience and appearance were sacrificed. He added, however, that 'occasionally a passage of communication is made at the back of the staircase, and by this arrangement the inconvenience is in some degree removed'. The houses of the 1770s in Queen Anne's Gate, Westminster and the two magnificent terraces at Wapping Pier Head (1811-13) have this same floor plan. 74

80. No.10 Bedford Square, ceiling, rear room, first floor, designed by Thomas Leverton. An identical ceiling was installed at No.1 Bedford Square (see fig.71 and colour plate VII).

the area railings at the side of the house), with an annual rent of £15 4s 6d. As with Nos.7-9, a plot of land at the rear was added to the garden at a rent of 2s per annum for 91 years from Michaelmas 1783 (see p.41).

This is a very important house because of its association with No.1, which Samuel's brother, Sir Lionel, commissioned Thomas Leverton to design. Leverton also designed the interior of this house but there is no particular individuality because many of the features are 'repeats' of his work elsewhere in the Square, particularly that at No.1.

A large proportion of the fine original details survive, in spite of extensive alterations, particularly to the ground floor, at the turn of this century – for example, the stained glass to the fanlight and sidelights at the entrance doorway and the canted bay to the rear of the side elevation. While looking at the outside, we should note the original
28 rainwater hopper and lead downpipes, and the height of the ground-floor windows which, unexpectedly, are the same height as those on the first floor. A glance at the other houses will quickly reveal that the first-floor windows (cut down to the string course or not) are all taller than those on the ground floor.

The staircase rises between the front and rear rooms (as in Nos.4, 6 and 11) and is lit by a circular lantern. The balusters are identical to those in No.1. In the rear 79
ground-floor room is an Edwardian ceiling, but the original cornice remains, composed of the miniature Doric columns Leverton used in Nos.1, 6 and 13.

On the first floor there are two most beautiful ceilings. In the rear room, which has rounded corners, the ceiling is identical to that found in the same location in No.1, 80, VII
with seven painted panels which are also exact versions of the seven in No.1. The main panel – in the centre – represents the Judgement of Paris, who chose Aphrodite as the fairest of the three goddesses brought him by Hermes; his reward was a free choice of lover. He chose Helen and thereby began the Trojan War.

In the front room is a barrel-vaulted ceiling (see No.6) with three painted panels plus one at either end in the 81
'tympanum'. The main panels depict the musical contest between Apollo and Pan; first Pan plays his pipes, then Apollo plays his lyre. Apollo is judged the winner and his prize is Daphne, priestess of Mother Earth. Crying out for help at her fate, Daphne is turned into a mountain laurel by Mother Earth. There is a marked similarity between this ceiling and the main centre section of that in the main room on the first floor of No.13. A flat version IV

81. No.10 Bedford Square, painted panel on ceiling, front room, first floor. Apollo, the Greek sun-god, plays the lyre to the nine Muses of artistic inspiration in the musical contest between him and Pan. In the background stands the Temple of the Arts on Mount Parnassus.

of this ceiling, without the painted panels, can be seen at Woodhall Park in the main bedroom (see p.73). The joinery on the first floor has carved details identical to that seen at No.1.

Number Eleven

Leased on 10 March 1783 for 99 years to Dr Michael Teighe, 'Doctor of Physic' of the parish of St George Bloomsbury. The plot was some 26 feet wide (increasing to 41 feet in the rear garden) by some 159 feet deep, with a ground rent of £13 3s per annum. A separate building agreement was signed between the Duke's trustees and William Scott and Robert Grews on 6 March 1781 for this house.

Although it has always been considered part of the
26 Square rather than Gower Street (in which it stands),
No.11 has no architectural tie with its associates – there
85 is no first-floor string course, the cornice is moulded but
82 lacks the dentils, the doorway is in stucco and bears no
relation to the Coade stone of the other houses, and the
83 ground-floor windows are actually taller than the first-
floor windows.

82. No.11 Bedford Square, entrance doorway. Although the canted bay is original, the stucco door surround appears to be much later.

This must have been a very good house, but now has little left that is of interest. The floor plan was well contrived, the entrance being at the 'side' of the house (in Montague Place), contained within a canted bay. Beyond
84 the entrance hall is the staircase with rooms on either side. At the basement- and ground-floor levels are two original wings which contain octagonal rooms – two per floor – above which rises a handsome full-height bow to the garden, with excellent window proportioning.

The main staircase rises all the way to the third floor, with two niches to each of the first two flights contained within the compartment's one curved wall. The balusters alternate between two straight and one fairly plain decorative type, ornamented with wrought-iron calyces, and the whole space is topped with a vaulted ceiling and circular lantern. Other than this, there are just a few friezes that are worth noting; all are standard off-the-peg mouldings encountered elsewhere, except for an excellent example in the rear room on the first floor, comprising griffin, vase and arabesque ornament in a far bolder relief than one would expect to see in a 1780s West End house. The basement retains its original wine cellar.

83. No.11 Bedford Square, front elevation to Montague Place.

84. No.11 Bedford Square, staircase.

85. Nos.11 and 12 Bedford Square, front elevations.

86. No.12 Bedford Square, cast-iron verandah dating from the early nineteenth century. There were at least three examples in the Square but this is the only survivor.

Number Twelve

Leased on 1 June 1781 for 99 years to Nathaniel Sanderson, mason of the parish of St Pancras. The plot was the second smallest granted in the Square trimmed down to a mere 60 feet in depth by the houses in Gower Street. The plot width was 28 feet, with an annual rent of £16 16s.

This house is at the east end of the north side and so possesses a balustrade parapet. Far more interesting,
85 though, is the early nineteenth-century cast-iron trellised
86 and tented balcony to the first floor. There are good cast-iron shoe scrapers at the entrance and an original fanlight over the door. The doorway itself is an imitation in stucco of the Coade stone examples. Inside is a standard floor plan, a stone staircase with S-scroll balusters and some good plasterwork – ornamental panels in the ground-floor front room and two good ceilings on the first floor.

Number Thirteen

This is a very important house because the 99-year lease, granted on 1 June 1781, was taken by Thomas Leverton, 'Surveyor of the parish of St Giles in the Fields', who was, by his own admission, responsible for finishing the interior (see p.91). Although occupation was first taken in 1782, Leverton was not to settle here until 1795. It then served as his London town house until his death in 1824, and continued in family occupation by his second wife, Rebecca, for a further nine years.

The plot was identical to its easterly neighbour (No.12) but six inches shorter, making it the smallest plot in the Square, and the rectangular house built on it – 28 feet wide by 41 feet 10 inches deep – is the smallest of any in the four palace-fronted blocks.

The house displays much individuality, inside and out, 88
which reflects Leverton's initial interest as original lessee and subsequent interest as resident. Outside, on both front and rear elevations, there is a profusion of Gothic 50
cast-iron balconies of the sort seen on London houses of the early nineteenth century. It is fairly safe to say that these were inserted by Leverton during his residency. There are nine of them overall, three to the second-floor windows at the front, three to the same windows at the rear, and three above these. The continuous first-floor balcony at the front is similar to the individual ones at No.6. The doorway, like that at No.12, is an imitation in stucco of the Coade stone examples elsewhere in the Square. The rainwater hopper on the party wall with No.12 is worthy of note and has a good overflow spout.

Inside, the most tragic thing has happened. The original

87. No.13 Bedford Square, painted panel in ceiling, front room, first floor. Fortuna, the goddess of good fortune, sits in triumph in her chariot, pulled at great speed by a pair of winged creatures with sea-serpent tails and dragon heads.

88. Nos.13 and 14 Bedford Square, front elevation. The only exception to the regular spacing of windows in each house in the Square is at No.13, where the width of the right-hand pier is greater than that on the left. This is due to the unusual floor plan which was designed by Thomas Leverton and can be seen in fig.89. Leverton took the lease of this house in 1781.

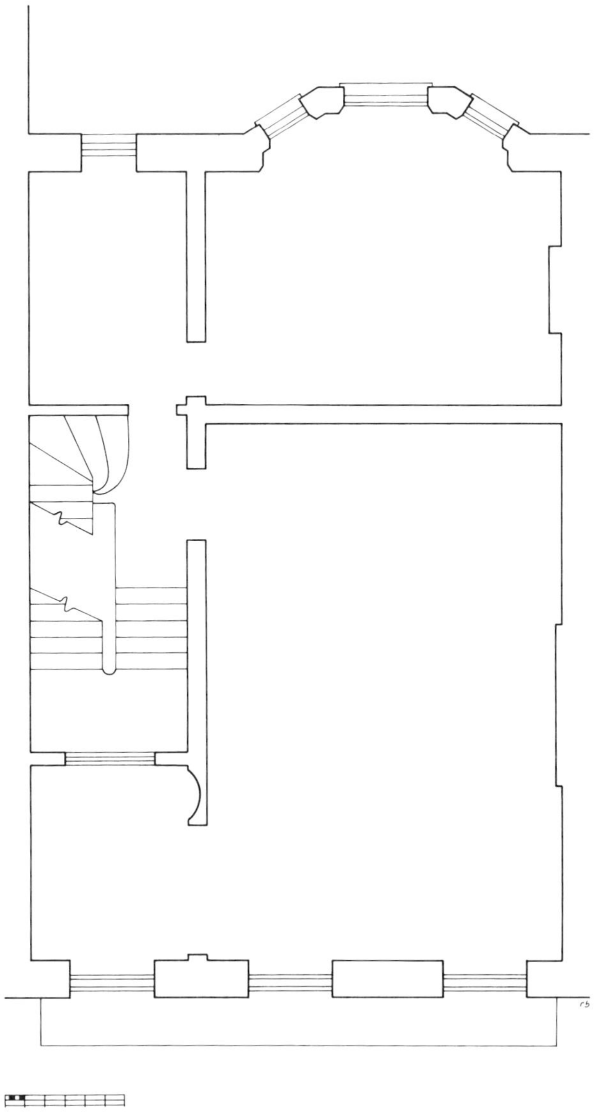

89. No.13 Bedford Square, first-floor plan.

90. No.14 Bedford Square, staircase baluster.

stone staircase was ripped out and replaced by a wooden version in the latter years of the Victorian period. It is the only house in the entire Square to have been affected in this way and we can only guess at the design and layout of the original. It probably would have had balusters similar to those in Leverton's other houses – Nos.1, 6 and
79 10. The front room on the ground floor has 'Leverton's cornice' – those miniature Doric columns hanging from their abacus (also seen at the other three houses).

The ground-floor plan appears to be standard (though not if the present staircase, which rises in one flight towards the front of the house, duplicates the original), but on the first floor Leverton twisted the front room
89 through 90° so that it took up just two windows. To the third window he planted a lobby, and at the rear there are two small rooms restricted in size by the depth of the
IV main room. This has an excellent ceiling, with sphinxes, arabesques and festoons, four cameos and three painted
87 panels. The lobby repeats the ceiling in miniature, with a cameo as the centrepiece. It is worth noting that the chimney-breast protrudes just five inches into the main room, as in those on the first floor of Nos.1 and 10. The rear elevation has a canted bay to the lower three floors (probably a later alteration) and tripartite windows to the main rear rooms of the top two floors. This could be the result of alterations by Leverton during his residency.

Number Fourteen

Leased on 1 June 1781 for 99 years to James Baillie esquire of Percy Street. The plot was 29 feet wide and 138 feet deep, with a rent of £15 4s 6d per annum. Baillie was one of only five first occupiers to whom the lease was granted (see also Nos.1, 2, 10 and 11).

This is one of the largest houses in the Square, stretching back 65 feet to the canted bay at the rear, and one 49
of the best; what I might call an 'architect's house'. If one is actively trying to seek more houses, in addition to the four certainties, where Leverton was involved, then this is a strong candidate. Not only is it just the sort of house where he would have become involved – first occupier being head lessee – but it bears the mark of his hand.

The ground-floor plan is fairly standard, but certain 46, 48
details distinguish it. The door to the front room, for instance, is curved and has a matching door opposite,

91. No.14 Bedford Square, cantilevered staircase and landing at second-floor level. The closed door leads to the third-floor staircase. The cantilevered staircase leads to the closet wing.

92 OPPOSITE. No.14 Bedford Square, ceiling, first-floor front room.

which serves a cupboard. The rear room has a curved end but set within a straight rear wall. At the ground to first floor half-landing of the staircase there are two semi-circular arches; one contains a niche, the other is an opening onto a small staircase that leads to the first-floor room of the full-height canted bay.

The main staircase itself is good, with an oval lantern
lined with decorative plasterwork. It has the sort of
90 ornamental baluster – S-scrolled – most commonly found
in the Square and rises, typically, to the second floor; at
the top, however, the landing continues on as an
ornamental balcony through to the rear wall, cantilevered
91 from the party wall with No.15. It gives a beautiful effect
to the whole compartment and is repeated at No.25.

There is good plasterwork in this house. An anthemion
and bucranea frieze adorns the entrance hall, which has
decorative plasterwork to the ceiling as does the staircase
hall beyond. In both rooms on this floor there are excel-
lent arabesque, griffin and vase friezes. On the first floor
are two ornamental ceilings. At the rear, an arabesque
and griffin frieze gives onto a good if plain ceiling, but
at the front an identical frieze introduces a beautiful
92 ceiling whose design has much of the Leverton style – the
almost rampant floral scrolls, the ribboned swags and
peltoid shields. These features bear a strong similarity to
those ceilings in the first-floor rear rooms of Nos.1 and VII
10, and the central feature resembles those in the entrance
hall of No.1 and at the top of the staircase in No.6. There 75
is a full-height canted bay at the rear of the house.

Number Fifteen

Leased on 20 August 1782 for 99 years to Thomas Martin, carpenter of the parish of St George Hanover Square. The plot was 28 feet wide by 138 feet deep, with an annual ground rent of £14.

The house has little of interest. The individual cast-iron balconies to the first floor are good and have moulded stone bases. Inside, the floor plan is standard, the staircase has straight balusters, there are a few ornamental friezes and cornices, and the decorative plaster ceiling in the main room on the first floor, although good, has been divided by a partition.

Number Sixteen

Leased on 20 August 1782 for 99 years to John Utterton, plasterer of the parish of St George Bloomsbury. The plot size and annual ground rent were identical to that of No.15.

The house is so similar in plan to No.15 that it is reasonable to assume one guiding hand to both houses

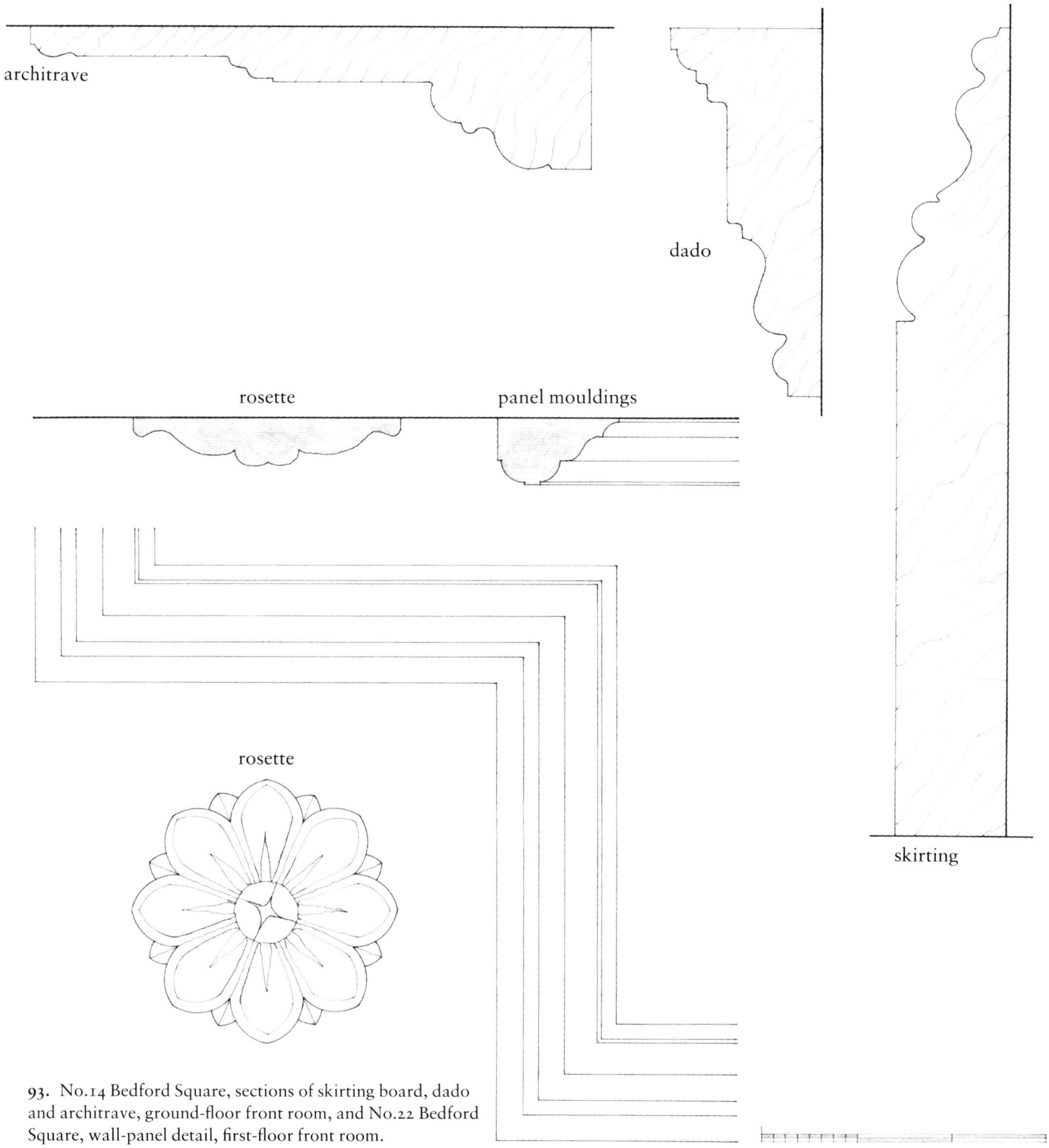

93. No.14 Bedford Square, sections of skirting board, dado and architrave, ground-floor front room, and No.22 Bedford Square, wall-panel detail, first-floor front room.

in spite of the different lessees (see also No.17). There is little of interest except the staircase, which has good S-scroll balusters and a carved dado rail, repeated in the ground-floor rooms, and decorative plaster cornices to these rooms and those on the first floor, all of which have been painted out.

Number Seventeen

Lease details as for No.16. The plot size, annual ground rent and house dimensions (the plan of the external walls as shown on the lease) are identical to Nos.15 and 16.

Outside, there is a good rainwater hopper shared with No.16, and a wrought-iron lampholder and link extinguisher to the right of the entrance. Inside, the floor plan is identical to that of No.16, as is the wrought-iron balustrading of the staircase (interestingly, the stonework of the staircase is unpainted).

There is a fine decorative plaster ceiling in the front

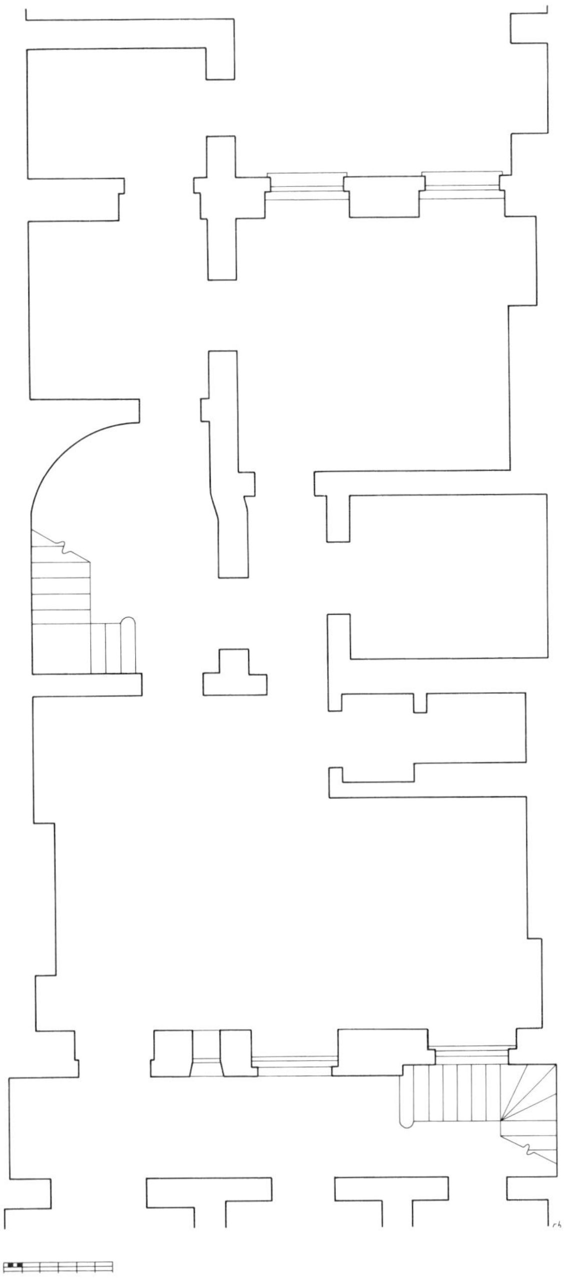

94. No.18 Bedford Square, basement plan.

room of the first floor with an arabesque, griffin and vase frieze and a dado carved with anthemion ornament. The front room on the second floor has an angle chimney-breast, again duplicating that found in No.16 and further proof that these houses were a pair but given a different decorative treatment.

Number Eighteen

Leased on 20 August 1782 for 99 years to Robert Grews, 'late of the parish of St Marylebone but now of the parish of St Giles in the Fields'. The plot was 30 feet wide by 138 feet deep, with an annual ground rent of £15. This is one of the two stuccoed centre houses on the north side, with a rusticated ground floor, and plain floors above with Ionic pilasters supporting the pediment. The middle pilaster on the party-wall line of Nos.18 and 19 was the cause of much criticism when the Square was completed (see p.20).

The floor plan is standard, but there are interesting variations similar to those found in No.14 – two curved doors to the front room on the ground floor within a rounded wall facing the Square, and a full-height bay at the rear entered from the half-landings. The staircase is excellent. It rises tightly around a curved rear wall, with several winders and no half-landings. It has fine wrought-iron S-scroll balusters (and an anthemion at each end of the scroll) and two string courses at second-floor level – guilloche and running scroll – and is lit by an oval lantern which has a decorative plaster soffit and lining.

Little else is of note except the basement – probably 94
the most interesting in the Square – which retains its silver vault with metal door, brick-vaulted wine cellar with metal-barred door, and an original storage cupboard.

Number Nineteen

Leased on 20 August 1782 for 99 years to William Scott. All other details are as for No.18. This house is the mirror image of its stuccoed neighbour and, like Nos.16 and 17, identical in every way except for the decorative finish treatment.

The staircase is therefore identical to the handsome 96
example in No.18, with its S-scroll and anthemion balus- 97
ters, decorative plaster bands at the second-floor landing,

95. No.19 Bedford Square, staircase lantern.

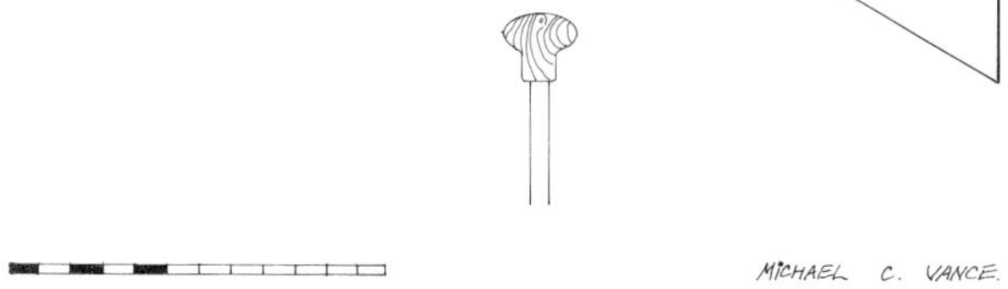

97 ABOVE. No.19 Bedford Square, staircase baluster.

96 LEFT. No.19 Bedford Square, staircase rising from the ground floor.

95 and ornamental work to the oval lantern. The front room
on the first floor has original decorative overdoors, but
the double set of doors through to the rear room are
probably slightly later.

34 At the rear there is a most interesting building, almost
98 certainly contemporary, with a beautiful and appropriate
stucco elevation facing the main house. It stands over two
floors and a basement, with a palm-leaf string course
below the top windows, and semi-circular arched ground-
floor windows, with guilloche imposts and female head
keystones identical to those shown in the Coade stone
35, catalogue of 1799. (See also the building at the rear of
99 No.21.)

Number Twenty

Leased on 20 August 1782 for 99 years to William Woolcott, carpenter of the parish of St Marylebone. The plot was 28 feet wide and 138 feet deep, with a ground rent of £14 per annum.

Outside is a good continuous late-Victorian cast-iron balcony with stone base at first-floor level, a rainwater hopper and an original radial fanlight over the doorway.

Inside, the house is plain with unusual balusters to the staircase. There is an interesting ornamental plaster frieze in the front room on the ground floor, composed of vases and rosettes with guttae.

Number Twenty-One

Leased on 20 August 1782 for 99 years to William Scott. One lease covered this house and Nos. 22 and 23.[116] Each of the three plots was 28 feet wide and 138 feet deep, except for an additional section at the rear of No.23 which was to terminate Gower Mews. The combined annual ground rent for the plots was just £3 13s 6d, which can only be seen as an incentive to Scott (and Grews) to finish off the Square, at a time of great decline in London's building trade, caused by the war in America.

Outside, there is an original fanlight over the doorway, and at first-floor level a fine continuous cast-iron anthemion balcony of the early nineteenth century, with a stone base. All ground-, first- and second-floor windows retain the blind boxes that are so prevalent on this south-facing side of the Square.

In the front room, on the ground floor, are two square Corinthian columns forming a screen across the rear wall; the original dado rail survives, carved with rosettes and flutes. The screen that divides the entrance and staircase hall contains the original fanlight. Also of interest is an excellent decorative plaster ceiling in the front room on the first floor. It contains motifs that can be found on the better ceilings in the Square, some of which are to the designs of Leverton. Perhaps this is another.

At the rear of the plot, beyond the courtyard, there is
an important pedimented two-storey brick outbuilding 35
with an excellent elevation; it is almost certainly con- 99
temporary with the house, and was probably used for
servant accommodation. It is three bays wide with flat-
headed ground-floor windows recessed within semi-
circular arches. The arch imposts continue as a string
course linking the openings. At first-floor level the
windows are square, and there is a blank oval bull's-eye
window in the tympanum of the pediment. This and the
outbuilding at the rear of No.19 are the only examples 34, 98
in the Square, and represent a building type that has all
but vanished from Georgian London.

Number Twenty-Two

Lease details as for No.21.

This is a plain house both outside and in. The staircase 93
has three cast-iron balusters per tread – two straight bars flanking a waving bar. On the first floor, the rear room has semi-circular headed windows with good surrounds and panelled reveals, the surrounds imitating the door-

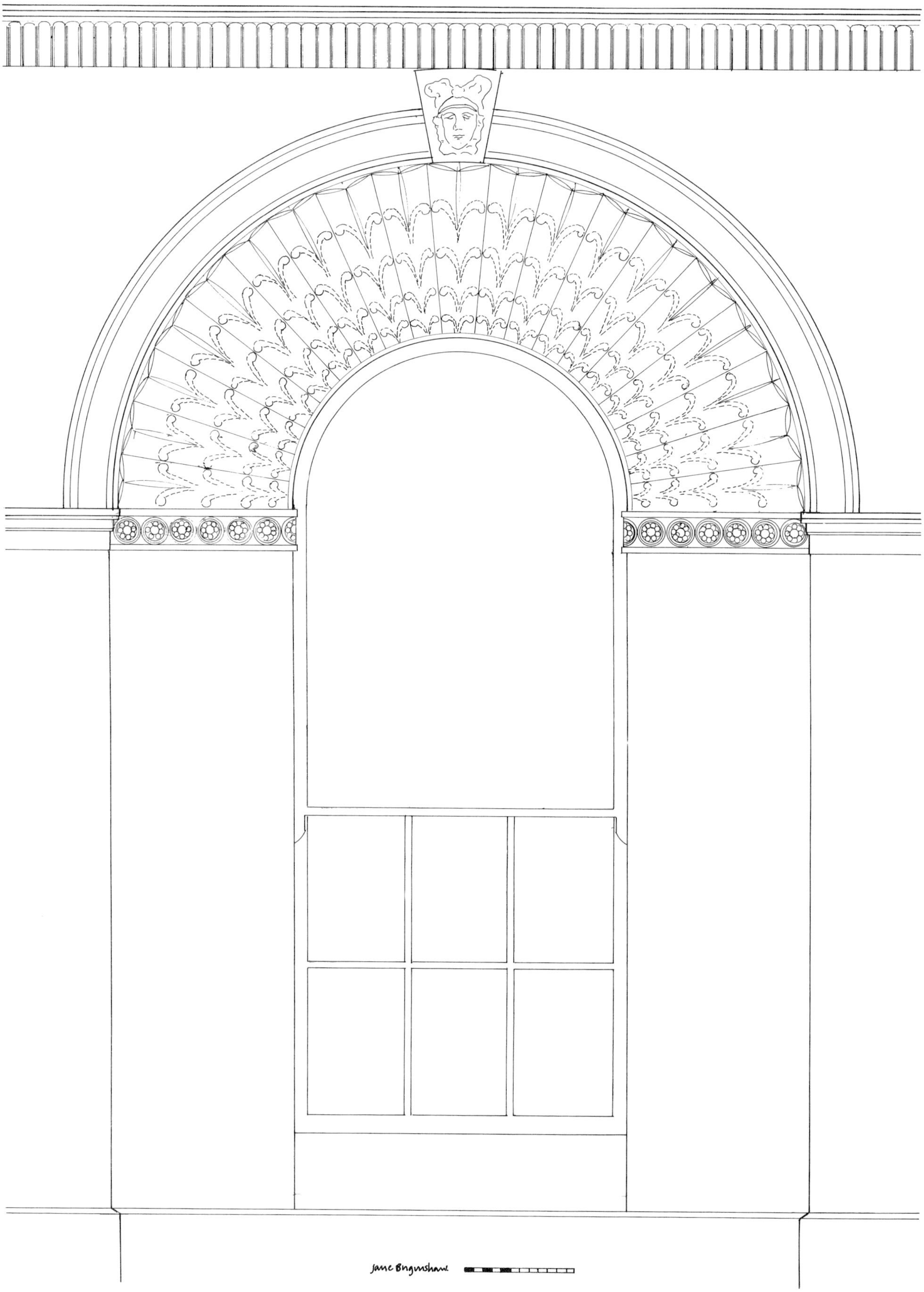

98. No.19 Bedford Square, detail of outbuilding facing rear elevation of main house.

99. No.21 Bedford Square, elevation of outbuilding facing rear elevation of main house.

case. The front room on this floor has a stark decorative ceiling, consisting simply of three rope and leaf panels, one within the other, with fan motifs to the corners of the middle panel.

Number Twenty-Three

Lease details as for No.21.

On the front elevation there is a fine lead rainwater
100 hopper and lead downpipes on the party wall with No.24, all of which are original, later individual cast-iron balconies to the first-floor windows, and an original radial fanlight over the door.

Inside, the floor plan is standard, but the staircase is
101 much wider than average, which reduces the width of the rear rooms on the three middle floors. There are three straight flights per floor with two landings, all lit by an oval lantern which has a dentilled cornice band, and bucranea, swag and rosette ornamental plaster lining. The ground-floor front room has a curved rear wall that takes in a central niche and two flanking curved doors, above each of which is a decorative plaster panel.

There are some good doors on the first floor, with leaf-moulded panels and fluted architraves taking the form of bound reed bands and corner blocks. In the front room there is a fairly good decorative plaster ceiling.

The flank wall of the coach house and stable block terminating Gower Mews has rosette panels (probably

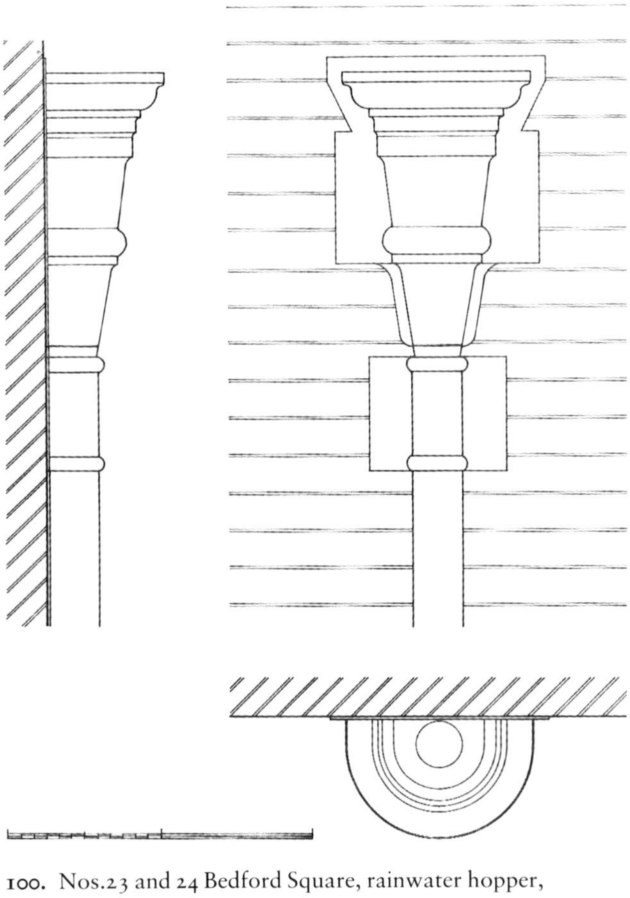

100. Nos.23 and 24 Bedford Square, rainwater hopper, elevation, plan and side elevations.

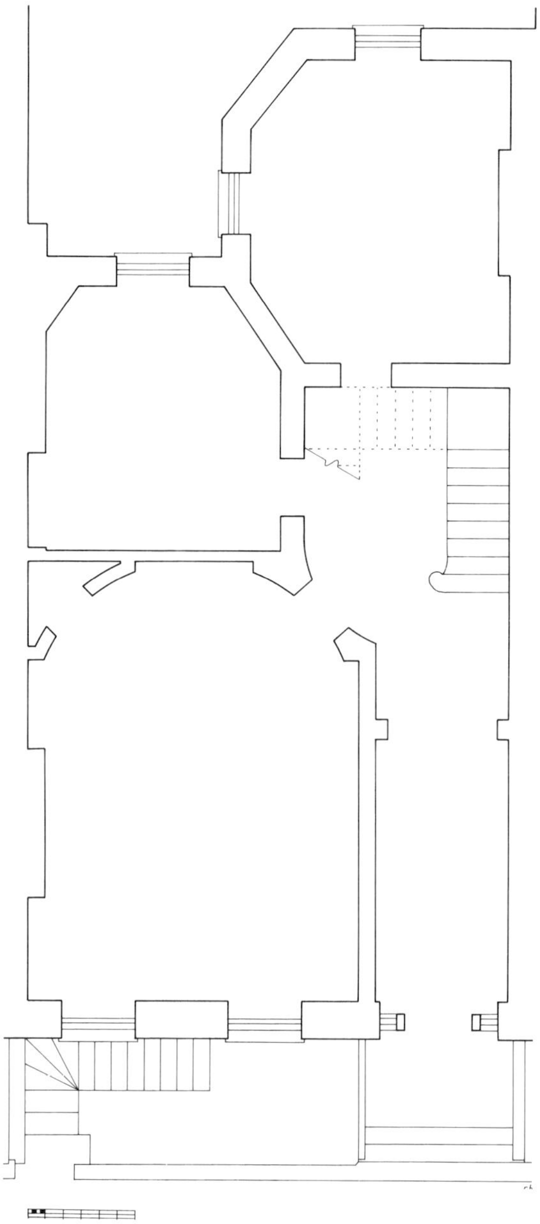

101. No.23 Bedford Square, ground-floor plan.

Coade stone) and arched blank windows. It appears to have been rebuilt about one hundred years ago with the decorative rosette panels set aside and re-used. This was the last house in Bedford Square to be occupied.

Number Twenty-Four

Leased on 20 November 1777 for 99 years to Robert Grews. This lease covered 'a piece of Ground on the North side of Bedford Square whereon three houses are built and another is to be built (being the 11th, 12th, 13th and 14th houses Eastward from Tottenham Court Road)'. The 14th house was this one, which was unbuilt
16 on the granting of the lease. This was the only house in the Square to have a lease granted before it was built (all other leases have an 'as built' floor plan appended in the margin). Here, although the plan is marked out (26 feet wide by 40 feet deep, though it was built much deeper than this), it is annotated 'Ground whereon a House is to be erected'. The overall plot size was 26 feet wide by 73 feet deep, at an annual ground rent of just £4 for all four houses.

As in so many houses on this side of the Square, the rear wall of the front room on the ground floor is segmental on plan, but here the door into the room and its matching cupboard door are straight, rather than curving with the wall as elsewhere. There are good plaster panels above these doors and a delicate ceiling with fan centrepiece surrounded by swags set within leaf-moulded panels. On the first floor there is a very heavy honeysuckle and arabesque frieze in the front room. In the rear room the spine wall is gently curved on plan, and the decorative plaster ceiling, though good, is fairly sparse, with thin vase and arabesque outer panels and a radial centrepiece to the main panel, surrounded by swags and rosettes with fan motifs to each corner. The garden elevation has a canted bay to the lower three floors, possibly a later alteration.

Number Twenty-Five

Leased on 20 November 1777 for 99 years to Robert Grews (see No.24). The plot was 29 feet wide by an average 71 feet deep, the boundary at the rear reducing to the west. This is the western end house of the palace-
fronted north side of the Square and so it has a 1
balustraded parapet and is stepped slightly forward from its neighbours. There are good individual cast-iron anthemion balconies of the early nineteenth century to
the first-floor windows. 102

This is one of the best houses in Bedford Square, with a floor plan similar to No.14 and some very fine interior details. Like No.14, Thomas Leverton may have had a hand in the finishing.

The staircase hall is divided from the entrance hall by

102. No.25 Bedford Square, balcony, elevation, plan and side elevation.

103. No.25 Bedford Square, ceiling, first-floor rear room.

a screen with a good radial fanlight to its semi-circular arch. The sidelights to the entrance door retain their internal shutters. The staircase itself is an open well dog-leg type, with no half-landings and a curved rear wall. An anthemion and palmette frieze decorates the soffit of the first-floor landing, from which runs a guilloche and anthemion ornamental plaster band around the compartment. At the second floor, the main staircase terminates but continues as a balcony cantilevered from the party wall of No.24 and leading to the rear closet room. A
91 similar arrangement occurs in No.14.
31 The front room on the ground floor has a curved back wall set within a 'screen' composed of two pilasters whose capitals are a variation of those of the Athenian Tower of the Winds. The curved wall contained by the 'screen' has a coved ceiling ornamented with swags. There is a beautiful plaster plaque framed by a floral festoon on the chimney-breast. Both the entrance door and opposing cupboard door are curved on plan, as at No.14.

There is some good wood carving on the first floor. In both rooms all the door and window architraves are carved with honeysuckle and the dadoes with leaf and egg. Most of our attention on this floor, though, must be directed to the plasterwork. The front room has an 11
arabesque frieze with a pair of sphinxes to the centre of each run, rising to a very good ceiling, with radial 33
centrepiece surrounded by swags and cameo panels flanked by wreaths and arabesques. The ornamental plaster in the rear room is altogether better, with a honeysuckle, rosette and swag frieze and a beautiful ceiling not dissimilar to that in the same room of No.24, but 32, 103
with a differing centrepiece (arabesque). For over 200

years this beautiful ceiling contained six painted panels, but on the night of Thurdsay 20 July 1989 these were cut out and stolen. The garden elevation has a full-height bow and full-height half-canted rear closet.

Numbers Twenty-Six, Twenty-Seven, Thirty-Seven, Thirty-Eight and Thirty-Nine

These five houses have been grouped together because they fall outside the palace-fronted north and west sides and because of their inferiority in every aspect when compared with the other houses in the Square. They have, however, always been treated as part of the Square and, if for no other reason, are worth a note or two because of their presence and the minor role they have assumed in its history.

No.26 was leased on 20 November 1777 for 99 years to Robert Grews, along with No.27 (see No.24 for details). It is the most interesting of the five houses because it contains some wonderfully exuberant plasterwork. On the ground floor, the front room has plaster
104 medallions above both doors and on the chimney-breast. The rear room is oval on plan, with an oval top-light set close to the rear wall, and a good decorative plaster frieze (arabesque and honeysuckle) and ceiling. The closet room behind the staircase is a remarkable little room, which has probably always served as the lavatory, and is almost certainly original. It has a drum skylight and lovely plaster
medallions on the walls: an unusually elaborate decora- 107
tive treatment of such a room. The front room on the first floor has a toned-down version of a 'typical' Bedford Square ceiling.

No.27 has nothing of interest except for an original and
most interesting basement door to the front area. It has 105
its original hinges and small pair of glass panels at the head – the glass is remarkably imperfect! – with iron bars across these, and the whole door is clad in metal.

Nos.37, 38 and 39 were leased on 1 November 1776 for 99 years to William Scott and Robert Grews, at an annual ground rent of £1 10s for all three. No.37 has little of interest except for its original wine cellar in the basement, with stone shelves on brick supports. At the rear
there is a full-height bow. No.38 has a later Victorian 106

104. No.26 Bedford Square, ground-floor plan.

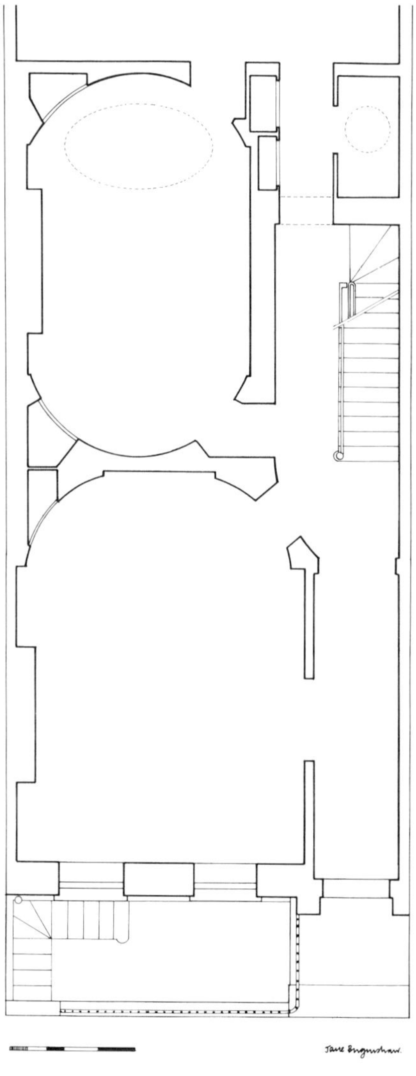

105. No.27 Bedford Square, door to front basement area. It is clad in metal.

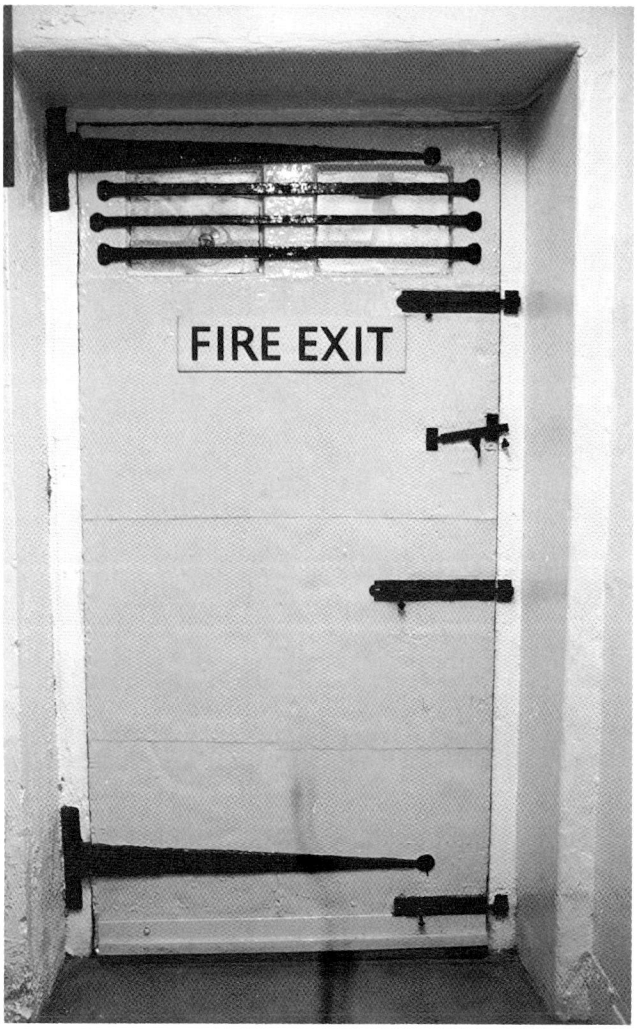

106. No.38 Bedford Square, Coade stone impost block to doorway, showing the depth of Coade blocks. The damage has now been repaired.

wooden staircase but nothing else of note. No.39 was demolished in the mid-1890s, probably shortly after Michaelmas 1895, when its second lease – for 21 years from Michaelmas 1874 – fell in. It was a remarkably small house, just 20 feet wide and 32 feet deep. The present-day No.39 (which because of the global listing of all the houses in Bedford Square is also listed Grade 1) was leased on 29 September 1899 on a much wider plot than that on which its predecessor stood.

Number Twenty-Eight

Leased on 1 November 1776 for 99 years to John Roberts, bricklayer of the parish of St George Hanover Square. The plot was some 29 feet wide and some 143 feet deep, at a ground rent of £14 10s per annum.

In 1910, there was a major renovation of this house, which involved among other things taking down and rebuilding the whole of the flank and rear walls 'on account of settlement due, as was discovered when the ground was opened up, to the footings having been laid upon irregular baulks of timber'.[117]

107. No.26 Bedford Square, plasterwork to water closet, ground floor. The decoration could well be original. The tablet depicts Cupid, the Roman god of love, and Psyche being led to the marital altar. Over the tablet a Roman couple framed by laurel leaves face each other below a dancing Bacchante celebrating with a tambourine. To the right, Venus rises from her bath, emblematic of profane love, and Fortitude leans on a pedestal. To the left, Diana, the hunter goddess, sacred to those who in the marriage vow are chaste, and emblematic of sacred love, is accompanied by a hound, and Erato, the muse of lyric poetry, sings love songs.

The floor plan is standard, with a good full-height bow to the garden elevation. The staircase is typical – in stone rising to the second floor – with good guilloched bucraneum and anthemion friezes to the ground- and first-floor landings, a fluted rosette example at the top of the compartment, and interesting balustrading – the standard alternating S-scroll and two straight uprights, except
131 for the ends of each scroll which extend out to connect to the adjacent straight bar.

The front room on the ground floor has original ornamental plaster panels. On the first floor, the rear room has a fine decorative ceiling that is in fact a reproduction. That in the front room is an original example. During the 1910 renovation two chimney-pieces were stolen. Two more were stolen in 1986 but fortunately were recovered.

Number Twenty-Nine

Leased on 1 November 1776 for 99 years to Thomas Wise, 45
brickmaker of the parish of St Marylebone. The plot was 28 feet wide by some 128 feet deep, at an annual ground rent of £14.

The front elevation is embellished with an original 108
fanlight, individual early nineteenth-century cast-iron anthemion balconies to the first-floor windows, and a lead rainwater hopper and downpipes to the party wall with No.30. Sadly, the glazing bars of the sash windows are missing.

The floor plan is standard, with a full-height canted bay at the rear (internally it is curved as for a bow). A screen with semi-circular fanlight divides the entrance and staircase halls, both of which have guilloched bucranea and anthemion friezes; the staircase is identical to that

108. No.29 Bedford Square, entrance doorway.

109. No.31 Bedford Square, ceiling, first-floor front room.

in No.28, but the S-scroll balusters are detached from their neighbouring upright bars. As at No.28, the top of the staircase is finished with a fluted rosette frieze. In the main room on the first floor there is a good decorative plaster ceiling with a vase and anthemion frieze.

Number Thirty

Leased on 1 November 1776 for 99 years to Charles Jacks, carpenter of the parish of St Anne Soho. The plot had a frontage to the Square of 28 feet and a depth of some 129 feet, at an annual ground rent of £14.

24 There are good individual early nineteenth-century cast-iron anthemion balconies to the first-floor windows, and shoe scrapers at the entrance.

Inside there is a standard floor plan. The staircase is identical to that in No.29, down to the fluted rosette frieze at the top of the compartment, and the entrance and staircase halls repeat the friezes also found next door. The ceiling in the front room on the first floor is a very good example, with eight cameo panels placed around the radial centrepiece. There are details in this ceiling that are identical to those in the ceiling of the rear room on
67 the ground floor of No.1. It is possible therefore that the ceiling here was also designed by Thomas Leverton.[118] In this same room, above the door that links with the rear room, is a long ornamental plaque with a painted central panel flanked by arabesques. In the rear room is a strange arabesque and anthemion frieze, with a rope and bay-leaf moulding to the perimeter of an otherwise plain ceiling.

Number Thirty-One

Leased on 1 November 1776 for 99 years to John Utterton, plasterer of the parish of St Marylebone. Utterton was later to take leases on Nos.16, 17 and 47. The plot was 29 feet wide by some 130 feet deep, at a rent of £14 10s per annum.

The façade is plain with no decoration and is rendered
17 austere by its Victorian sashes. Inside, there is so much that is identical to the interiors of Nos.29 and 30 (and to an extent No.28) that it is reasonable to assume an overall guiding hand in their finishing. The floor plan, staircase and friezes to the entrance and staircase halls and ground-floor front room are all as for No.30.

There are two excellent decorative plaster ceilings on
109 the first floor. In the front room there are griffin and vase, arabesque, anthemion and palmette motifs and cameo panels. The whole ceiling is repeated in the same room at No.47. In the rear room, the ceiling has arabesque panels with a radial centrepiece, swags and four cameo panels. In both rooms the ceilings have octagonal panels formed by the arrangement of the ornament. This is a different form to most examples in the Square, where four-sided and circular panels are the norm. The two ceilings are probably the work of an architect, and the name of Thomas Leverton must be considered, especially as the outermost circular band to the front-room ceiling is composed of a variation of his flowing anthemion bands seen in Nos.1 and 6.

Number Thirty-Two

Leased on 1 November 1776 for 99 years to Daniel Mawley, painter of the parish of St Giles in the Fields. The plot was the widest granted in the Square (with the obvious exception of No.6, the centre house on the opposing east side) with a width of 32 feet, a depth of some 131 feet, and a ground rent of £16 per annum.

Being the centre house on this side of the Square, it is in stucco, with a rusticated ground floor and plain upper
floors with four Ionic pilasters and a pediment. The whole 18

110. No.32 Bedford Square, ground-floor plan.

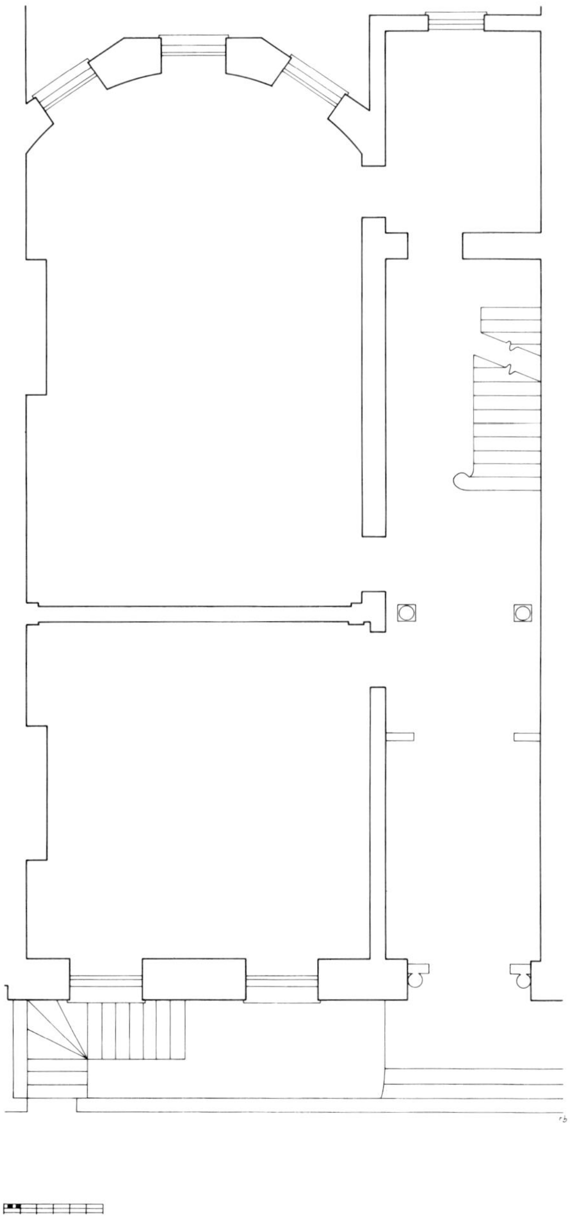

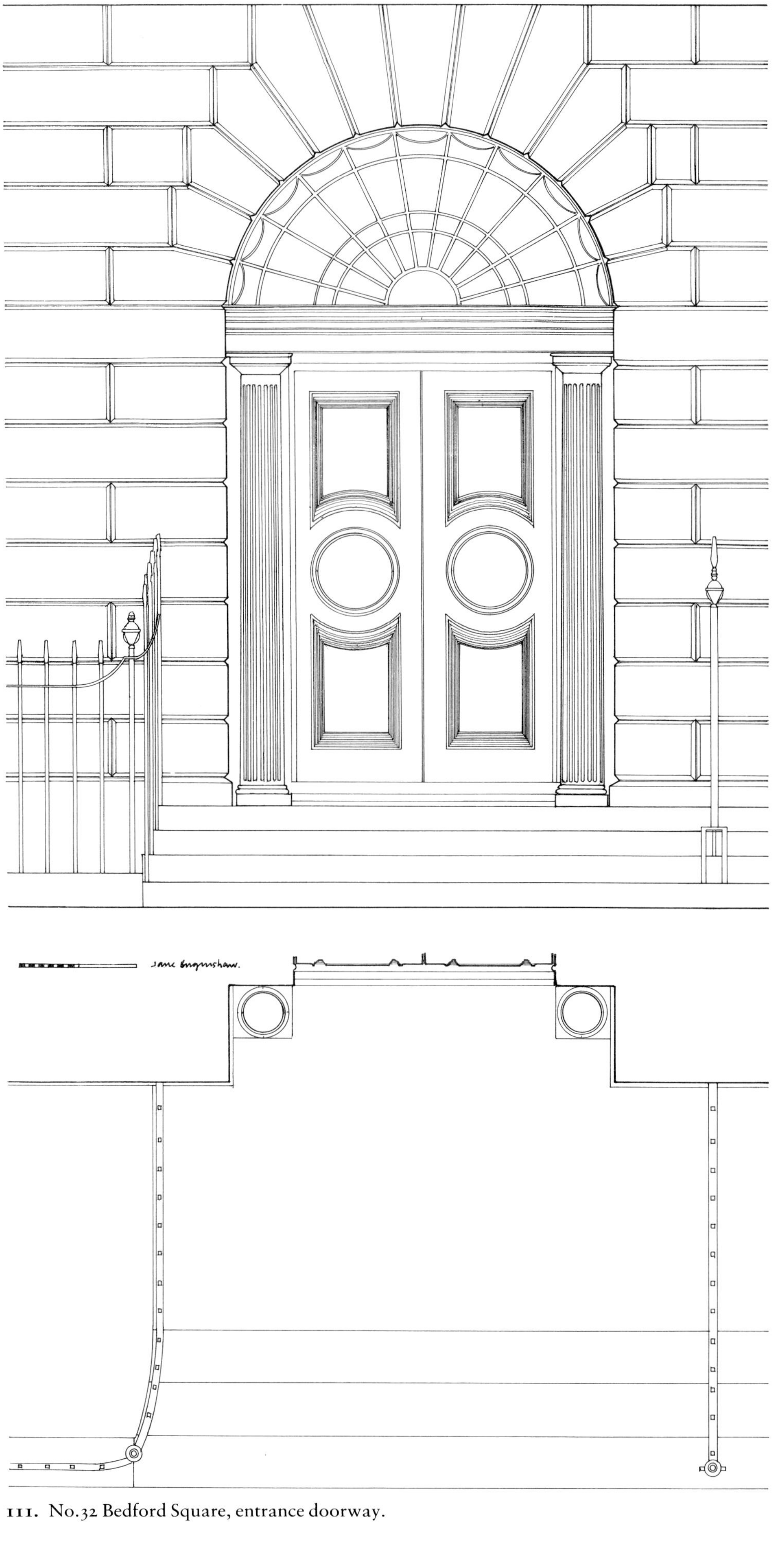

111. No.32 Bedford Square, entrance doorway.

112. No.32 Bedford Square, screen between entrance and staircase halls. The decoration to this house dates from the late 1770s. It is very fine but somewhat old-fashioned, having a 1760s appearance.

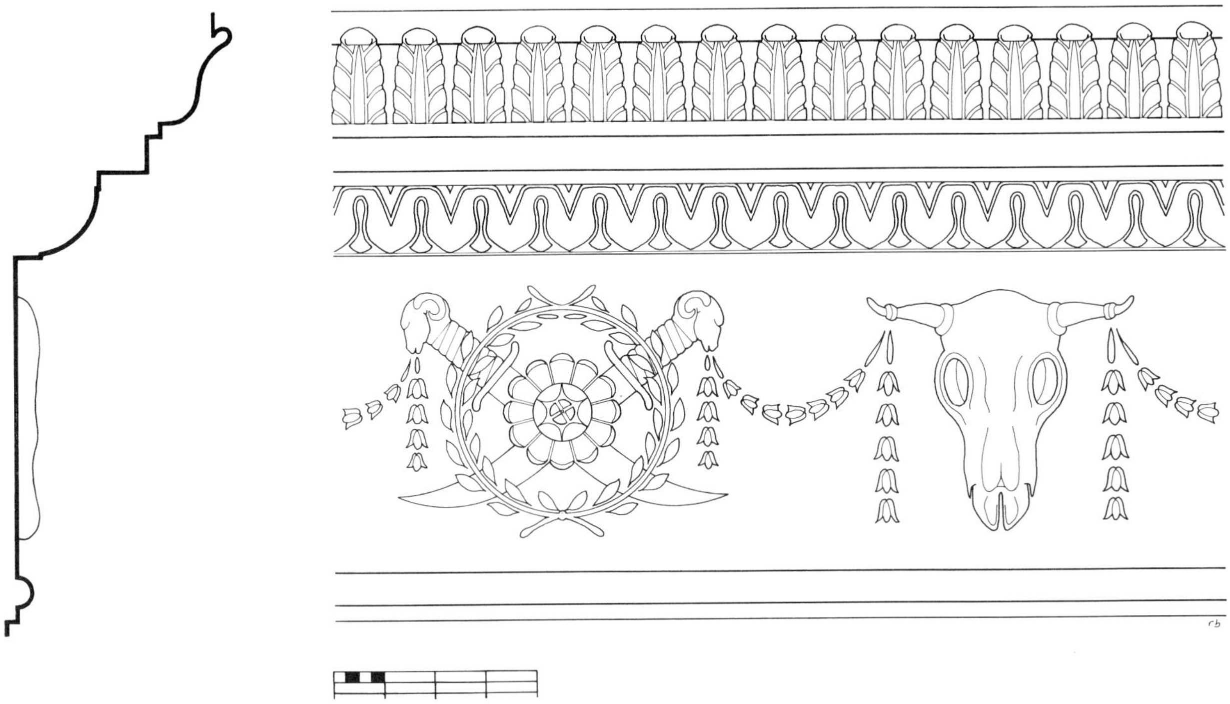

113 TOP. No.32 Bedford Square, entrance-hall frieze and cornice, elevation and section.

114 LEFT. No.32 Bedford Square, staircase baluster.

115 ABOVE. No.32 Bedford Square, staircase baluster.

116 OPPOSITE. No.32 Bedford Square, staircase around first-floor landing, showing the moulded staircase soffit.

117 ABOVE. No.32 Bedford Square, ceiling, rear room, first floor. The octagonal arrangement of the ceiling is rare for the Square.

43 façade bears a striking resemblance to the Royal Society of Arts building at the Adelphi (Robert Adam, 1772-4), although here the entrance is to one side and the massive Venetian window of the Adam building is missing; interestingly, though, the unfluted pilasters are here spaced as
111 if to accommodate one. The doorway is similar to that at No.15 St James's Square (James Stuart, 1763-6), with fluted Roman Doric columns (unfluted, at St James's Square) supporting a plain entablature and large fanlight.

110 This is one of the finest houses in Bedford Square, with some particularly good interior detailing. The excellent entrance and staircase halls are divided by two screens; the first contains a semi-circular fanlight, the second has
112 two detached, fluted, wooden Ionic columns with a fluted frieze and bracketed cornice that links the screen to the walls. The cornice itself acts as an impost from which springs a semi-circular arch. This arch duplicates that over the doorway and first screen, and has decorative plasterwork in its spandrils. Throughout there is an excel-
113 lent plaster frieze, with bucranea, swags and rosettes encircled by laurel wreaths and pierced with crossed daggers. This is one of the few houses to retain its original stone floor to the entrance and staircase halls.

116 The staircase is a very fine example, with beautifully moulded soffits – these are usually left plain and often plastered over – and a wonderfully elaborate wrought- 114
iron S-scroll baluster (only at landings and mid-flight). 115
The plaster ceiling at the top of the staircase compartment has decoration that borders on the Rococo. 118

The front room on the ground floor has a good overdoor, carved rope and bay-leaf panel mouldings to the window-shutters, and a fluted dado that continues as the surround to the windows. The ceiling in this room is unusually austere for the type generally seen in the Square, with very heavy mouldings.

The rear room has two overdoors similar to that in the front room, a fluted dado, carved window-shutters and architraves, and an interesting decorative plaster ceiling with some unusual motifs, especially the radial centrepiece and the four plain circular panels that were perhaps intended to have (or indeed had) painted panels. The cornice is bracketed with an egg-and-dart band and is of a type more frequently seen in a house of 1730-60. These rooms were probably originally connected, as there is a pilastered screen that continues on the same line as the columned screen in the entrance hall but which is now contained within a partition.

On the first floor there is more good joinery – all the dadoes, shutter-mouldings and skirtings are carved – and an excellent decorative ceiling in the rear room. 117

118. No.32 Bedford Square, ceiling over staircase.

Number Thirty-Three

Leased on 1 November 1776 for 99 years to James Higley, carpenter of the parish of St Clement Danes. The plot was 29 feet wide and some 131 feet deep, at an annual ground rent of £14 10s.

The front elevation has a radial fanlight identical to that at No.29, a continuous cast-iron balcony, and a lead rainwater hopper and downpipes on the party wall with No.34.

Inside, the entrance hall is divided from the staircase 119 hall by a screen with an original semi-circular fanlight. The staircase has S-scroll balusters and a mahogany handrail and rises to the second floor, where a semi-circular arched opening with rosettes to the spandrils leads to the separate staircase to the third floor.

The ground-floor front room has a screen – distyle *in* 44 *antis* – with capitals derived from the Athenian Tower of the Winds. The rear room has curved walls at either end. There is a decorative plaster ceiling in the front room on the first floor, with an anthemion and rosette (at the 120 corners only) cornice. The whole composition lacks the merit of most in the Square. At the rear is a full-height bow to the garden which has at one stage been entirely rebuilt. It is virtually all in header brickwork.

119 TOP. No.33 Bedford Square, fanlight and screen to entrance hall. The hallway at the rear is a much later addition.

120 BOTTOM. No.33 Bedford Square, ceiling, front room, first floor. The perimeter soffit moulding suggests that the ceiling is slightly later, perhaps from the 1790s. It lacks the elegance of original examples.

121. No.34 Bedford Square, plaster panel to staircase landing. This tablet depicts the art of bacchanalian festivities, with a goat being sacrificed at the altar of love. Two putti hold torches of love – one alight and aloft, the other extinguished, perhaps symbolising the life-cycle. A companion holds a staff bearing fruit. To the left, another putto bears a myrtle branch and his companion carries a basket of offerings.

Number Thirty-Four

Leased on 1 November 1776 for 99 years to William Barlow, slater of the parish of St George Hanover Square. The plot was 28 feet wide by some 132 feet deep, at a ground rental of £14 per annum.

There are heavy individual late-Victorian cast-iron balconies to the first-floor windows and scaled-down versions to the windows above, a lead rainwater hopper and downpipes on the party wall with No.35, and a strange bracket to the left-hand area railings, adjacent to the doorway, which probably served as a shoe scraper.

There are two screens in the entrance and staircase halls. The first encloses an area 7 feet by 7 feet, with a fine semi-circular fanlight above; the second area is the same width but longer, and has two plaster plaques. The screen consists only of a semi-circular arched opening that leads to the staircase hall. The staircase itself is interesting as it rises to the third floor, but the dog-leg flights from the second floor are in wood rather than stone. The balusters on the last two flights are square section, but to the first two floors are of the S-scroll type so frequently encountered, and placed on alternate treads between two square-section uprights. Strangely, though, the scrolls are connected to the uprights on both sides by a straight horizontal bar (a similar arrangement can also be seen at
121 No.28). There is an ornamental plaster panel depicting putti at the half-landing of the first flight.

The front room on the first floor has a decorative plaster ceiling which is, however, a copy of that in the same room in No.35, installed after the original collapsed.

The garden elevation has a full-height bow, with Gothic cast-iron balconies to the second-floor windows and plain examples to the third-floor windows. Both sets are probably later than the house.

Number Thirty-Five

Leased on 1 November 1776 for 99 years to John Berry, glazier of the parish of St George Hanover Square. The plot had a frontage to the Square of 28 feet and a depth of some 132 feet, with an annual ground rent of £14.

Individual cast-iron balconies adorn the first-floor windows, and scaled-down versions the windows above. The entrance has been blocked off by railings, and the door has been turned into a window. The severe structural movement on the party-wall line with No.36 should be noted.

There is a handsome fanlight over the screen in the entrance hall. The staircase has been taken out of this 122
house and not replaced. In the first-floor front room there is a griffin, vase and arabesque frieze, and a good decorative ceiling of swags, anthemions and arabesques. This was used to take a mould for the copy in the same room in No.34.

The garden elevation has a full-height bow, with small individual decorative cast-iron balconies to all ground-, first-, and second-floor windows. They are all straight on plan (in spite of the bow) and probably much later than the house.

Number Thirty-Six

Leased on 1 November 1776 for 99 years to James Bramble, smith of the parish of St Anne Soho. The plot was 29 feet wide with a depth of some 133 feet, at an annual ground rental of £14 10s.

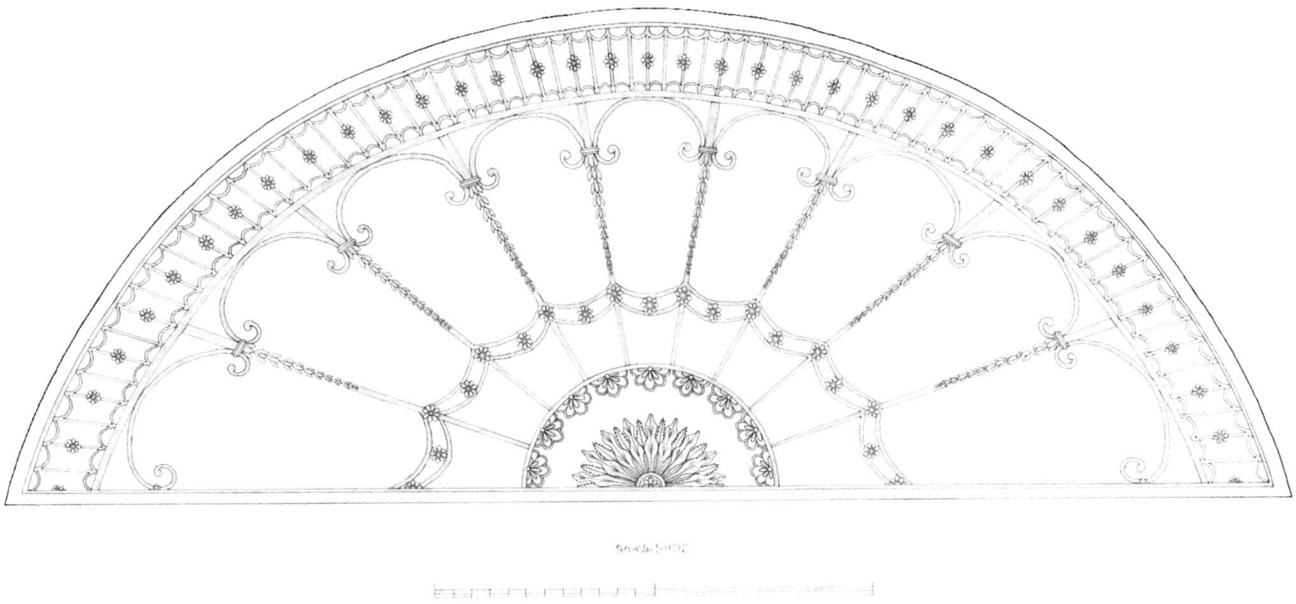

122. No.35 Bedford Square, entrance-hall fanlight.

123 BELOW. No.36 Bedford Square, staircase baluster.

This is the southern end house of the palace-fronted
22 west side, and typically has a balustraded parapet, as well as a good radial fanlight over the entrance door, and individual cast-iron balconies to the first-floor windows.

The staircase has an excellent wrought-iron decorative
123 baluster of a type unique to this house in the Square; on the dog-leg first flight it alternates with two straight balusters, but on the next flight only appears at the landings.

The front room on the first floor has a good decorative ceiling, fairly sparse in detail, and a honeysuckle and palmette frieze, the latter repeated in the rear room. There is a full-height bow at the rear.

Number Forty

Leased on 20 November 1777 for 99 years to Robert Grews, at a ground rent of £6 per annum. On 1 December 1777, Grews subleased the property to William Scott for 99 years less 21 days, at a peppercorn rent for four years (instead of five years on his head-lease) and a ground rent of £20 6s per annum for the remainder of the term. On 8 June 1778, Grews surrendered the leasehold interest to the trustees of the Duke of Bedford's Estate for the sum of 5s. Five days later, Grews was granted a lease on a slightly reduced plot (see p.40).

This is the western end house of the south side. There 126
are good, late-Georgian, individual cast-iron key pattern balconies to the first-floor windows. An important point
to note is the Coade stone door surround, which has been 51
stripped of its paintwork; this has revealed the word
'COADE' stamped twice on the soffit of the right-hand 124
impost block.

The entrance and staircase halls have a good frieze – fluted with oval rosettes and guttae – and cornice-block with rosettes to the soffit. The staircase is top-lit by an
oval lantern, and has decorative wrought-iron balusters 125
to each tread up to the first floor, and two straight balusters to each tread up to the second floor, where it terminates.

In the front room on the ground floor, there is an excellent oval plaster plaque on the chimney-breast and

124. No.40 Bedford Square, entrance doorway detail, with 'COADE' stamped twice on the soffit of the impost.

125 RIGHT. No.40 Bedford Square, staircase baluster.

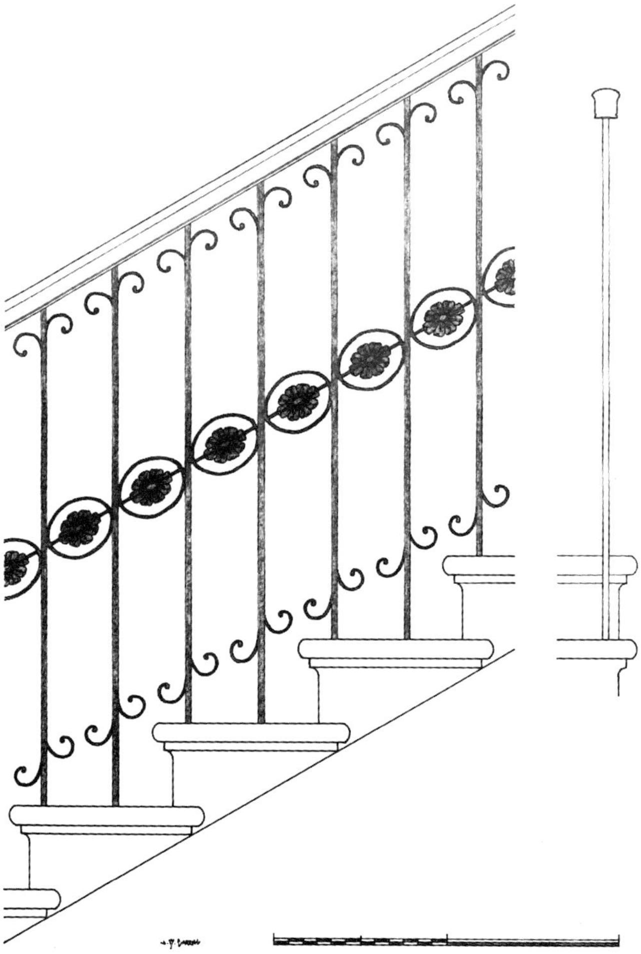

a further decorative panel beween the windows. There is a carved dado and two fluted square columns serving as a screen to the rear wall. The room above has a carved dado of flutes and rosettes, with the walls above formed into panels by plaster rope and bay-leaf mouldings terminating at a vase and anthemion frieze, and an excel-
v lent decorative plaster ceiling with five painted panels (these have been completely over-restored).

The garden elevation has a full-height canted bay, also canted internally (this is usually translated into rounded walls internally).

Number Forty-One

Leased on 20 November 1777 for 99 years to William Scott, at an annual ground rent of £6. On 1 December 1777, Scott subleased to his partner Robert Grews for 99 years less 21 days, at a peppercorn rent for four years and a ground rent of £18 4s for the remainder of the term. The plot had a frontage of 26 feet and a depth of 130 feet.

The balconies to the first-floor windows are in cast-iron with good stone bases. Inside, this house is very plain. The stone staircase rises, strangely, all the way to the third floor, with two straight cast-iron balusters per tread. It is lit by an oval lantern. Elsewhere, only the rear room on the first floor is of note, with original doorcases and a very good decorative plaster ceiling.

126. No.40 Bedford Square, side elevation.

Number Forty-Two

Leased on 20 November 1777 for 99 years to William Scott, at a ground rental of £8 14s per annum. On 1 December 1777, Scott subleased to William Grant, carpenter of the parish of St Marylebone, for 99 years less 21 days, at a peppercorn rent for the first four years and £20 6s for the residue. The plot was 29 feet wide by 130 feet deep.

There are beautiful individual cast-iron 'spider's web'
127 balconies on stone bases to the first-floor windows at the front, dating probably from the early nineteenth century.

Inside, the entrance and staircase halls are divided by a screen with a semi-circular radial fanlight within the arch. Both halls have a bucranea and rosette frieze and a leaf cornice. The staircase has good S-scroll balusters and is lit by an oval lantern with an ornamental plaster lining. The front room on the grund floor has stucco panels above the door, and an off-the-peg griffin, vase and arabesque frieze.

On the first floor, the frieze seen in the rear room of the ground floor is repeated in both rooms. The front room has a good doorcase with Corinthian pilasters, a

127. No.42 Bedford Square, cast-iron spider's web balcony from the early nineteenth century.

carved dado and a very good decorative plaster ceiling, with scrolled arabesques, trophied panels and swags. The room behind has an elliptical back wall (externally this is straight) and a decorative ceiling of swags and putti.

Between the second-floor landing and the lantern of the staircase compartment, there is a bucranea and anthemion decorative plaster string course defining the third-floor level and set within a guilloched band.

There is an interesting original staircase within the canted bay at the rear of the house. It starts at both half-landings of the main staircase and leads to the closet rooms at first- and second-floor levels. These rooms in turn connect via a doorway to the main rear rooms at these levels.

Number Forty-Three

Leased on 20 November 1777 for 99 years to William Scott, at a ground rent of £8 8s per annum. On 1 December 1777, Scott subleased the property to John Roberts, bricklayer of the parish of St George Hanover Square, for 99 years less 21 days, at a peppercorn rent for the first four years and a rent of £19 12s per annum for the remainder of the term.

The plot had a frontage of 28 feet and a depth of 130 feet. Inside, the house is rather plain. The staircase is original, but the balusters are heavy, late-Victorian, cast-iron replacements. The only important item of interest is an excellent decorative plaster ceiling in the front room on the first floor. There is a full-height bow at the rear.

Number Forty-Four

Leased on 20 November 1777 for 99 years to William Scott, at a ground rent of £8 11s per annum. On 1 December 1777, Scott subleased the property to Charles Jacks, carpenter of the parish of St Anne Soho, for 99 years less 21 days, at a peppercorn rent for the first four years and £19 19s for the remainder of the term. On 13 December 1777, Jacks assigned his lease to Joseph Harrington, an employee at the Bedford Estate office. The plot was 28 feet 6 inches wide by 130 feet deep.

There is some good detailing inside this house. The entrance and staircase halls are divided by a screen with an excellent fanlight and carved softwood transom of anthemion and palmette. Both halls have a standard ornamental plaster frieze of alternating bucranea and 129
anthemion in a guilloche band. The staircase rises to the second floor and has an apsed rear wall and a splendid lantern light which has a decorative lining of swags and rosettes.

The decorative plaster ceiling in the front room on the first floor is a fine example of its type. There are also good consoled doorcases on this floor with carved friezes of 128
flute and palmette. The basement is reached via a windered staircase (they are usually straight) and has an original vault. At the rear, there is a full-height canted bay.

Number Forty-Five

Leased on 20 November 1777 for 99 years to Robert Grews, at a rent of £8 11s per annum. On 1 December 1777, Grews subleased to James Tomes, bricklayer of the parish of St Marylebone, for 99 years less 21 days, at a peppercorn rent for the first four years and £19 19s for the remainder of the term. The plot size was identical to its western neighbour (see No.44).

There is very little of interest in this house, except for a good fluted cornice with applied lion heads in the staircase and entrance halls, and a staircase identical on plan to that in No.44. At the rear elevation there is a full-height canted bay.

Number Forty-Six

Leased on 20 May 1782 for 99 years to Robert Grews 'late of the parish of Saint Marylebone but now of the parish of St Giles in the Fields', at a ground rent of £8 12s per annum. It is difficult to understand quite why this house was granted a lease five years after every other house on this side of the Square. The plot size was 30 feet by some 131 feet deep, an exact mirror image of its neighbour to the east (No.47), as is the 'as-built' floor plan hatched on the lease.

This is one of the two centre houses on this side of 54
the Square, in stucco, and shares, with the two centre houses on the north side, the classical solecism of a pilaster beneath the apex of the pediment. There are individual cast-iron balconies to the first-floor windows and an original fanlight over the doorway.

Although the floor plans of the two houses differ, the staircases have the same arrangement, which is of great

128. Nos.44 and 50 Bedford Square, doorcases, first-floor front rooms.

129. No.44 Bedford Square, entrance-hall frieze and cornice, elevation and section.

interest because it is only seen in this pair. Instead of the usual dog-leg, the staircase here does not return back on itself, but terminates with a series of winders at the head of a straight flight (at the back wall of the house), and returns with a long landing leading to the front room on the first floor, and the flight up to the second floor. The balusters are an excellent variation on the standard S-scroll, and the whole compartment is lit by an oval lantern with a very good lining of arabesques, swags and rosettes. A string course defines the level of the third floor, as at Nos.42 and 47.

The ground-floor front room has the curved entrance door and matching curved cupboard door more usually associated with the later houses on the north side, and this rather bears out the delayed completion of this house and perhaps explains the difference in its layout from that of No.47. Aside from some good friezes, a curved door from the rear room, and the closet, there is little else in this house of note.

Number Forty-Seven

19, 54 Leased on 20 November 1777 for 99 years to Robert Grews, at an annual rent of £9. On 1 December 1777, Grews subleased to John Utterton, plasterer of the parish of St Marylebone, for 99 years less 21 days, at a peppercorn rent for the first four years and £21 for the remainder of the term. See No.46 for the plot size.

The staircase is identical in form and decoration with that in No.46, except for a slightly different decorative baluster detail. The front room on the ground floor has a fluted pilaster screen with capitals derived from the Athenian Tower of the Winds.

There are two splendid decorative plaster ceilings on the first floor. The one in the front room is identical to 109
that in the same room in No.31. In the rear room, there is a similar frieze to the adjacent room – anthemion and vase with a rope and leaf architrave – and a restrained ceiling of honeysuckle and swags.

Number Forty-Eight

Leased on 16 January 1777 for 99 years to Robert Grews, at a ground rental of £8 8s per annum. On 25 January 1777, Grews subleased to Henry Sumpter, mason of the parish of St John Westminster, for 98 years less 21 days from the Feast of St Michael the Archangel 1776 (the lease would therefore fall in in 1874 with all the other houses), at a peppercorn rent for the first two years and £19 12s for the remainder of the term. On 22 February 1777, Sumpter 'bargained sold assigned transferred and set over unto the said William Scott' the benefit of his sublease. The plot had a width of 28 feet and a depth of 130 feet.

The staircase and entrance halls have a very good frieze, comprising vases and vine leaves in the form of a wreath crossed by pine-cone-tipped staffs. There is 130

130. No.48 Bedford Square, entrance-hall frieze and cornice. The frieze is dedicated to Bacchus, the Greek god of wine. A Grecian wine vase is bound by festive drapery to trophies of thyrsae – the staffs tipped with pine cones borne by Bacchus and his train – garlanded with vine leaves and centred with a bunch of grapes.

another good example, at the soffit of the staircase on the first floor, of an arrowed guilloche with alternating bucranea and vase. The same frieze is repeated in the rear room on this floor. The staircase itself, lit by an oval lantern, rises all the way to the third floor with plain iron balusters.

In the front room on the first floor there is a fine decorative plaster ceiling of anthemions, swags, palmettes, vases and small plaques. There is a full-height canted bay to the rear elevation which is curved on the room side.

Number Forty-Nine

Leased on 16 January 1777 for 99 years to Robert Grews, at a ground rental of £8 8s per annum. On 25 January 1777, Grews subleased to James Tomes, bricklayer of the parish of St Marylebone, for 98 years less 21 days from the Feast of St Michael the Archangel 1776, at a peppercorn rent for the first two years and £19 12s for the remainder of the term. On 22 February 1777, Tomes 'bargained sold assigned transferred and set over unto Reverend Richard Walter, clerk of Portsmouth in the County of Southampton' the benefit of his sublease. The plot had a width of some 28 feet and a depth of 130 feet.

The front elevation has been rendered very plain by the removal of the original sashes and their replacement with Victorian sashes.

The staircase and entrance halls have an identical frieze to those in No.48. The dog-leg staircase has good scrolled balusters, with a ten-inch diameter metal dish cantilevered from one of these at the half-landing of the first flight. I have not discovered exactly what this was for, but it may have been a candle-holder. There are two good decorative plaster ceilings on the first floor. At the garden elevation there is a full-height canted bay.

Number Fifty

Leased on 16 January 1777 for 99 years to William Scott, 128
at ground rent of £8 14s per annum. On 25 January 1777, Scott subleased to Philip Woodham, sawyer of the parish of St Marylebone, for 98 years less 21 days from the Feast of St Michael the Archangel 1776, at a peppercorn rent for the first two years and £20 6s for the remainder of

131. No.50 Bedford Square, staircase baluster.

132. No.50 Bedford Square, ceiling, first-floor front room.

the term. On 24 February 1777, Woodham 'bargained sold assigned transferred and set over unto Robert Grews' the benefit of his sublease. The plot had a frontage to the Square of 29 feet and a depth of 130 feet.

The entrance hall is divided from the staircase hall by a screen with a good semi-circular radial fanlight. The rooms on the ground floor have been greatly altered at some time around the turn of this century.

The staircase is very good in this house. The S-scroll
balusters are standard, but the ends are stretched out to 131
connect with the adjacent straight bar (as at No.28). The rear wall of the compartment is apsed, and the whole
space is lit by an oval lantern, with arabesques to the soffit 133
and a swag and rosette lining.

The rear room on the first floor has a good decorative ceiling with a honeysuckle and vase frieze. Above the

133 TOP. No.50 Bedford Square, staircase lantern.

134 BOTTOM. No.51 Bedford Square, door surround, front room, first floor.

dado rail, the walls are panelled with stucco mouldings, and the same treatment is seen in the room above, which has a simple ornamental ceiling of rope and bay-leaf mouldings. There is a very good decorative plaster ceiling 132
in the front room on the first floor. The garden elevation has a full-height canted bay with a rounded face inside.

Number Fifty-One

Leased on 16 January 1777 for 99 years to William Scott, 10
at a ground rent of £8 14s per annum. On 25 January 1777, Scott subleased to William Grant, carpenter of the parish of St Marylebone, for 98 years less 21 days from the Feast of St Michael the Archangel 1776, at a peppercorn rent for the first two years and £20 6s for the remainder of the term. On 21 February 1777, Grant 'bargained sold assigned transferred and set over unto Robert Grews' the benefit of his sublease. The plot had a width of 29 feet and a depth of 130 feet.

The line that divides the parishes of St Giles in the Fields and St George, Bloomsbury runs along the party wall of this house and No.50, and is marked by two 135
plaques immediately below the first-floor string course. There is also good leadwork – hopper and downpipes – on this party wall. The staircase is identical in layout and VI, 47
detail to that of No.50.

On the first floor, there are two splendid decorative plaster ceilings, both with similar vase rosette and swag friezes. The front room has a fluted dado and carved shutter-mouldings and good doorcases. The garden eleva- 134
tion has a full-height canted bay – curved inside – which looks out onto a courtyard that retains its original Yorkstone paviors.

Number Fifty-Two

Leased on 4 August 1777 for 99 years to Robert Grews, 136
at a ground rent of £6 per annum. On 11 August 1777, Grews subleased the property to William Scott for 99 years less 21 days, at a peppercorn rent for the first four years and £18 4s for the remainder of the term. The plot had a frontage to the Square of just over 26 feet and a depth of 130 feet.

This is a very plain house. The main staircase rises to the third floor with square-section iron balusters throughout. Elsewhere only the friezes are of interest. There is a full-height canted bay to the rear.

Number Fifty-Three

Leased on 4 August 1777 for 99 years to William Scott, at a ground rent of £6 per annum. On 11 August 1777, Scott subleased to Robert Grews on the same terms that Grews subleased to Scott at No.52, except that here the ground rent was £20 6s per annum. The plot had a width of almost 29 feet 6 inches and a depth of some 139 feet.

This house is at the eastern end of the south side of

51

20 the Square, and has a good balustraded parapet and very good individual mid-Victorian cast-iron balconies to the first-floor windows.

The house is plain inside but the staircase is good. As at No.52, it rises to the third floor with good S-scroll balusters to every other tread, with a plainer decorative baluster at each half- and main landing. The flank wall to Bloomsbury Street has a stucco doorcase numbered 54, but there is no evidence of sub-division within this house. There is a full-height canted bay to the rear.

135 OPPOSITE, TOP. Nos.50 and 51 Bedford Square, front elevations. The plaques on either side of the downpipe mark the parishes of St George Bloomsbury and St Giles-in-the-Fields, the boundary between which runs along the party wall of both houses.

136 OPPOSITE, BOTTOM. No.52 Bedford Square, Coade stone detail to doorway. The transom – beneath the fanlight – is wooden.

A selection of chimney-pieces
from houses in Bedford Square

137. A ground-floor chimney-piece. The insert is slightly later and takes into account the improved efficiency of fireplace design that took place in the 1780s and 1790s.

138. A first-floor chimney-piece.

139. A second-floor chimney-piece. The whole cast-iron insert is later and the hob grate has water vessels.

140 TOP. A first-floor chimney-piece. An identical hob grate can be seen in fig. 142.

141 BOTTOM LEFT. A first-floor chimney-piece.

142 BOTTOM RIGHT. A second-floor chimney-piece. An identical hob grate can be seen in fig. 140.

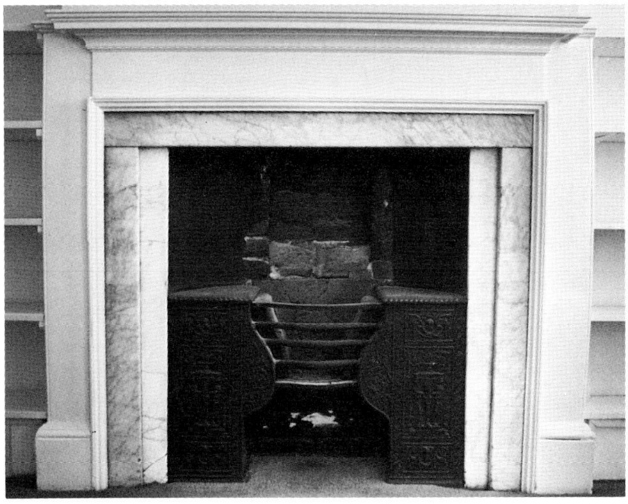

143 TOP. Centre panel of a first-floor chimney-piece. The youthful Bacchus – his curly locks wreathed with vine – embraces the panther that accompanies him at his triumphant wine festivities. The panther rests his paw on Bacchus's wine tazza. This panel was probably inspired by the engraving of the Bacchic frieze at the Temple of Lysicrates, published by Stuart and Revett in their *Antiquities of Athens*, 1762. Appropriately, this chimney-piece is in the dining parlour.

144 BOTTOM. Detail of a first-floor chimney-piece. The central panel depicts Flora, the goddess of fertility, holding a bunch of flowers and framed by Grecian drapery. The frieze has quatrefoils enclosed in libatian plates and framed by a Greek fret. On the lintel block a wine ewer depends from a laurel garland.

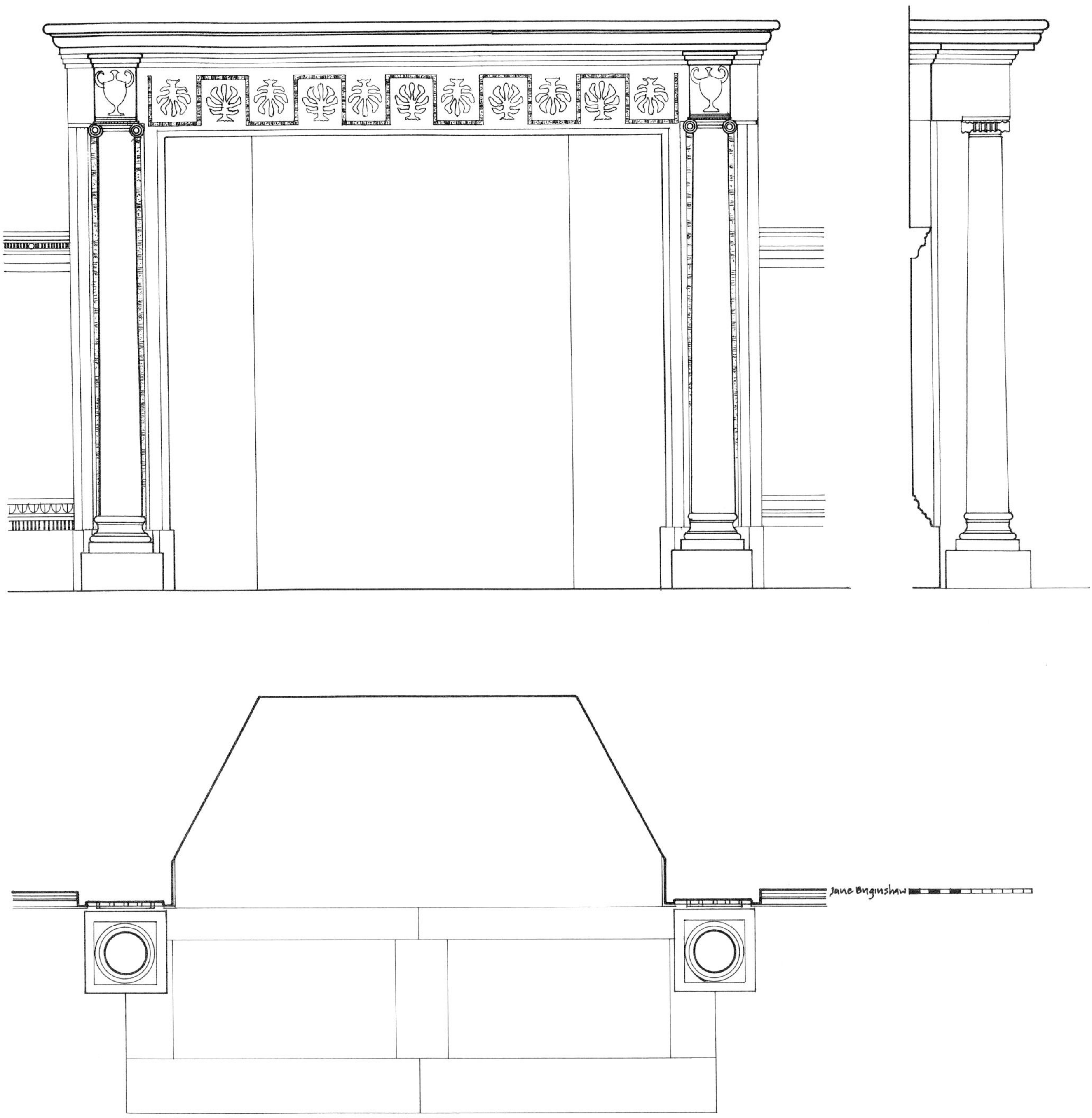

145 ABOVE. A first-floor chimney-piece, elevation, section and side elevation.

146 LEFT. Detail of a first-floor chimney-piece.

Principal Residents of Bedford Square

Number One

1782-91 Sir Lionel Lyde (1724-91), born Bristol, son of sometime Mayor of Bristol. Tobacco merchant and a director of the Bank of England. Made Sheriff of Hertfordshire in 1768 and created baronet in 1772. Buried at Ayot St Lawrence, Hertfordshire, under one of the pavilions of the church he built in 1778-9.

1791-1820 George Gostling, Admiralty proctor at Doctors' Commons.

1820-36 Mrs Gostling

1836-61 Miss Lydia Gostling

1861-96 Jabez Hogg (1817–99), born Chatham, opthalmic surgeon. Published a *Manual of Photography* in 1843. Joined the staff of the *Illustrated London News* shortly after and edited the *Illustrated London Almanack* for fifty-one years. Admitted a member of the Royal College of Surgeons in 1850. Concentrated chiefly on diseases of the eye and became opthalmic surgeon to both the Royal Westminster Opthalmic Hospital and the Hospital for Women and Children at Waterloo.

1896-1903 Louis Marcey

1903-19 Walter Weedon Grossmith (1854-1919), actor and playwright.

Number Two

1780-92 John Addison

1792-1813 James Bennett

1813-15 Rowson Parke

1815-23 James Flower

1823-44 Haskett Smith

1844-56 William Smith

1856 Sarah Smith

1857 Empty

1858-74 Farmery John Law, banker

1875-8 William Charles Lancaster

1878-85 Walter Knight, auctioneer and surveyor of 104 Great Russell Street (see No.16, 1893-1904)

1885-1912 Joseph Higham Hill, surgeon

Number Three

1781-5 James Bland Burges (1752-1824), politician, created baronet and knighted in 1795. Latter years spent as a poet and playwright.

1785-1808 Joseph Shrimpton, possibly of Shrimpton, Grenfide & Co, corn factors, of 26 Mark Lane in the City of London (see No.16, 1784-5).

1808-32 Mrs Shrimpton

1832-5 Richard Foster

1835-43 Mrs Foster

1843-60 Dr Theophilus Thompson (1807-60), born Islington, physician. Appointed physician to the Northern Dispensary in London early in his career. Elected a fellow of the Royal Society in 1846. Introduced cod-liver oil into England and researched its effects on the blood.

1860-7 David Davis

1867-8 — Pickard

1868-73 Mrs Blakey

1873-7 Frederick Wilhelm Gerber

1877-9 Edward Christian

1879-93 Collard Augustus Drake

1894 Empty

1895-1905 William Hornibrook

The current occupier is Laporte Industries

Number Four

1780-8 John Franklin

1788-97 Joseph May, merchant

1797-9 Mrs May

1799-1807 Henry Lushington, barrister

1807-13 Walter Shairp, of Walter Shairp & Co, Russia merchants, of 87 Old Broad Street in the City of London.

1813-24 Sir George Wood (1743-1824), born Roystone, near Barnsley, Yorkshire, judge. Was engaged by the Crown for all state prosecutions in 1792. Became MP for Haslemere in 1796. Appointed a baron of the Exchequer and was knighted in 1807. Died at his house in Bedford Square on 7 July 1824.

1824-40 Lady Sarah Wood

1840-9 Richard Edward Arden, solicitor

1849-56 Benjamin Willoughby, solicitor

1856-90 Mrs Willoughby

1890-1912 George Philip Willoughby, solicitor and magistrate

Number Five

1780-92 Robert Baker, a director of the South Sea Company

1792-5 Dr Nicholls

1795-1816 Robert Williams MP for Wootton Bassett, Wiltshire

1816-23 Andrew Loughnan

1823-5 John Loughnan

1825-42 Sir Joseph Littledale (1767-1842), judge, called to the bar 1798. Knighted 1824. Left £250,000.

1842-58 Lady Hannah Littledale

1858-61 Thomas Buckmaster

1861-7 Dr John Rose Cormack (1815-82), born Stow, Midlothian. Graduated in medicine at Edinburgh in 1837 and the same year was president of the Edinburgh Royal Medical Society. Moved to London in 1847 and to France in 1867. Knighted in 1872. Spent his last years in Paris. Edited the *Association Medical Journal*, 1852-5, forerunner of the *British Medical Journal*.

1867-9 Mrs Ambrose

1869-73 William Wright

1874 Empty

1875-6 George Stammery Webb

1876-80 James Raynor

1880-1 James Johnson, publisher

1881-4 Henry James Byron (1834-84), born Manchester, dramatist and actor. Prodigious playwright with some 130 plays to his name between 1858-82.

1885-92 Seward Brice, barrister
1892-3 Albert Leutner
1894-6 Empty
1897-1916 John Hopper Baker, physician and surgeon

Number Six

1782-99 Alexander Wedderburn, Lord Loughborough and first Earl of Rosslyn (1733-1805), born Edinburgh, Lord Chancellor. Son of an advocate. Called to the English bar in 1757. Elected MP for the Ayr burghs in 1761 and later for Richmond, Yorkshire, Bishop's Castle, Shropshire and Okehampton, Devonshire. Appointed Chief Justice of the Common Pleas in 1780 and was raised to the peerage as Baron Loughborough. Made Lord Chancellor in 1793, a post he held until 1801 when ousted by Lord Eldon.
1800-19 John Scott, Lord Eldon (1751-1838), born Newcastle-upon-Tyne, Lord Chancellor. Came to London in 1775. Called to the bar 1776. Returned to Parliament as member for Weobley, Herefordshire in 1783. Appointed Solicitor-General and was knighted in 1788. In 1799 became Lord Chief Justice of the Common Pleas and was appointed Lord Chancellor in 1801, a post he held until 1806 and from 1807-27. He exerted great political influence in the first quarter of the nineteenth century.
1820-54 George Shedden, merchant (see No.53, 1803-20)
1854-74 Lewis Jordan, merchant
1874-5 Mrs Jordan
1876-81 Empty

In 1880-1 the house was divided into two dwellings. No.6 was the southern of the two and retained the main staircase.

Number Six

1881-90 Sir George Donaldson, art expert
1890-1902 Dowager Countess of Winchelsea and Nottingham

Number 6A

1881-2 William Richard Stevens
1882-4 Lew Shi Ting, proprietor of the Shaou Shing Company, Chinese Merchants, of 9 New Broad Street, London EC
1885-6 Empty
1887-8 William Richard Stevens
1888-94 William Thomas Holmes Spicer, surgeon
1895-6 Empty
1897-1904 Leonard Smithers

The 1861 Census shows a household of twenty-five – thirteen family and twelve servants. Lewis Jordan was the head of the household; the other members were his wife, son-in-law, six daughters, son, two granddaughters and grandson. There was a governess, three male servants and eight female servants.

Number Seven

1781-9 Samuel Hartley, possibly of Samuel Hartley & Co, merchants of 33 Swithin's Lane in the City of London.
1789-91 Benjamin Boddington (1730-91), West India merchant. A director of the South Sea Company and the Million Bank. Treasurer and governor of the City of London Lying-in-Hospital.
1791-1807 Duncan Davidson MP for Cromartyshire
1807-12 Mrs Davidson
1812-13 Henry Garnell
1813-26 Joseph Butterworth (1770-1826), born Coventry, philanthropist and law bookseller, established his business in Fleet Street. MP for Coventry (1812-18) and Dover (1820-6).
1826-7 — Brady
1828 Empty
1829-34 Newman Knowlys, barrister, Recorder of London and a director of the Equitable Insurance Office.
1834-55 Sir Robert Harry Ingliss (1786-1855), born London, politician. Called to the bar 1818, but did not practise. Succeeded his father as baronet in 1820. MP for Dundalk (1824-6) and Ripon (1828) and represented Oxford University in Parliament (1829-54), until he retired.
1855-73 Lady Mary Ingliss
1873-87 Archdeacon Benjamin Harrison (1808-87), son of Benjamin Harrison, who was treasurer of Guy's Hospital. Archdeacon of Maidstone (1845-87). Inherited this house from Lady Ingliss.
1887-95 Mrs Isabella Harrison, daughter of Henry Thornton MP, philanthropist and economist. Isabella, along with her eight brothers and sisters, was placed under the guardianship of Sir Robert Harry Ingliss, a family friend, after the early death of both her parents.

Number Eight

1780-7 George Stainforth, possibly of Stainforth Giberne & Stainforth, wine merchants of 21 Old South Sea House, Broad Street in the City of London.
1787-1800 John Raymond
1800-4 Miss Snow
1804-20 Robert Dallas (1756-1824), judge. Called to the bar 1782. Made a king's counsel in 1795. MP for St Michaels, Cornwall (1802-5) and Kirkcaldy (1805-6). Knighted and appointed Solicitor-General in 1813.
1820-5 William West
1825 Miss West
1826-30 Huntley Bacon
1831 John Raine MP and a director of the Law Life Assurance Society.
1831-51 Peregrine Dealtry, barrister and a director of the Law Life Assurance Society
1851-9 Miss Dealtry
1859-62 Samuel Mart, fruit merchant
1862-9 Frederick Maynard
1869 Mrs Thorne
1870-1901 Frederick Warne (1825-1901), born Westminster, publisher. Started as a bookseller with his brother-in-law, George Routledge. In 1851, Warne became a partner in Routledge's publishing business. Published Edward Lear, Kate Greenaway, Disraeli, Beatrix Potter and Mrs Frances Hodgson Burnett. Died at his house in Bedford Square on 7 November 1901.

Number Nine

1780-97 James Haughton Langston, partner of Langston, Towgood, Amory & Cazalet, bankers of 29 Clement's Lane in the City of London. Also a director of the Sun Fire Office. His son John was MP for Bridgwater, Somerset.

1797-1805 Mrs Langston

1805-11 Peter Cazalet, partner of Langston, Towgood, Amory & Cazalet, bankers

1811-18 Mrs Cazalet

1818-40 Andrew Spottiswood

1840-1 Dr Michael Hue

1841-61 Dr Clement Hue (1779-1861), physician. Physician to St Bartholomew's between 1823 and 1860.

1861-75 John Clement Hue, physician, and Clement Berkeley Hue, clergyman. Clement Berkeley Hue exhibited at the Royal Academy in 1857.

1875-1909 Jonah Jonas, diamond merchant, partner of Jonas Brothers, wholesale jewellers, diamond brokers, precious stone dealers, etc, of 34 Ely Place, Holborn.

The current occupier is the Association of Anaesthetists.

Number Ten

1782-9 Samuel Lyde, merchant, younger brother of Sir Lionel (see No.1).

1789-91 Charles Shaw Lefevre, barrister and MP for Reading (1802-20). Also a director of the Sun Fire Office. His eldest son, also Charles, became Viscount Eversley in 1857.

1791-7 John Lefevre, of Hartfordbridge, Hants, gentleman of Huguenot descent. Helena, his daughter and heiress, married Charles Shaw who assumed the name Lefevre.

1797-9 Charles Lefevre, see above – Charles Shaw Lefevre

1799-1818 Henry Davidson, merchant

1819-20 Empty

1821 Joseph Chitty (1776-1841), legal writer, called to the bar 1816

1822 Empty

1823-44 Luke Graves Hansard (1777-1851). Son of Luke Hansard, printer, who in 1774 became manager and partner in the printing office of John Hughes of Great Turnstile, Lincoln's Inn Fields, printer to the House of Commons. In 1800 he became sole proprietor of the business and subsequently took his three sons, the middle of whom was Luke Graves, into partnership, trading as Luke Hansard and Sons.

1844-51 George Herbert Kinderley, solicitor

1851-7 Edmund Calvert

1858-75 Charles Gilpin, Secretary to the Poor Law Board and MP for Northampton

1875 Thomas Webb

1876 Empty

1877-1907 Agostino and Stefano Gatti, restaurateurs and wine merchants. Proprietors of the Grand Café restaurant, Strand and the Adelphi Theatre restaurant, Strand.

The current occupier is D L Taffner UK Ltd

Number Eleven

1783-4 Dr Michael Teighe, physician

1784-1810 Henry Cavendish (1731-1810), born Nice, eldest son of Lord Charles Cavendish, the fifth son of the second Duke of Devonshire. Natural philosopher and scientist. He discovered latent heat and the compound nature of heat. In 1798 he determined the density of the earth (*ie* the weight of the world) which made the law of gravitation complete. Left a fortune of £1,175,000.

1810-20 Charles Potts

1820-2 James Bowden

1822-42 George Henry Gibbs, merchant

1842-9 William Gibbs, merchant

1849-74 Henry Rosher, brick, lime and cement merchant. Depots at Limehouse; Blackfriars; Kingsland Basin, Hackney; Westminster and Northfleet, Kent

1874-93 Thomas Underwood, dental surgeon

1894-6 Empty

1896-1913 Thomas Ayscough Hodgkinson

The current occupier is the Royal Holloway and Bedford New College

Number Twelve

1783-4 Richard Richardson

1784-1804 John Chalie, director of John and Matthew Chalie, wine merchants of 29 Mincing Lane in the City of London. Chalie was also a director of the Sun Fire Office.

1804-10 Mrs Chalie

1810-50 Dr John Scott, physician

1850-62 Mrs Maria Scott

1862-7 Sir George Smart (1776-1867), born London, musician. Began life as a chorister at the Chapel Royal, St James's. Knighted in 1811. Became an original member of the Philharmonic Society in 1813. In 1822 he was appointed joint organist at the Chapel Royal and composer in 1838. He conducted the music at the funeral of George IV and the coronations of William IV and Queen Victoria. He died at Bedford Square on 23 February 1867.

1867-70 Lady Smart

1870-98 Miss Margaret Rose Smart, only child of Sir George and Lady Smart

Number Thirteen

1782-4 Richard Walker

1784-91 Marchant Tubb

1791-5 Mrs Royal

1795-1824 Thomas Leverton (1743-1824), born Woodford, Essex, architect. Important works were in the 1770s and 1780s. He worked in the Adam style with flair and originality but his output was never prodigious. Designed at least four interiors in Bedford Square. Latter years spent as a JP. His country house was at Purley, Surrey.

1824-33 Mrs Rebecca Leverton, second wife of Thomas Leverton. Married in 1803. Her country residence was Grove House, Blackheath.

1833-9 Henry Willoughby, solicitor, moved here from Charlotte Street (present day Bloomsbury Street)

1839-52 Dr Patrick Black (1813-79), born Aberdeen, physician. Elected assistant physician to St Bartholomew's Hospital in 1842 and chief physician in 1860.

1852-68 Joseph Collyer, landowner

1868-74 Mrs Ann Collyer

1875 Empty

1876-82 Clarence Harcourt, solicitor

1882-1927 Halsey Ralph Ricardo, architect, exhibited at the Royal Academy (1883-1903).

The current occupier is the Associated Board of the Royal Schools of Music

Number Fourteen

1782-93 James Baillie, moved here from Percy Street. Possibly of James Baillie & Co, merchants of 3 New Court, Swithin's Lane in the City of London. A director of the West India Dock Company. (See No.46, 1796-1823)
1793-1812 Sir Alexander Munro, a Commissioner of His Majesty's Public Offices of Revenue, at the Custom House
1813 Empty
1814-18 Sir William Fraser
1818-31 Edmund Larken
1832-3 Empty
1834-8 Sir John Key (1794-1858), Lord Mayor of London in 1830 and, unusually, re-elected the following year. Created a baronet in 1831 and elected MP for the City of London in 1833, serving for 20 years.
1838-55 Mrs Ann Larken, boarding-house keeper
1855-6 Edward Miles
1856-66 Benjamin Woolf
1866-95 Thomas Fenn, stockbroker, member of the Stock Exchange
1896 Empty
1897-1905 William Anastasius Jones

The current occupier is the Associated Board of the Royal Schools of Music

Number Fifteen

1783-90 John Cologan, possibly of Cologan, Pollard & Cooper, merchants of 20 Swithin's Lane in the City of London
1790-4 John Stephenson (1710-94), MP for Tregony. Died at his house in Bedford Square.
1794-5 Mrs Stephenson
1795-8 Robert Tubbs
1798-1807 James Williams
1807-13 John Crawford
1813-31 Charles Warren, barrister
1831 Richard Roshwell
1832 Empty
1833-44 Mrs Amelia Warren
1844-8 Peter Stafford Carey
1849 Empty
1850-86 Dr John Waters, born Limerick, Eire, physician
1886-95 George Charles Lea, solicitor

The current occupier is the Associated Board of the Royal Schools of Music

Number Sixteen

1784-5 Joseph Shrimpton (see No.3, 1785-1808)
1785-95 Thomas Wildman, solicitor
1795-1814 Sir Soulden Lawrence (1751-1814), judge, son of Thomas Lawrence MD, president of the College of Physicians. Called to the bar 1784. Knighted 1794. Succeeded Sir Francis Buller (*q.v.*) at the Court of the Common Pleas in 1795 and was succeeded by Sir Vicary Gibbs (*q.v.*) at the same Court in 1812 on his retirement. Had a small collection of pictures, including works by Sir Joshua Reynolds.
1814-19 Philip Dauncey, judge
1819-24 Robert Bill, barrister
1824-39 Sir James Burroughs (1750-1839), judge. Called to the bar in 1773. In 1792 he was appointed a commissioner of bankruptcy and in 1816 was raised to the Bench of the Common Pleas whereupon he was knighted. Retired in 1829.
1839-47 Miss Ann Burroughs
1847-57 Henry Charles Chilton, solicitor
1857-67 Reverend Anthony Wilson Thorold (1825-95), bishop of Rochester and, later, of Winchester. Rector of St Giles-in-the-Fields during his years at Bedford Square.
1867-93 Reverend James Marjoribanks Nisbet, Canon of Norwich, Rector of St Giles-in-the-Fields.
1893-1904 Walter Knight (See No.2, 1878-85)

Number Seventeen

1784-6 Samuel Gardiner, merchant of Bishopsgate Street in the City of London.
1786-94 Thomas Greenough
1794-1801 Mrs Greenough
1801-2 Job Mathew, a director of the Bank of England. Also a director of the Sun Fire Office.
1802-19 John Currie
1819-23 Dr Parke
1823-34 Richard Woodhouse, solicitor
1834-6 Francis Woodhouse
1836-49 Edward Bellasis (1800-73), born Basilden, Berkshire, serjeant-at-law. Called to the bar 1824. From 1836 until 1866 he was, as a barrister, employed solely in parliamentary business. He was employed in many of the railway and navigation bills and the laws regulating water supply to the major cities of the United Kingdom.
1849-71 John Pryor, landowner, merchant and underwriter at Lloyds
1872 Empty
1873-84 Reuben Brooks, dealer in works of art
1884 Edwin Oldfield
1885-7 Reverend William Panckridge, rector of St Bartholomew the Great, West Smithfield
1887-8 Mrs Panckridge
1888-92 Lieutenant-Colonel William Henry Allsopp
1892-9 Frederick Anstiss

Number Eighteen

1783-6 Reverend Frederick Hamilton
1786-1800 Thomas Hankey
1800-30 Mrs Hankey
1830-4 John Bernard Hankey
1834-44 Edgar Corrie
1844 John Merivale (1779-1844), born Exeter, scholar and poet. Called to the bar 1804. Appointed a commissioner in bankruptcy in 1831. Published many poems and contributed articles to several magazines.
1844-51 Reverend James Endell Tyler (See No.24, 1829-44)
1851-63 Mrs Jane Tyler, second wife of Reverend James Endell Tyler and daughter of Divie Robertson (*q.v.*)
1863-8 Henry William Hemsworth
1869 Empty
1870-1 Michael Gedge, solicitor
1872-9 Manuel De la Quintana, consul-general of the Peruvian Consulate

1879-1906 Henry Skipper Ryland, solicitor

The current occupiers are Europa Publications and the Chartered Accountant Students Society of London

Number Nineteen

1784-6	Henry Grant
1786-8	John Hanney
1788-1814	Thomas Everett MP for Ludgershall, Wiltshire
1814-30	Mrs Everett
1830-67	Miss Ann Everett
1868	Empty
1869-71	John Black
1871-6	Henry Morris, surgeon
1876-82	Thomas Dolling Bolton, solicitor
1883	Empty
1884	– Hollander
1885-1918	Arthur John Eden

The current occupier is The Publishers Association

Number Twenty

1784-6	Francis Wright
1786–1805	Thomas Brooks
1805-8	Thomas Smith
1808-12	Thomas Orm
1813-23	John Cowell
1823-36	John Bell (1764-1836), born Kendal, Westmorland, barrister. Called to the bar 1792. Lord Eldon (*q.v.*) thought him to be the best lawyer at the equity bar although he suffered from severe disabilities. Bell was lame, spoke with a broad Westmorland accent, had a severe stammer and appalling handwriting. He died at Bedford Square on 6 February 1836.
1836-46	Sir William Erle (1793-1880), born Fifehead-Magdalen, Dorset, judge. Elected MP for Oxford in 1837. Became serjeant-at-law and was knighted in 1844. Retired in 1866.
1846-57	Sir William Bovill (1814-73), born Allhallows, Barking, judge. Called to the bar 1841. Elected MP for Guildford in 1857. In 1866 he succeeded Sir William Erle (*q.v.*) as Chief Justice of the Common Pleas.
1857-61	Nathaniel Bridges
1861-2	Henry De Briou, physician
1862-6	Edward Rouse
1866-76	James Blythe Stephens, wine merchant
1876-87	Reverend John Russell Stock, rector of Allhallows, Upper Thames Street, City, and prebendary of St Paul's Cathedral
1887-92	Samuel Hart
1892-6	John Davis

The current occupiers are Greenwoods, solicitors and Sodagars, chartered accountants

Number Twenty-One

1784	– Reade
1784-5	John Tyson
1785-9	Mrs Drummond
1789-93	John Drummond
1793-1813	John Vernon, solicitor
1813-31	James Carden, solicitor
1831-56	Robert Walker, Registrar to the Court of Chancery
1856-63	Samuel Barker, solicitor
1863-74	Robert and Edward Low, soap manufacturers
1875-8	General Pedro Romulo Negrete, envoy extraordinary and minister plenipotentiary of the Legations of the Salvador and Guatemala Republics
1879-80	Empty
1881-8	Michael Samuel Nathan, fine art dealer
1888-91	Dr John Henry Nicholson, aural surgeon
1891	Nicholsons Patent Limited, Robert Cramp
1892	Empty
1893-1905	Mary Campbell

The property is currently undergoing renovation

Number Twenty-Two

1784-6	Corbet Corbet
1786-92	Richard Heaton, barrister
1792-1800	John Vivian, barrister
1800-7	James Langham, MP for St Germain
1807-10	John Cobb, solicitor
1810-51	Divie Robertson, born Scotland, wine merchant. Daughter Jane was second wife of Reverend James Endell Tyler (*q.v.*)
1851-68	Jacob E Goodhart, sugar refiner and magistrate
1868	Mrs Goodhart
1869-73	Jonah Leslie
1873-81	Henry Deverson Clark
1881-9	Sir Wilmot Parker Herringham (1855-1936), physician. Vice-chancellor of London University 1912-15; knighted 1914.
1889-1937	Sir Johnston Forbes Robertson (1853-1937), born Crutched Friars, London, actor. Knighted 1913.

The property is currently undergoing renovation

Number Twenty-Three

1784-1812	Thomas Burn
1813-28	Michael Nolan, barrister
1829	Empty
1830-4	Bonamy Dobrée
1834-8	Mary Ann Stevens
1838-40	George Smith
1840-50	Thomas Moore
1850-5	Reverend Thomas Nolan, minister of St John's Episcopal Chapel, Bedford Row, Holborn
1855-60	James Davis
1861	Empty
1862-83	Beare Falcke, silver and diamond merchant
1883-5	Florence Gerard
1885-8	Madam Winifred Nicol
1888-1907	Edward Pool

The property is currently undergoing renovation

Number Twenty-Four

1782-3	– Bond
1783-8	N Bishop
1788-1811	Robert Storey
1811-13	Thomas Lewin, barrister
1813-27	George Courthorpe, barrister
1827	Macrae Callon
1828	F Lewin
1829-44	Reverend James Endell Tyler (1789-1851), born Monmouth, rector of St Giles-in-the-Fields between 1826 and 1828. Endell Street, Covent Garden, is named after him. (See also No.18, 1844-51)

1844-7 William Strickland Cookson, solicitor
1847-54 Reverend Alexander William Black
1854-7 Frederick Thomas Pratt
1857-69 Sir Henry Ellis (1777-1869), born London, principal librarian of the British Museum. On graduating from Oxford he was appointed one of two assistants at the Bodleian Library. That same year, 1798, he published his *History and Antiquities of the Parish of St Leonard Shoreditch and Liberty of Norton Folgate*. Became temporary assistant at the British Museum in 1800 and rose to head-keeper of printed books in 1806. Knighted in 1833. Resigned in 1856 and spent his retirement in Bedford Square where he died on 15 January 1869.
1869-74 Banister Fletcher (1833-99), architect. Came to London from Newcastle in 1869 and established a large practice. MP for North-west Wiltshire (1885-6). In collaboration with his son, later Sir Banister Fletcher, he wrote *A History of Architecture on the Comparative Method*, (1896), a monumental standard work of reference which has run to many subsequent editions.
1875-95 William Charles Day

The property is currently undergoing renovation

Number Twenty-Five
1782-6 John Boddington, perhaps related to Benjamin Boddington (see No. 7, 1789–91)
1786-99 Cuthbert Fisher, possibly agent to the Royal Engineers
1799-1813 Mrs Wilbraham Bootle, wife of E Wilbraham Bootle, MP for Newcastle-under-Lyme, Staffordshire
1814 Empty
1815-36 Basil Montagu (1770-1851), legal and miscellaneous writer, and philanthropist; son of fourth Earl of Sandwich. Called to the bar 1798. Montagu was a great friend of Coleridge and Wordsworth and his house in Bedford Square was a meeting place for London's literary society.
1836-42 Edward Jacob, barrister
1842-69 John Douglas Hopkins, architect. Pupil of J B Papworth. Unsuccessful with his design for Houses of Parliament in 1835. Died at his house in Bedford Square.
1869-72 Mrs Hopkins
1873-5 Empty
1876-7 Eugene Pavey
1877-95 Abraham Andrews

The property is currently undergoing renovation

Number Twenty-Eight
1779-1800 George Drake, merchant
1800-18 Sir Charles Price, one of the four MPs for London
1819 Empty
1820-36 Thomas Fowler Ellis (1796-1861), barrister and law reporter. Graduated from Trinity College, Cambridge in 1818, and was elected a fellow. Called to the bar 1824. From 1839 until his death he was Attorney-General for the Duchy of Lancaster. Died at his house in Bedford Place.
1836-46 John Herbert Koe, barrister, equity draftsman
1846-52 George Darby Dermott, surgeon
1852-74 Mrs Charlotte Dermott, boarding-house keeper
1874-88 James Martin, solicitor
1888-1908 William Cecil Marshall, architect

The current occupier is the Nuffield Foundation

Number Twenty-Nine
1779-84 George Foyle
1784-6 Dr Compton
1786-1804 George Shum, MP for Honiton, Devon. Also a director of the Phoenix Fire Office.
1804-19 Mrs Ann Shum
1819-30 William Draper Best (1767-1845), born Haselbury-Plucknett, Somerset, judge. Called to the bar 1789. Became serjeant-at-law in 1799 and elected MP for Petersfield in 1802 and Bridport in 1812. Was appointed Solicitor-General to the Prince of Wales in 1813. Knighted in 1819 and made Chief Justice of the Common Pleas in 1824. Called to the House of Lords in 1829 and took the title of Baron Wynford.
1830-1 Henry Thompson
1832-4 Empty
1835-7 Robert Bell
1837-41 Paul Francis Stratford
1842 Empty
1843-6 James Bourdillion, solicitor
1847 John Goodwin
1847-59 Henry Harrison (*c.*1785-*c.*1865), architect and surveyor. Had a large practice, designing small country houses and London town houses. His works include Richmond Terrace in Whitehall and the Lying-in-Hospital, York Road, Lambeth, both of the 1820s.
1859-74 William Cutler, solicitor
1875-6 Empty
1877 Frederick Cooper
1877-80 Charles William Schwaben
1880-95 Hugh Frederick Jackson, solicitor
1895-1923 Dilnot Dibley Pankhurst

The current occupier is the Chartered Society of Designers

Number Thirty
1779-80 James Lee, Turkey merchant
1780-93 Robert Cooper Lee, merchant
1794-1818 William Tatnell, merchant
1819-44 John Frederick Pike
1845 Empty
1846-53 George Alexander, architect and surveyor
1853-62 George Lennox, iron cable and anchor manufacturer
1862-74 Harry Hanslip Lawrence, solicitor
1875-6 Empty
1877-84 Alexander Cochrane, banker
1884-1910 Thomas Gibson Wilson

Number Thirty-One
1780 – Scott
1780-3 Sir Richard Perryn (1723-1803), judge. Called to the bar 1747. Appointed baron of the Exchequer in 1776 and was knighted in the same year.
1783-9 Sir Samuel Hannay, of Sir Samuel Hannay & Co, drug merchants of 3 Philpot Lane in the City of London and MP for Camelford.

1789-94 Silvester Douglas (1743-1823), politician. Called to the bar in 1776 and acquired a considerable practice. In 1793 he gave up his legal career for politics. Became a member of the Irish parliament for Irishtown, Co. Kilkenny in 1794 and became MP for Fowey, Cornwall in 1796, and later that year for Midhurst, Sussex. Appointed Lord of the Treasury in 1797. Created Baron Glenbervie of Kincardine in 1800.
1794-8 George Newnham, barrister
1798-1813 John Godfrey, a director of the Sun Fire Office
1813-25 Nicholas Pearce
1826-8 Empty
1829-31 John Adolphus, barrister and writer
1831-48 Thomas Starkie (1782-1849), born Blackburn, legal writer and lawyer. Called to the bar 1810. Elected professor of law at Downing College, Cambridge in 1823. Became judge of Clerkenwell County Court in 1847.
1848-56 James Lord, barrister
1856-74 Reverend George Rust, master of the Lower School, King's College
1874-7 Mrs Emily Mary Rust
1877-85 John Sloane Carter, provisions merchant
1885-95 Mrs Charlotte Carter

Sir Edwin Landseer Lutyens, architect, and Lady Emily Lutyens lived here between 1915 and 1918.

Number Thirty-Two

1780-92 Sir John Skynner (1724-1805), born London, judge. Called to the bar 1748. Elected MP for Woodstock, Oxfordshire in 1771. Appointed Lord Chief Baron of the Exchequer and was knighted in 1777.
1792-5 James Jackson
1795-9 Mrs Jackson
1799-1816 Sir Simon Le Blanc (1748-1816), judge. Called to the bar 1773. Created serjeant-at-law in 1787; knighted in 1799. Died at his house in Bedford Square.
1816-18 John Lumsden
1819-21 Empty
1822-38 Sir James Allen Park (1763-1838), born Edinburgh, judge. Called to the bar 1784. Appointed Vice-chancellor of the Duchy of Lancaster in 1791, Recorder of Preston in 1795, Recorder of Durham in 1802 and Attorney-General of Lancaster in 1811. Knighted in 1816 on his promotion to the bench of the Common Pleas, where he stayed until his death in Bloomsbury on 8 December 1838.
1839-42 Empty
1843-9 Dr Charles Von Lang, physician
1849-74 Frederick Kelly, Inspector of Letter Carriers at the General Post Office
1875-8 Godfrey Davis
1878-95 Dr James Pattison Walker, surgeon-general

Number Thirty-Three

1782-1813 Oliver Farrer, barrister
1813-15 Mrs Farrer
1815-29 James William Farrer, barrister
1830-1 Thomas Glanville
1831-51 Sir John Patteson (1790-1861), born Coney Weston, Suffolk, judge. Called to the bar 1821. Worked alongside Sir Joseph Littledale (*q.v.*). Appointed judge in the Court of the King's Bench in 1830 and was knighted
1852 Empty
1853-61 John Dawson, solicitor
1861-74 Mrs Maria Dawson
1875-7 George Brocklebank
1878 Empty
1879-82 Edmund Meredith Cross, merchant of preserved meats, etc
1882-1902 Charles Best

The current occupier is Gardiner & Theobald, chartered quantity surveyors

Number Thirty-Four

1779-84 Mary Jurin, wife of Dr Jurin. Died at her house in Bedford Square on 5 July 1784.
1784-8 James Watson
1788-93 George Hardinge, the Queen's Solicitor-General and MP for Old Sarum, Wiltshire (see No.35, 1779-81).
1793-5 Mrs Lee
1795-8 Henry Gawler, barrister
1798-1804 Alexander Cuthbert
1804-13 William Curtis
1813-15 Duncan Campbell
1815-18 Mrs Campbell
1818-28 Thomas Yuille, moved here from Percy Street
1828-31 Miss Yuille
1832 Empty
1833-50 Charles Hensch
1850-4 Sarah Hensch
1854-67 Frederick John Reed, solicitor
1867-1912 Hasler Harris, dental surgeon

The current occupier is the Architectural Association, which has been here since 1917

Number Thirty-Five

1779-81 George Hardinge (see No.34, 1788-93)
1781-6 John Heath (see No.36, 1786-1816)
1786-92 Jacob Bosanquet, a director of the East India Company
1792-6 James Wildman
1796-9 Samuel Young
1799-1804 Alexander Willock, merchant of 4 Tokenhouse Yard, Lothbury in the City of London.
1804-7 Sir Thomas Manners Sutton, Solicitor-General to the King
1807-8 Sir Edward Carrington
1808-15 John Wedderburn
1815-26 Matthew White
1827 Empty
1828-48 Thomas Wakley (1795-1862), born Membury, Devon, reformer. Early years spent as a surgeon. Founded *The Lancet* in 1823, mainly to disseminate recent medical knowledge. Was returned as MP for Finsbury in 1835 and made a great impression in his seventeen years in the House. An early speech spared six Dorset labourers from fourteen years transportation after they combined to resist a reduction in their wages. Was an opponent of the Corn Laws and an advocate for the repeal of the Irish Union. Died in Madeira.

1849-66 Thomas Hodgkin (1798-1866), born Tottenham, physician. Worked at Guy's Hospital and was a member of the Senate of University of London from 1837 until his death. In later years he gave his time to philanthropic pursuits and his house in Bedford Square became a meeting place for philanthropists, ethnologists and geographers. Worked hard for persecuted Jews and the badly-housed poor. Died on a visit to Palestine with Sir Moses Montefiore.
1866-8 Mrs Sarah Francis Hodgkin, married to Thomas Hodgkin in 1850
1868-72 Howard Holden, building contractor
1872-4 General George Campbell
1875-94 Frederick Battam Pankhurst
1895 Empty
1896-1913 John Melton Drummond Black

The current occupier is the Architectural Association

Number Thirty-Six
1779-83 Edward Bearcroft, barrister
1783-6 John Allen
1786-1816 John Heath (1736-1816), judge; son of Thomas Heath, alderman of Exeter. Called to the bar 1762. Became a serjeant-at-law in 1775 and recorder of Exeter in the same year. Refused a knighthood. (See also No.35, 1781-6)
1816-36 Sir Robert Graham (1744-1836), born Hackney, judge. Graduated from Trinity College, Cambridge in 1766 and entered the Inner Temple, where he was called to the bar. Appointed Attorney-General to the Prince of Wales in 1793. Knighted in 1800.
1837 Empty
1838-43 Dr Abraham Toulmin, physician
1843-7 Thomas King, surgeon
1848 Empty
1849-81 Dr Samuel Richards, physician
1881-8 Dr Smith Richards, surgeon, son of Samuel Richards
1888-1906 Edward Augustus Harbord, surgeon

The current occupier is the Architectural Association and, in the basement, a specialist architectural bookseller, Triangle Bookshop

Number Forty
1779-92 William Dickey, army and general clothier of 9 Caroline Street, Bloomsbury
1792-1811 Thomas Green
1811-44 Mrs Martha Green
1844-54 John Braithwaite (1797-1870), born London, civil engineer. In 1820 he ventilated the House of Lords by means of air-pumps and in 1822 made the donkey-engine. Was introduced to the Stephensons in 1827 and with John Ericsson, in 1829, he constructed *The Novelty*, the first locomotive to run a mile within a minute. At the same time, he manufactured the first practical steam fire-engine which attended the burning of the English Opera House in 1830 and the Houses of Parliament in 1834. From 1834 he practised as a civil engineer and became involved in the laying out of railways at home and on the Continent. In 1837 he co-founded *The Railway Times*. Elected a member of the Institution of Civil Engineers in 1838.
1854-67 Reverend Charles Fynes-Clinton
1867-91 Ellis Williams, stockbroker, member of the Stock Exchange
1892 Edmund Sheriff
1892 Emma Dando
1893-1901 Reverend Henry William Parry Richards, vicar of St Giles-in-the-Fields and prebendary of St Paul's Cathedral

The current occupier is Gardiner & Theobald, chartered quantity surveyors

Number Forty-One
1779 Mr Serjeant Glynn (1722-79), born Cornwall, politician and lawyer. Called to the bar 1748. Created serjeant-at-law in 1763. Entered Parliament in 1768. Elected Recorder of London in 1772. Died at his house in Bedford Square on 16 September 1779.
1779-81 William Lushington
1781-1819 Robert Peers, barrister
1819-43 Richard Richards, barrister, MP for Merionethshire between 1832 and 1852. Eldest son of Sir Richard Richards, judge.
1844-61 William Rogers, barrister
1861-5 Benjamin Alexander
1865-84 John Woolf, stockbroker
1884 Mrs Jewell
1884-94 Joseph David Barnett
1894-5 Jeremiah McVeagh
1896 Empty
1897-1902 Dugald Clerk, patent agent

The current occupier is Gardiner & Theobald, chartered quantity surveyors

Number Forty-Two
1781-7 Richard Buller, possibly of Richard Buller & Co, merchants of 12 Copthall Court in the City of London
1787-95 William Watson, barrister
1795-1811 Dr Henry Revell Reynolds (1745-1811), born Laxton, Nottinghamshire, physician. Came to London in 1772 and was elected a fellow of the College of Physicians in 1774. Was physician to the Middlesex Hospital (1773-7) and St Thomas's Hospital (1777-83). Appointed physician-extraordinary to George III in 1797, and physician-in-ordinary in 1806. Died at his house in Bedford Square on 22 October 1811.
1811-35 Sir John Bayley (1763-1841), born Elton, Huntingdonshire, judge. Called to the bar 1792. Made a judge of the King's Bench in 1808, replacing Sir Soulden Lawrence (*q.v.*). Knighted in the same year, created baronet in 1834 and at the same time was admitted to the Privy Council.
1835-55 John Swarbreck Gregory, solicitor
1856-7 Empty
1858-83 Edward Gilbert Highton, barrister
1884-6 Empty
1887-1900 William Butterfield (1814-1900), born London, architect. His early architectural training had a mediaeval bias which helped him establish a very large practice in the Gothic Revival of the Victorian era. Concentrated mainly on ecclesiastical

buildings; his most important early commission was All Saints, Margaret Street, Marylebone (1849-59). Died at his house in Bedford Square on 23 February 1900.

Katherine and Helen Asquith, daughters of Herbert Henry Asquith's first marriage, lived here between 1928 and 1931.

The current occupiers are Edward Arnold Ltd, publishers, and *The Lancet* medical journal

Number Forty-Three

1782-9 James Richardson
1789-91 Mrs Folley
1791-6 John Elliot, MP for Liskeard, Cornwall
1797 Empty
1798-1800 Sir Francis Buller (1746-1800), born Downes, Devon, judge; son of Lady Jane Bathurst. Called to the bar 1772. On the recommendation of Lord Mansfield he was made a puisne judge of the King's Bench in 1778; at the time he was the youngest man ever created a judge. Died at his house in Bedford Square.
1800-9 Sir Vicary Gibbs (1751-1820), born Exeter, judge, son of the chief surgeon to the hospital at Exeter. Called to the bar 1783. Became one of the most eminent judges of the day, though a humourless and caustic manner acquired him the nickname 'Vinegar Gibbs'. MP for Totnes in 1804 and afterwards for Great Bedwin and the University of Cambridge. Knighted in 1805. Died at his house in Russell Square.
1810 Empty
1811-14 Samuel Joseph
1814-16 Mrs Joseph
1817-18 Empty
1819-27 Alexander McDonald
1827-41 Sir John Richardson (1771-1841), born City of London, judge. Called to the bar 1803. Succeeded Sir Robert Dallas (*q.v.*) at the Court of Common Pleas in 1818 and was made serjeant-at-law. Knighted by the Prince Regent at Carlton House in 1819. Died at his house in Bedford Square on 19 March 1841.
1841-55 Thomas Coates, solicitor and parliamentary agent. Secretary of the Society for Diffusion of Useful Knowledge, based here.
1855-75 Peter Marshall, surgeon and general medical practitioner
1875-88 Charles James Partington, solicitor
1889-90 Empty
1891-8 Dr John Oswald Auchinleck Browne, physician

The property is currently undergoing renovation

Number Forty-Four

1781-4 Thomas Hibbert. Possibly the founder of a Jamaican mercantile house and uncle of Robert Hibbert (1770-1849), merchant and founder of the Hibbert Trust.
1784-95 Thomas Scott Jackson, a director of the Bank of England
1795-1827 Henry Gregg, barrister
1827-46 Sir Nicholas Conyngham Tindal (1776-1846), born Coval Hall, Chelmsford, judge. Called to the bar 1809. Entered Parliament in 1824 and became Solicitor-General in 1826. Knighted in the same year. Succeeded William Draper Best (*q.v.*) as Chief Justice of the Common Pleas in 1829.
1846-54 Eleanor Blackburn
1854-6 Joshua Blackburn
1856-84 Dr William Smiles, surgeon
1884-9 Dr William Saul, surgeon
1889-95 Dr Robert Henry Coall, surgeon

Philip Morrell, politician, and Lady Ottoline Morrell, socialite, lived here between 1906 and 1913. Lady Ottoline was patroness of the intellectual social circle that included Bertrand Russell, D H Lawrence, W B Yeats, T S Eliot, Augustus John, Virginia Woolf and Aldous Huxley.

Herbert Henry Asquith, first Earl of Oxford and Asquith (1852-1928), born Morley, Yorkshire, statesman, lived here between 1921 and 1928. His second wife, Emma Alice Margaret (known as Margot), Countess of Oxford and Asquith (1864-1945), writer, died at her house in Bedford Square on 28 July 1945, having spent the war in London, unperturbed by air raids.

The property is currently undergoing renovation

Number Forty-Five

1781-90 Samuel Pole, a director of the Sun Fire Office
1790-1802 Sir Alexander Thomson, judge
1802-5 James Heseltine, King's Proctor and Register to the Dean and Chapter of Westminster of Doctors' Commons
1805-7 Mrs Heseltine
1807-27 Joseph Ward, solicitor
1827-42 William John Ward, solicitor
1843-52 Phineas Nathan, wholesale jewellery and watch manufacturer
1852-3 Mrs Nathan
1854-9 Benjamin Solomon
1859-61 Jacob Marks, merchant
1861-88 Robert James Moser, iron merchant and artist. Exhibited at the Royal Academy between 1871 and 1885.
1889-1906 Samuel Eyres Wilson

The property is currently undergoing renovation

Number Forty-Six

1782-90 Samuel Castele
1790-6 Andrew Reid
1796-1823 James Baillie, merchant (See No.14, 1782-93)
1823-30 John Baillie
1830-54 George Frere, barrister and magistrate and a director of the Law Life Assurance Society
1854-94 Bartle John Laurie Frere, solicitor

The current occupier is Hodder & Stoughton Ltd, publishers

Number Forty-Seven

1780-99 John Raymond Barker, a director of the South Sea Company and the Million Bank
1799-1814 Peter Pole
1815-18 Thomas Willimott
1818-46 James Parkinson, merchant
1846-56 Octavius Smith, malt distiller
1856-89 Moses Joseph, merchant
1889-91 Mrs Rosetta Joseph

1891-5 Oliver Rhys Williams, artist

The current occupier is Hodder & Stoughton Ltd, publishers

Number Forty-Eight

1782-3 — Bevan
1783-9 Samuel Gaussen, a director of the South Sea Company
1789-1812 Robert Parnther, barrister
1813-25 Sir Christopher Robinson (1766-1833), admiralty lawyer. Studied maritime law at the College of Advocates. Knighted 1809, appointed King's advocate in the same year. As part of the Admiralty Court he was engaged in many cases involving prizes captured on the seas. Elected MP for Callington, Cornwall, 1818.
1827-40 Dr Thomas Edwards
1840-8 Josiah Wathen, solicitor
1849 Empty
1850 Reverend Dr James Booth
1851-69 Ladies College
1869-74 Bedford College
1875-6 Empty
1877-1913 James Orrock, artist, member of the Institute of Painters in Water Colours

The current occupier is Heald Nickinson, solicitors

Number Forty-Nine

1781-2 Robert Sanderson
1782-4 — Higginson
1784-6 William Hornby, solicitor
1786-97 Francis Hawkins
1797-1822 John Reid, merchant
1822-32 Janet Hare
1832-9 Joseph Hare
1839-40 John Plummer
1841-51 William Henry Cotterell, solicitor
1851-62 Richard Creed, landlord
1862-9 Ladies College
1869-73 Bedford College
1873-4 Miss Thomas
1875 Empty
1876-9 Mrs Ann Jordan
1880 Empty
1881-4 George Gomperty Barber, stockbroker
1885 Empty
1886-1902 Christopher Knight Watson, fellow of the Society of Antiquaries

Raymond Asquith, eldest son of Herbert Henry Asquith, lived here between 1909 and 1913. He was killed in action in 1916. The current occupier is Gardiner & Theobald, chartered quantity surveyors

Number Fifty

1781-1803 John Hunter, a director of the East India Company and MP for Leominster, Herefordshire
1803-27 John Walker
1827-56 Mrs Walker
1856-66 Alfred Price, property owner
1866-93 Solomon Beyfus, scrivener and landlord
1894-6 Alexander Leveson

The current occupier is Gardiner & Theobald, chartered quantity surveyors

Number Fifty-One

1779-91 John Boldero, partner of Boldero, Adey, Lushington & Boldero, bankers of 30 Cornhill in the City of London
1791-1816 Mrs Boldero
1816-51 Miss Sarah Edwards, ran a ladies school at this house in the 1840s with Letitia Edwards. It had nine pupils according to the 1841 Census.
1852 Empty
1853-60 Henry Wallis
1861 Joseph Gillott
1862-7 John Andrews
1868 Empty
1869-74 Prosper Leopold Everard & Co, picture dealers
1875-6 Empty
1877-85 Barlase Hill Adams, barrister and magistrate
1885-6 Mrs Adams
1886-93 Frederick Bosher Henson
1893-1905 John Passmore Edwards (1823-1911), born Blackwater, Truro, philanthropist. Came to London in 1845, earning his keep as a journalist and lecturer. Launched and purchased several newspapers and magazines including *Building News* and the *Echo*, the first halfpenny newspaper, which made him his fortune. Elected MP for Salisbury in 1880. His latter years were devoted to philanthropy. He established schools, hospitals, homes and libraries, most of which were either in Cornwall or London.

The current occupier is Gardiner & Theobald, chartered quantity surveyors

Number Fifty-Two

1779-1831 John Morgan, barrister
1831-69 Francis Morgan, landowner
1869-74 Reverend Henry Morgan
1875-6 Empty
1877-82 Robert Seymour Bridges, physician
1883 Empty
1884-5 James Martin
1886 John Ashford
1887-91 Lieutenant-Colonel Charles Lindsay
1891-5 John Francis Holcombe Read
1896-8 Empty
1899-1908 Reverend William Covington, rector of St Giles-in-the-Fields and prebendary of St Paul's Cathedral

The current occupier is Dechert Price & Rhoads, lawyers

Number Fifty-Three

1779-93 Dr Monro
1793-6 Thomas Wildman
1796-1803 George Rous, barrister
1803-20 George Shedden (See No.6, 1820-54)
1820-3 — Taylor
1823-33 Charles Gibbs
1833-4 Mr Serjeant Jones, judge
1834-47 David Atcherley, barrister, serjeant-at-law and attorney-general of the county palatine of Lancaster
1847-9 Charles Henry Lacey
1849-67 Lewis Cubitt (1799-1883), architect. The youngest of the Cubitt brothers; apprenticed to his eldest brother, Thomas, in 1815 as a carpenter and received architectural training as a pupil of Henry

	Edward Kendall. Appears to have designed many of the houses in Bloomsbury and Belgravia that were built by the Cubitts in the 1820s. Designed King's Cross railway terminal (1851-2). Died in Brighton, aged 84.
1867-9	S Kisch
1869-70	William Day
1871	Empty
1872-5	Thomas Hutchinson Baylis
1875	Thomas Barrow
1876-7	Empty
1878-9	Richard Evered
1879-82	Frederick Brodie, magistrate
1883	Empty
1884-95	Henry Spencer Ashbee

Appendix 1

Letter from Robert Grews to Robert Palmer dated 4 February 1784

Permit me to remind you, that in the year 1776 I, in conjunction with Mr William Scott, engaged to build the West and North sides of Bedford Square, and formed and prepared Plans and Elevations of the whole Square at a very considerable expence, which being submitted for the perusal of Her Grace the Dutchess of Bedford and yourself met with approbation.

As the Business might have been impeded, or the Plan deviated from had more persons been concerned, we were induced to engage for the Completion of the whole Square and the several Streets leading into the same.

The great scarcity of Money, occasioned by the unhappy American War, so severely affected many of the persons concerned under us, that some were compelled to stop, and we found ourselves under the unfortunate necessity of taking back the Ground, and completing the Houses thereon, which their inability had rendered them incapable of doing, several of which when finished we were obliged to sell for less than they cost us, and to let others considerably under their value.

By seven years constant and unwearied attention, and combating the Calamities of the times, I am however happy to find that, with the ready and chearful assistance which you gave us from time to time whenever required, we have been enabled to fulfil our Engagement and to complete (at an Expence of two hundred Thousand pounds and upwards) a Work, which I hope the Trustees and all the World allow to be a very Capital Improvement upon the Estate, comprehending, (besides several regular well built Streets) one of the completest Squares in Europe, but which I am sorry to add, does not produce those advantages to us, which I think we are entitled to, from a Work of such Magnitude.

Sir, my hope is, that knowing my situation and the difficulties I have laboured under, you will see the propriety of representing these Circumstances in such a manner to Her Grace the Dutchess of Bedford and His Grace the Duke of Bedford, that, upon any future occasion I may be thought worthy their Graces favour and preference.

I am bound, Sir, before I conclude, to express my sincere Thanks to you, for the attention and ready assistance which you have from time to time offered me, during the course of so arduous an undertaking, and to subscribe myself with great respect.

Store Street, Bedford Square
4th February 1784

Sir
Your most obliged, obedient and very humble Servant
Rob[t.] Grews

Appendix 2

The account of Her Grace the Duchess of Bedford Her Grace the Duchess of Marlborough and Robert Palmer Esq as devisees in trust of the real estate of the late Most Noble John Duke of Bedford showing the date on which loans were granted to builders to finance building work, names of borrowers, value of loans, and the houses concerned.

DATE	BORROWER	£	HOUSE
1777			
26 Nov	Charles Jacks	400	?44
13 Dec	Charles Jacks	1,000	44
17 Dec	William Scott (principal money advanced by him to Henry Sumpter on 22 Feb 1777 on a mortgage of a house on the south side of the Square)	600	48
17 Dec	Henry Sumpter (further mortgage)	400	48
1778			
16 Jan	Stephen Mear & Thomas Dalston	1,000	8
22 Jan	William Scott	2,000	52
22 Jan	Robert Grews	1,500	53
4 Mar	Daniel Mawley	1,200	32
4 Mar	William Grant	1,000	42
29 Apr	Charles Jacks (further mortgage)	300	44
20 Jun	James Higley (this house was by indenture dated 8 Jan 1777 mortgaged to James Hardy of Eaton, Bucks, Gentleman for £500	500	33
22 Jun	John Utterton	1,000	47
18 Jul	William Jacques	600	4
23 Jul	Robert Phillips	500	9
30 Jul	Henry Sumpter (further mortgage)	300	48
23 Oct	William Grant (further mortgage)	500	42
25 Nov	Charles Jacks (further mortgage)	300	44
1779			
18 Jan	William Jacques (further mortgage)	400	4
6 Mar	William Scott	600	49
25 Mar	Robert Grews	500	41
11 May	Robert Phillips (further mortgage)	300	9
27 May	Stephen Mear & Thomas Dalston (further mortgage)	250	8
23 Nov	Charles Jacks (further mortgage)	200	44
3 Dec	Robert Phillips (further mortgage)	200	9
14 Dec	William Grant (further mortgage)	200	42
1780			
19 Feb	Daniel Mawley (further mortgage)	500	32
30 May	Robert Phillips (further mortgage)	300	9
2 Nov	John Hakewill	500	5
21 Nov	Charles Jacks (further mortgage)	100	44
1781			
24 May	Robert Grews (further mortgage)	1,000	41
22 Jun	William Scott (on an assignment of a mortgage from James Bramble)	1,200	36
31 Jul	Robert Grews	800	50
1782			
24 Mar	Robert Grews (further mortgage)	700	50
24 Sep	Thomas Martin	500	15
14 Oct	William Woolcott	500	20
4 Nov	Alexander Hendy	500	21
26 Nov	William Jacques	750	22
1783			
5 Mar	Charles Jacks	1,900	30
25 Apr	Thomas Martin (further mortgage)	500	15
31 May	Charles Jacks (further mortgage)	100	30
31 May	John Hakewill (further mortgage)	200	5
14 Jun	William Grant (further mortgage)	300	42
1785			
1 Jun	John Drummond	1,000	21
1786			
21 Feb	William Jacques (further mortgage)	400	?4

Notes

1. A T Bolton, *The Architecture of Robert and James Adam*, vol.2, 1922, p.112.
2. F Sheppard, V Belcher and P Cottrell, 'The Middlesex and Yorkshire Deeds Registries and the study of building fluctuations', *The London Journal*, vol.5, 1978.
3. J Mordaunt Crook, *The Greek Revival*, 1972, p.71.
4. Tall houses – four storeys over basements – were common in the City after 1700 but not in the West End until after the Adelphi. In Dublin, however, five-storey houses were the norm after the Palladian revival reached the Irish capital in the 1720s, *eg* Henrietta Street, 1720s-40s and Dominick Street and Parnell Square, 1750s and 1760s.
5. John Gwynn, *London and Westminster Improved*, 1766, p.14.
6. Sir John Summerson, *Georgian London*, 1978 edition, p.70.
7. Dorothy Stroud, *George Dance, Architect*, 1971, chapter 7 and plates 41 and 42.
9. John Gwynn, op cit, preface.
10. The development of the Bedford Estate is discussed in Donald J Olsen's *Town Planning in London in the Eighteenth and Nineteenth Centuries*, 1982 edition, chapter 2, section 4.
11. Thomas Malton, *A Picturesque Tour Through the Cities of London and Westminster*, 1792, vol.2, p.100.
12. James Ralph, *A Critical Review of the Public Buildings, Statues and Ornaments, in and about London and Westminster*, 1783. Ralph had written the 1734 edition but had died long before the 1783 edition; this was printed for John Wallis by whom it was probably written.
13. Sir John Soane, *Lectures on Architecture*, edited by A T Bolton, 1929, Lecture XI, p.179.
14. Ibid, Lecture X, p.156 (both quotes).
15. Isaac Ware, *A Complete Body of Architecture*, 1756, p.347.
16. Thomas Malton, op cit, pp.98-9.
17. E B. Chancellor, *The History of the Squares of London*, 1907, pp.202-10.
18. *Builder*, 25 August 1855, p.400. A letter from an 'Old Subscriber' recounts: 'I believe several houses about there were built by Sir William Chambers: they bear marks of his hand.'
19. Letter from Thomas Leverton to the Duke of Bedford, dated 17 July 1797, at the Bedford Estate archives.
20. *Survey of London*, vol.39, p.106.
21. At the Bedford Estate archives.
22. Sir John Summerson, op cit, p.166.
23. A T Bolton, op cit, pp.103-7 states that although the earliest plan of Portland Place was of 1773-4, work was not in progress until 1776 with about a dozen houses covered in during 1777, the year it first appears in rate books. Bedford Square on the other hand had a dozen houses covered in during 1776 and a further twenty-two during 1777.
24. Vol.1, p.32.
25. An article on the Shire Hall appears in *Architectural Review*, 1 April 1918, pp.68-73, by Arthur T Bolton.
26. At the Bedford Estate archives.
27. Marylebone Local History Library, 124/3, Lease dated 5 March 1772.
28. Bloomsbury Rental books at the Bedford Estate archives.
29. Grews died on 5 September 1794. His obituary in the *Gentleman's Magazine*, 1794, p.868 states that he had 'by a life of industry and economy, joined to the most perfect integrity, realised a fortune upwards of £70,000'.
30. Marylebone Local History Library, 97/33, will dated 6 June 1783.
31. Letter dated 4 February 1784. Reproduced in Appendix 1.
32. Thomas Malton, op cit, pp.98-9.
33. John Matthews, *An Abstract of the Act of Parliament made in the fourteenth year of his present Majesty King George III*, 1774. This information appears at the rear of the book. Mecluer's address is given as Carnaby Street, Carnaby Market.
34. The agreements and leases for Bedford Square are at the Bedford Estate archives.
35. See note 31.
36. This is an assumption because the names that appear in the rate books for the Square are Gorges Foyle and Margaret Turin. The houses were Nos.29 and 34 respectively.
37. Rowland Dobie, *History of the United Parishes of St Giles in the Fields and St George Bloomsbury*, 1829.
38. Measurement taken at No.5 Stratford Place.
39. No.28 has no balconies.
40. *Survey of London*, vol.21, p.24. Also H M Colvin, *A Biographical Dictionary of English Architects, 1660-1840*, 1954.
41. John Matthews, op cit.
42. The subleases are at the Greater London Record Office and generally appear next but one to the original lease.
43. See note 31.
44. Quoted by Frank Kelsall, *Architectural History*, vol.27, p.125.
45. *Gentleman's Magazine*, 1787, p.94.
46. Letter dated 22 May 1775 at the Bedford Estate archives.
47. See note 31.
48. John Holliday, *A further Appeal to the Governors of the Foundling Hospital*, 1788, p.17.
49. Lease at the Bedford Estate archives.
50. A letter at the Bedford Estate archives from Thomas Rowe to Robert Palmer, dated 9 May 1775, regarding raising funds for an Assembly Room at Okehampton mentions Palmer and Wedderburn 'having expressed their wishes when here, for having an Assembly Room in this town, and that they would promote such an undertaking'.
51. At the Bedford Estate archives.
52. Page 125.
53. Ibid, p.122.
54. Ibid, p.121.
55. Quoted by Damie Stillman, *English Neo-classical Architecture*, 1988, p.39.
56. Quoted by Dan Cruickshank, *A Guide to the Georgian Buildings of Britain and Ireland*, 1985, p.22.
57. Isaac Ware, op cit, pp.345-7.
58. *Survey of London*, vol.27, p.201.
59. *Particulars composing the Prizes in the Adelphi Lottery*, 1774. Pamphlet in the British Library.
60. *Survey of London*, vol.40, p.136.
61. Quoted by Donald Olsen, op cit, p.110.
62. *Gentleman's Magazine*, 1791, p.781.
63. Quoted in *Anaesthesia*, vol.41, pp.726-30.
64. Donald Olsen, op cit, pp.147-9.
65. There were examples of non-residential use in the nineteenth century but these appear to be casual; *eg* The Society for Diffusion of Useful Knowledge was based at No.43 Bedford Square during the residency of its secretary, Thomas Coates, between 1841-55.
66. Information from Post Office directories.
67. Isaac Ware, op cit.
68. Grosvenor Square is covered by vol.40 of the *Survey of London*.
69. John Gwynn, op cit, p.77.
70. Ibid, p.5.
71. Johann Wilhelm von Archenholz, *A Picture of England*, 1789, pp.126-33.
71a. The words crossed out are 'when made', 'are to' and 'to be'.
72. James Ralph, op cit.
73. Page 556.
74. Maurice Craig, *Dublin 1660-1860*, 1980 edition, p.338.
75. Letter dated 15 December 1889 at the Bedford Estate archives.
76. *Building News*, 18 November 1910.
77. *Building*, 22 March 1985, pp.39–46.
78. Batty Langley, *The London Prices of Bricklayer's Materials and Works*, 1749, p.9.
79. Ibid, p.94.
80. See note 75.
81. Alison Kelly, *Architectural History*, vol.28, pp.71–91.
82. *A Descriptive Catalogue of Coade's Artificial Stone Manufactory.*
83. Page x.
84. John Gwynn, op cit, p.83.
85. Mr Dunning, *Observations on Two Trials at Law respecting Messieurs Adams's new-invented Stucco*, 1778.
86. John Liardet, *An Appeal to the Public on the right of using Oil-Cement, or Composition for Stucco, etc.*, 1778, p.32.
87. Ibid, pp.73-4.
88. Frank Kelsall, op cit, vol.27, p.123.
89. Mr Wallace, *A Reply to Observations on Two Trials at Law*, 1778, p.7.
90. Frank Kelsall, op cit, pp.118-26.
91. James Ralph, op cit.
92. *Dictionary of National Biography*, see entry under Hartley.
93. David Hartley, *An Account of some Experiments made with the Fire Plates ...*, 1776, p.3.
94. Ibid, p.3.
95. Hartley published a pamphlet following the Pantheon fire, arguing

that the plates had been installed contrary to his instructions and that only a screen between stage and auditorium would work as an aid to fire prevention in such buildings.

96. George Herbert Guttridge, *David Hartley M.P.*, 1926, p.239.
97. Ibid, p.240.
98. Bedford Square Correspondence files at the Bedford Estate archives.
99. *Gentleman's Magazine*, 1784, p.237.
100. *Victoria County History, Essex*, vol.6, p.268.
101. *Architectural Publications Society Dictionary*, see entry under Leverton.
102. Ibid.
103. Letter dated 29 September 1785 at the Bedford Estate archives.
104. See note 28.
105. *Gentleman's Magazine*, 1824, p.469.
106. Leverton designed a dwelling house and warehouse in St Mildred's Court, Poultry, for Matthew Bloxam, a stationer of Harley Street. He charged 3 per cent of the estimated building cost for unexecuted designs, and 5 per cent of cost for design and supervision of executed work (ex inf. Frank Kelsall).
107. Letter dated 31 July 1807, Bodleian Library, MS. Eng. Misc.c.40 (ex inf. Peter Meadows).
108. Renumbering Order, 6 April 1866, at the Camden Local History Library, Holborn.
109. *Survey of London*, vol.1 (1900), Introduction, p.XIX includes Bedford Square in a list of 'Buildings, etc., destroyed during the last six years'. The entry reads: 'Many Adam interiors destroyed.' This would certainly have included some lost chimney-pieces.
110. Information on Lyde from J P F Broad, 'The Building of the New Church of Ayot St Lawrence in the Eighteenth Century', *Hertfordshire Past and Present*, No.4, 1964, and the *Gentleman's Magazine*, 1779, p.374; 1789, p.972; 1791, p.374; 1791, p.682.
111. The ceiling is not recorded in the *Survey of London*, vol.5 of 1914 but is recorded in *Small Houses of the late Georgian Period*, vol.2, 1923, by Stanley Ramsey and J D M Harvey. If it is original then the ceiling of the first-floor front room of No.30 is almost certainly by Thomas Leverton as many details are identical in both ceilings.
111a. Edward Croft-Murray, *Decorative Painting in England (1537-1837)*, Vol.2, 1970, pp.55–6.
112. *Builder*, 3 November 1860, p.702.
113. *Country Life*, 13 February 1932, p.189.
114. See note 19.
115. At Sir John Soane's Museum, Adam Collection.
116. No.21: Scott subleased to Alexander Hendy, painter and glazier of John Street, St Pancras on 16 September 1782. The same day Hendy assigned his lease to Joseph Harrington of St George Bloomsbury, an employee at the Bedford Estate office. No.22: Scott subleased to William Jacques, carpenter of St George the Martyr on 16 September 1782. No.23: Scott subleased to Thomas Burn esquire of St George Bloomsbury on 16 September 1782. (ex. inf. Nancy Edwards).
117. See note 76.
118. See note 111.

Bibliography

There are obviously very few books that concentrate on Bedford Square. The most important of these is Volume Five of the *Survey of London* (1914) which covers the parish of St Giles-in-the-Fields, taking in all of the Square. Although the text is not always reliable, the illustrations are excellent. I have taken advantage in this study of using ten photographs commissioned for the Survey, eight of which were not published in 1914. Donald J Olsen's *Town Planning in London* (1964, revised 1982) is a study of the development and management of the Bedford and Foundling Estates, more social than architectural. Gladys Scott Thompson's *The Russells in Bloomsbury 1669-1771* (1940) gives a history of the Estate before the development of Bedford Square.

There are three nineteenth-century works on the area: John Parton, *Some Account of the Hospital and Parish of St Giles-in-the-Fields Middlesex* (1822); Rowland Dobie, *The History of the United Parishes of St Giles-in-the-Fields and St George Bloomsbury* (1829) and George Clinch, *Bloomsbury and St Giles's: Past and Present* (1890).

Concerning individual houses, much attention is given to Bedford Square interiors by Stanley C Ramsey and J D M Harvey in *Small Georgian Houses and their Details, 1750-1820* (1972), and in W Shaw Sparrow's *The British Home of Today* (1904) there are four interior photographs of No.48.

Adam, Robert and James, *The Works in Architecture*, London 1773

Archenholz, Johann Wilhelm von, *A Picture of England*, London 1789

Bolton, A T, *The Architecture of Robert and James Adam*, 2 vols, London 1922

Byrne, Andrew, *London's Georgian Houses*, London 1986

Colvin, Howard, *A Biographical Dictionary of British Architects 1600-1840*, London 1978

Cruickshank, Dan, *A Guide to the Georgian Buildings of Britain and Ireland*, London 1985

Cruickshank, Dan and Wyld, Peter, *London: the Art of Georgian Building*, London 1975

George, M Dorothy, *London Life in the Eighteenth Century*, London 1925, revised 1976

Gwynn, John, *London and Westminster Improved*, London 1766

Malton, Thomas, *A Picturesque Tour Through the Cities of London and Westminster*, 2 vols, London 1792

Pevsner, Nikolaus, *The Buildings of England*, 3 vols for London, 1952, 1973 and 1982

Ralph, James, *A Critical Review of the Public Buildings, Statues and Ornaments, in and about London and Westminster*, London 1734, revised 1783

Rasmussen, Steen Eiler, *London: the Unique City*, London 1932

Rudé, George, *Hanoverian London, 1714-1808*, London 1971

Sheppard, Francis, *London 1808-1870: The Infernal Wen*, London 1971

Stillman, Damie, *English Neo-classical Architecture*, London 1988

Summerson, Sir John, *Georgian London*, London 1945, revised 1988

Survey of London, 42 vols., LCC/GLC/Athlone, London 1900-86

Ware, Isaac, *A Complete Body of Architecture*, London 1756

Information on the residents has come from numerous reference sources, chief of which are the *Dictionary of National Biography*, *Boyles Court Guides*, *Post Office Directories*, Census Records and Rate Books.

In addition, No.1 Bedford Square has a full description in a *Country Life* article of 6 February 1932. There are photograph collections of the Square at the National Monuments Record Library in Savile Row and the Greater London Photograph Library in Northampton Road, Clerkenwell.

Illustration acknowledgements

With the exception of the illustrations acknowledged below, the photographs reproduced were taken by the author.

The author and publishers wish to thank the following for permission to reproduce the black and white illustrations and colour plates indicated (the numbers refer to illustrations and colour plates):
The British Library 52
Greater London Photograph Library 1, 73, 75, 84, 92, 103, 109, 118, 132, 138
London Borough of Camden Local History Library 7, 8, 9, 11
Marquess of Tavistock and the Trustees of the Bedford Estates 2, 3, 4
Royal Commission on the Historical Monuments of England 31, 32, 33
The following subjects are reproduced by courtesy of the Trustees of the British Museum (29, 30) and the Trustees of Sir John Soane's Museum (5, 6 plate III).

Drawings and measured drawings were specially commissioned, and the authors and publishers are grateful to the following for their contributions:
Ali Bernstein 46, 48, 49, 76, 90, 93, 102, 108, 122, 129, 131
Rupert Bound 19, 20, 23, 24, 89, 94, 101, 110, 113, 114, 141
Jane Briginshaw 17, 77, 79, 83, 98, 99, 104, 111, 126, 145
Jim Carroll 16, 27, 44, 60, 64, 65, 100, 123, 125, 128, 146
Michael Vance 97
Jamie Whitehead 43
Ted Cullinan frontispiece
Glynn Boyd Harte plate I
Plate II is reproduced from a London private collection, and Prudence Cuming Associates were responsible for photography for plates IV - VIII and the jacket illustration.
John Flower prepared the map on page 8.

Index of Principal Residents

In this index, numbers refer to the houses inhabited by the principal residents. These appear in numerical sequence on pages 144-154

General Index

References in this index are to page and figure numbers